MEMORIES OF AN OLD ACTOR.

Ever yours.
Walter M. Leman

MEMORIES

OF

AN OLD ACTOR

BY

WALTER M. LEMAN

"They are the abstract and brief chronicles of the time"

SHAKESPEARE

SAN FRANCISCO

A. ROMAN CO., PUBLISHERS

1886

Republished by
Scholarly Press, 22929 Industrial East, St. Clair Shores, Michigan 48080

Standard Book Number 403-00199-4

Library of Congress Catalog Card Number: 70-106905

This edition is printed on a high-quality,
acid-free paper that meets specification
requirements for fine book paper referred
to as "300-year" paper

DEDICATION.

To the Memory of

NATHAN PORTER,

Whose human sympathies embraced not kindred and friends alone, but went out to and beyond the circle of the legal profession which he dignified by his virtues and adorned by his talents, and to that great brotherhood which found in him the truest exemplar of their motto: "Friendship, Love and Truth," and took in mankind at large; who dared oppose Wrong though it were clad in silk and purple, and befriend Right though groveling in wretchedness and rags; upon whose escutcheon as husband, brother, father, friend and man there is neither spot nor blemish—this volume is dedicated by the writer who knew him long and loved him well.

CONTENTS.

CHAPTER I.

CHAPTER II.

CHAPTER III.

CHAPTER IV.

CHAPTER V.

CHAPTER VI.

CHAPTER VII.

CHAPTER VIII.

Contents.

CHAPTER IX.

CHAPTER X.

CHAPTER XI.

CHAPTER XII.

CHAPTER XIII.

CHAPTER XIV.

CHAPTER XV.

CHAPTER XVI.

CHAPTER XVII.

MEMORIES OF AN OLD ACTOR.

CHAPTER I.

WITH the opening of the Tremont Theatre,
in the city of Boston, in the year 1827,
commenced my theatrical life; but my remembrances of the theatre and the players antedate
that event by some three years, when, a restive
youth of fifteen, I returned to my parental home
from Bradford Academy, which, under the direction of the distinguished mathematician and

scholar, Benjamin Greenleaf, held a high rank among the schools of New England sixty years ago.

I had been bitten by the stage mania before I went to Bradford, had nursed the craze while there, and hence found the duties of a subordinate clerk, which position was obtained for me soon after my return home, each day more and more irksome—for an actor's life was in my excited imagination the summit of earthly bliss.

In my younger schoolboy days I had reveled with lads of my own age in the garret and cellar theatricals, which have ever been so fascinating to youth.

There were two little girls, the daughters of Mrs. Drummond, the actress—better known at a later day as Mrs. Geo. Barrett—residing during their mother's absence, at the house of a neighbor, and their half-brother, Samuel Stockwell, who subsequently became a scenic artist of eminence, was a school and playmate of mine. His family associations had familiarized him, even at that early age, with the paraphernalia and adjuncts of the theatre, and, as a matter of course, he was our stage manager.

Our performances were a combination of the dramatic and equestrian, our chief reliance in the ring department being a highly intelligent dog belonging to Sam Tapley, who could leap

banners and jump through hoops with vigor, if
not with grace ; but, truth to say, *Spring*—that
was his name—by some unlucky dog perversity,
often did as much to spoil as to *perfect* our grand
Saturday and Wednesday afternoon matinees—
which were fashionable because school didn't
keep—and on one occasion, when we had a grand
performance in the upper story of a house which
stood upon ground where, some years before, the
famous circus of Pepin and Breschard was located,
Spring, inspired perhaps by some canine instinct
with the feats of his biped predecessors, dashed
out of the ring with his triumphal chariot bearing a black cat, designated on our written play-
bill as Madame Clawrine Squallerini, and the
whole outfit tumbled head over heels down stairs
to the infinite alarm and terror of Mrs. J——,
the lady of the house. This untoward effect
brought our season to an abrupt close.

As with actors of mature growth, there was
contention for the best parts. My especial fitness, in my own eyes, was for Tragedy—the
more pronounced the better, and if a tragic
tyrant, better still. At a later period I felt
highly aggrieved when my teacher selected as
my theme for declamation, Lucius' speech for
peace, when I particularly wanted Sempronius'
speech for *war*. When the other boy stepped on
the platform and, striking an attitude, began

with " My voice is still for war !" the burning
envy I felt when those words fell from his lips,
in tones not half as loud as I would have used,
was but slightly modified by pity for my teacher's lack of judgment. To speak with candor,
my juvenile efforts at school were not a success,
and my elocutionary record at the academy was
the reverse of flattering. At the graduating
exhibition I selected for delivery a fugitive poem,
the theme of which was the imprisonment and
death of Napoleon at St. Helena. At this day I
do not remember a word of the poem, excepting
the last line, typifying the excitement among
the nations of the earth when news of the great
event should be spread abroad like—

" A thunder shock from that lone rock."

I intended to be impressive, but the inattention
with which my commencement was received,
made all the worse by what seemed to me an
inclination to laugh as I progressed, utterly dis-
concerted me. Many of the auditors were young
· lady pupils, three or four years my senior, and
to have my sounding periods greeted with laughter broke me down completely. I struggled
through after a fashion, but my disgust was
intensified when, on the following day, one fair
girl, in whose eyes I especially desired to stand

well, told me that she " felt so sorry for me, for I appeared very stupid."

Such a "thunder shock" as that ought to have cured me, but it didn't.

The status and personal appreciation of the theatre and players in the United States, sixty years ago, were in marked contrast with the opinions of to-day. Outside of a half dozen of the larger cities on or near the seaboard, and a few of the State capitals, the acted drama was almost unknown. Only a few of the interior towns boasted a theatre, and many so-called theatres were simply halls where the drama occasionally found a temporary footing. In the New England States, apart from Boston, which contained two theatres, there were but two others, one each in Providence and Newport, and neither of these were open more than two or three months in a year. In the city of New York there were, I believe, some five or six, only three of which were kept open with any permanence ; and there was also a theatre in Albany. Philadelphia had three, Pittsburgh one, Baltimore two and Charleston one. There was also a theatre in Mobile and three in New Orleans, one of which was exclusively devoted to French drama and opera. In the political capitals of some of the Middle and Southern Commonwealths the drama had occasionally a fitful existence during the legislative sessions.

In the then almost unknown West, the embryo stage was dominated by Ludlow and Smith, and the Chapman Family floated down the placid stream of the Ohio and the turbid waters of the Mississippi in a temple of the muses erected upon a flat-boat, where the study of Shakespeare alternated with the perusal of Izaac Walton. And unremunerative acting was often supplemented by profitable fishing, bites at the hook in the water bringing in more plunder, as it was termed in western phrase, than bites at the bait in the box office.

I heard Mr. Cooper say in 1828 that he had played in sixty theatres in the Union, and certainly there was in the United States hardly a theatre in which Thomas A. Cooper had not played. I do not think that buildings devoted to the purposes of the drama could have exceeded sixty in number in the year 1825.

The managerial power was held in New York, at the "Park" by Price and Simpson, and by Gilbert at the "Bowery." In Boston, by Kilner and Finn, with James A. Dickson—the "power behind the throne." Warren and Wood controlled the theatres in Philadelphia and Baltimore; James H. Caldwell, magistrate and merchant, politician and player, wielded the managerial sceptre in the South, and Ludlow and Sol. Smith had the wide, wide West to themselves—a boundless kingdom all their own.

The starring system, so called, had been in vogue for many years, but the " stars " of that era far exceeded in magnitude and effulgence most of the blinking luminaries of to-day. Every theatre of any importance had its permanent dramatic corps, in which the local favorites were continued from season to season ; this was of mutual advantage to the manager and actor, and changes were infrequent. It was the day of established *stock companies* of *actors*, not of *traveling combinations* of *performers*. And the stars of that period carried around with them no *queues* of feeble satellites merely to give *cues*, for they were, in general, sure of efficient support. Relatively to the population and number of playgoers the recognized stars of the theatrical firmament were in number far less than to-day ; but they shone with their own light and not with the borrowed glimmer of many of those who now shoot through the theatrical sky. The stage was a profession, and men would not have been accepted as *stars* because they had failed in trade, didn't want to go to work, and had succeeded in borrowing enough money to start "on the road" with a " grand combination." Such " Stars " would have had to begin at the bottom — and would have ended where they began.

Theatrical advertising did not then run riot as now. Kean and Cooke and the Kembles and their compeers were announced to the public by three-sheet posters, not by three hundred square feet of printer's ink, with colored "picters-to-match," in all the hues of the rainbow, with their names emblazoned in type exceeding in magnitude, on every dead-wall in our cities, that which recounts the miraculous virtues of "Rough on Rats" or proclaims the triumphs of Sullivan the Slogger.

We go sometimes one night, perhaps, to see one of these foggy orbs, endure the evening's torture with what patience we can, and sadly wend our homeward way, recalling the child's couplet—

> "Twinkle, twinkle, little star,
> How we wonder what you are."

In my early days there were in the theatres of the North not more than five or six weekly performances. English comedy and farce were popular, and the standard tragedies, if well acted, were attractive. Musical comediettas were in favor, as was ballad-opera. What is in our day called English opera was almost unknown, and Italian opera had been *heard of* but never heard or seen. If there was no *American Drama*, there was what was called the *Yankee Drama*. The *Irish Drama* was just born, but the *Ethiopian Drama* had not yet seen the light.

With the play-goers of the time the brilliant and versatile Hodgkinson, the "Admirable Crichton" of his day, whose death was so sudden and so tragic, was a vivid remembrance. Mrs. Merry, afterwards Mrs. Warren, the Miss Brunton of the London stage, who, at the age of sixteen, flashed into view with a splendor that almost rivalled that of Siddons, had passed away but was not forgotten. The erratic Fennel, another of the magnates of the mimic world, had departed—as had Cooke, a mightier spirit still—never to return. John Howard Payne, the wonderful boy, whom the harshest criticism acknowledged an actor of remarkable power, was on a foreign shore; but there was a shining galaxy of luminaries before the American public: James Wallack, Senior, the first and "greatest of his tribe," made periodical visits to the States; Kean had made his first visit, and was then in the agony of his last, fighting at disadvantage with an angry public; Macready had been twice over the sea to our shores; Hamblin had began to shine, but with a lesser light; Cooper had a little passed the zenith of his fame; Conway's brilliant but fitful course was nearing its fatal close; Forrest's successful career had just begun; and Junius Brutus Booth—THE Booth—stood forth, in the opinion of men of wisest censure—the more than peer—the very foremost man of all.

There were not so many starring aspirants among the gentle sex half a century ago as now. Miss Lydia Kelly, a dashing actress, and a very handsome woman, was much before the public of the Atlantic cities. Mrs. J. Barnes and Mrs. Drake occasionally made starring tours; both of these ladies were tragediennes. Miss Kelly was a comedienne. Mrs. Sloman, was another tragic star of superior merit. Mrs. Knight starred in the lyric drama. But Miss Clara Fisher's popularity far exceeded that of any starring actress of the period. Wherever she appeared the public patronage was liberally bestowed.

The period of time between my leaving school at Bradford and entering the theatre, seems in memory to be surrounded with a halo of brightness which no after-time has equalled.

I was only a store boy, to be sure, but I lived in a realm of dreams, bright with anticipations of a great future, when I should cast my shell and be an actor. I read every play-book good and bad, that I could lay my hands upon, and obtained access to the theatre by any and every means in my power. When I could not raise the necessary *half-dollar* for the pit, I would patronize the gallery, if I had the necessary quarter; books of theatrical biography had more attraction than the day-book or ledger. My employer had no taste for the drama, and looked

with marked disapprobation on my growing fondness for the theatre. The store being kept open
during evening hours, it was difficult to see the
play in its entirety — but I could always see the
after-piece — and the enforced delay lessened the
expense, for it was an easy matter to obtain
the return-check of some retiring auditor. The
meagre salary of a lad of fifteen would not admit
of a large out-lay for polite amusements — but
the theatre got the half of my small income all
the time.

With what delight I used to sit in the pit of
the Old Federal St. Theatre, and *drink in,* so to
speak — Kilner, Finn, Dan Reed, John Mills
Brown, Mrs. Powell. Mrs. Pelby, and the other
" good ones " of those days, whose features, notwithstanding the sixty years 'that have whitened
my hair and dimmed my vision, seem familiar
as a thing of yesterday. I shall have something
more to say of these ladies and gentlemen, but
will here refer to but two of the company. Mrs.
Powell was the widow of Mr. Snelling Powell,
the first manager of the Boston Theatre ; in her
youth she had played with Mrs. Siddons, and as
a Shakespearean actress, was entitled to a high
rank. She was the original representative in
Boston of many characters which still hold a
position among the popular representations of
to-day, " Meg Merriles " is one of these. I was

not more startled, years after, by Miss Cushman's creation of " Meg," than by that of Mrs. Powell, but I was but a boy when I saw Mrs. Powell, and had been familiarized by long experience of the " trick of the scene," and personal acquaintance with Miss Cushman, it was perhaps the glamour of a first impression. Mrs. Powell was an exemplary mother, and stood in the highest social regard — her annual benefits often netted $1,000.

Mrs. Papanti was another member of the old Boston Company, and was one of my chief idols. She was a piquante and fascinating actress, and esteemed as of a higher order of merit as a vocalist than any predecessor for many years. I remember her first appearance as Rosalvini, in the opera of " The Devils Bridge." Her husband, Signor Papanti, was a member of the orchestra. He became subsequently a teacher of dancing, and for several seasons managed the celebrated Boston " Almacks," these famous assemblies were composed of the crême-de-crême of Boston society. The lady patronesses were as rigid in their rules of admission to the charmed circle as their London predecessors. Signor 'P. subsequently married a Boston lady of dazzling beauty, an aunt of the present wife of Mr. Laurence Barrett.

The Kean riot which occurred in the fall of 1825, is one of the vivid memories of my early

·days — it was the parallel in many respects of the Astor Place riot, which occurred many years later, but unlike that it was attended with no loss of life. Mr. Kean is one of the great actors of old, whom I can not boast of having seen act, for on that stormy night the *acting* was monopolized by his opponents. He appeared upon the stage in citizens private apparel, but met by the howling tempest of popular fury was driven with every species of opprobrium from the boards.

Another great remembrance of my stage-struck era, was the production of the romantic spectacle play, " Cherry and Fair Star." I could never, if I would, forget " Cherry and Fair Star." Perhaps not one of my readers ever saw " Cherry and Fair Star " — great their loss if they chanced to be boy or girl in their " teens " ! When the great gilded galley swept the circle of the stage on the billowy surface of that ocean of cotton cloth (it was to my charmed eyes an ocean of real water), whose waves beat higher and wilder than any I have since seen in the theatre. When " Sanguinbeck " (Sanguinbeck, does not the very name bespeak what kind of a man he was), when " Sanguinbeck " flourished his bloody dagger; when " Topac " ran after his enchanted snow-ball; when " Cherry " thridded the forest glade with hunters horn and boar spear, and woke the echoes for the charming " Fair Star."

Oh ! how I envied Mrs. Pelby and Mrs. Finn —
Messrs. Finn and Reed — the luxury of living
and being part and parcel of a world which I was
as yet, but permitted to look upon, but not to
enter.

The amphitheatre in " Washington Gardens,"
opposite the Mall, had been opened to the public
under the name of the " City Theatre," by Mr.
Cowell — familiarly known as Joe Cowell — (of
whom more anon) two years prior to the time of
which I now speak. In May, 1825, it was opened
under the management of Watkins Burroughs,
who was a melo-dramatic actor of rare abilities.
The representation of a rather turgid play, dram-
atized from Lord Byron's poem, " The Bride of
Abydos," was another of the well-remembered
milestones of my stage-struck days. The piece
was produced with great splendor, and when the
handsome Burroughs, playing " Selim " to the
" Zulicka " of Mrs. Robertson, a fascinating member of his corps, entered on the scene with that
lady, both superbly costumed, they seemed the
very beau-ideal of Oriental splendor. The gossip of the day was very busy with the names of
the lady and gentleman, which was probably not
lessened by the dashing four-in-hand drives in
which they indulged. When the young bloods
of the town saw the magnificent turnout, I do
not know but they envied the popular actor as

much for his good fortune off as on the boards. I know that for myself it made my stage mania all the stronger. I believe that Mrs. Robertson afterwards became the wife of Mr. Geo. Coppin, the well-known actor and manager of the Australian theatres, and prominent, also, in colonial politics. The " Selim" and " Zulicka" of my boyhood admiration have both gone to the far beyond.

Another of the remembrances of the long-ago, is Thomas Flynn. He was brought out from the Haymarket for the Federal St. Theatre, and announced as principal tragedian. Although a clever actor, he was never much of a tragedian. His career was a remarkable one, and his voyage of life grew very dark towards its close. Involved in continual managerial squabbles, he did not always adhere to the strict line of truth, and when under the *influence*, which was too often the case, would draw largely upon his imagination for his facts. He married a Miss Twibill, a lady of great personal beauty, who was, I think, a member of the Albany company. Tom always had a high opinion of his own merits, but a still higher one of his wife's—his " Tilly," as he always called her. A friend of his, who had lost sight of him for some months, chanced to meet him unexpectedly while travelling, in an apparently prosperous condition, clad in glossy black, with an air of contentment and sleek self-satis-

faction in his face. " Tom, old friend," said he,
" how glad I am to meet you ; you look finely.
What are you doing here ? playing, I suppose."
—" Playing," replied Tom, " no, thir,"— Tom
spoke with a slight lisp—" No, thir ; I've done
with playing. I play no more, thir."—" And
what are you doing, Tom ? "—" Doing, my boy ?
I'm delivering temperance lectures. I've hit my
right line of business, at last."—" And *how* are
you doing ?"—" Thsplendidly ; thsplendidly, my
boy. Come and hear me ; crowded houthes all
the time."—" And how is Mrs. Flynn ? Does
she lecture, too ?" — " Tilly ? Oh no! Tilly's
playing, and doing thsplendidly, too. Such an
im-mense favorite ; we're both of us *raking 'em
in*. All the old women in town are *stuck* after
me, and Tilly's got all the *young men* by the
hair." Poor Tom's a " cold " now ; he has been
dead many a year. Be his virtues remembered
—his frailties forgotten.

CHAPTER II.

MY fondness for the theatre, was, as I have
said, very distasteful to my employer, and
the relation of master and servant became unsatisfactory to both, not that I neglected the
honest performance of duty while *on* duty ; but he
knew that my heart was far away from my business, and rightly thought that a stage-struck boy
was not so likely to advance his interests behind
the counter or in the office as one who had a
real love of trade. The growing dissatisfaction
on both sides culminated in an abrupt manner,
which may be told in a few words ; there was a
lad, a townsman of mine, employed in the store
of a gentleman, with whom my principal had
intimate, personal and business relations, both
establishments were kept open in the evening.

2

I had been sent over to the store of Mr. T——
which was in that part of the city then known as
Cornhill or New Market St., with a message, and if
Mr. T——was absent, was told to await his return.
Mr. T—— *was* absent, and young Thompson,
who, as well as myself was stage-struck, although
in a lesser degree, suggested that it would be a
favorable time to rehearse.   It was just between
the daylight and dark of a summer evening, when
few customers were abroad, and I gladly seconded
his proposal.   The raised floor in the rear part
of the store made an admirable stage, and when
after a desperate conflict (with yardsticks), I had
been overthrown as Richard, and had got as far
in my dying speech as — " Now let the world no
longer be a stage, etc.," I chanced to glance
towards the front door of the store, and there in
a crowd of street-passers, who had stopped to
enjoy our amateur performance, I saw the angry
face of my employer, and his entrance stopped
the play and dropped the curtain ; within a week
I prudently " retired with a good grace " from a
position which in military phrase was no longer
" tenable."

The corner-stone of the Tremont Theatre was
laid on the 4th of July, 1827 ; as the handsome
granite front approached completion it was looked
upon by Bostonians of the day, with admiration
and pride, and I lingered around the building,

and wondered if I should ever be an actor beneath
its roof. Mr. Pelby had offered in the previous
May a premium of money or plate to the author
of the best poem for the opening night, and that
opening night was now approaching. I had
failed by epistolary efforts to get into the "Federal St." My letters to Mr. Kilner perhaps un-
read, or, if read, committed to the waste basket,
and I dared not venture a personal application,
for I had hung around the entrance to the theatre
in the Washington Gardens in vain effort to
interview Mr. Burroughs, until I had exhausted
the patience of the gate-keeper, who looked upon
me as a nuisance, but perhaps, with the new
theatre my opportunity had come, and I desperately resolved upon another trial; with a timid
hand I knocked at the door of the manager's
residence, which was opened by the servant,
"Was Mr. Pelby within?" "No! but Mrs.
Pelby was," and as he answered, that stately lady
approached from the hall, with a scrutinizing
glance which said as plainly as words could have
done — " I know your complaint, young man."
She politely informed me that Mr. Pelby could
be seen at a certain hour; and at that hour on
the day following I went to know my fate. Mr.
Pelby received me with courtesy, and talked to
me with candor. "His company was engaged."
Novices were ineligible, and no more actors were

wanted, but what was wanted was a call boy or prompter's assistant. Would I be willing to engage as call boy ? Willing — indeed I was willing ; in was removing the first obstacle in my path ; it was unbarring the stage-door; it was lifting the veil of the green-room ; *it was getting into the theatre.* The rest lay with myself—I should be an actor at last. I instantly answered, " yes ! " I was told to wait upon the manager on the following morning, and be ready for the opening within a week, and thus commenced my theatrical career — as call boy of the Tremont Theatre, on a salary of three dollars a week, fifty-nine years ago.

Mr. William Pelby was, I believe, a native of western New York. A difficulty between him and the managers of the old theatre, ended with his withdrawal. His friends rallied around him and proposed the building of a new theatre, to " see him righted." The quarrels of actors and managers, then as now, were often exaggerated into a fictitious importance. Mr. Pelby was an actor of judgment, had frequently played as a star, and had appeared once before a London audience in the interest of some public charity, for which he had been presented with a handsome gold medal. He was handicapped by very weak lungs, and sometimes his best tragic efforts were utterly marred by the failure of his voice. He was in latter years intimately associated with the Boston stage both as actor and manager.

The prize address delivered on the opening night was as O'Dedimus says, a "mysterious mystery" at the time, and has ever remained so; none of the pieces sent in were deemed by the Committee of Judges, to possess much poetical excellence; but the poem by "Theron" was thought to be the most worthy, and to *that* the prize was awarded. The sealed envelope accompanying the poem contained the name of "J. Jamieson, Hartford, Conn." From all quarters came the inquiry, who is J. Jamieson? Hartford was searched through and through, the postmaster, the clergyman, the undertakers even, were consulted as to the missing man, but no J. Jamieson was ever found. The topic was discussed for months, but, after the lapse of more than half a century, it is a matter of no consequence who he was or may have been. The prize money was paid to the Rev. John Pierrepont, who received it as the agent of the author. That eminent divine, who then, and afterwards, filled so large a space in the public eye as a writer and poet, was well-known to be a man of advanced liberal views, and there were many who thought that J. Jamieson was no other than John Pierrepont; indeed, the charge was publicly made, but Mr. Pierrepont never either admitted or denied the accusation, and to this day J. Jamieson of Hartford, remains the " great unknown."

I append a passage or two from this much-disputed address:

" Friends of the stage, the friends of virtue too,
The suppliant drama brings her cause to you.
Long has she borne reproach ; for, though her brow
Of old was luminous, and burns e'en now
With heaven's own fire, the intense and hallowed flame
That genius kindles round a deathless name,
We hear her still denounced as virtue's foe,
Still round her shrines is muttered many a woe,
Still, at her name the superstitious sigh
The grave look graver as she passes by,
The bigot's ban on all her priesthood falls
And pulpit thunders shake her temple walls.
    *   *   *   *   *   *   *
Oh, were the stage as pure as Dian's fane
When pearled with dew and washed with vernal rain ;
Let honest zealots call it Belial's throne ;
Let pulpits fulminate—let presses groan
Their woes and warnings—and what need they more
To *cause* the curse they piously deplore ? "

If Mr. Pierrepont was the author of those lines, and were now living, I have no reason to think that he would regret the transformation of the old Hollis St. Church, in which he officiated for many years, into a theatre, which change has been made within a twelve-month.

The curtain drew up on the opening night to a brilliant and crowded house, and from the rear of the stage, which represented a handsome palace, William Rufus Blake, in full dress, and enveloped in the ample folds of a rich black silk toga, advanced to the front and spoke the address.

Mr. Blake had been for some time before the public. He was a light comedian of great ability. He had a compact and shapely form, a face of manly beauty, and an irrepressive hilarity, which combined with a pleasant voice and graceful bearing made his acting peculiarly pleasing in genteel comedy—in serious parts he was not so effective; in his later years he was an admirable representative of the "old men" of the drama, and his performance of "Bonus," "Kit Cosey," "Lord Duberly," "Sir Peter Teazle," and the like characters, was far superior to his contemporaries. There was a ripeness, an unctuousness, so to speak, that captivated his auditors, and in the "old men," he exercised the same power, which in his youth had made his "Floriville," "Young Rapid" and "Charles Surface" the delight of theatre-goers.

In private Mr. Blake was a delightful companion. He was not especially noted for prudence in money matters; he loved life and loved to enjoy it, and loved to see others enjoy it. If he had been a millionaire he would have spent his income like a prince. When he could command money he spent it like a gentleman, and, truth to say, he sometimes spent it like a gentleman when he had none to spend (save in expectancy).

From the first he took a great fancy to me, and in after years would pleasantly recall the days when he first knew " Walter," in Boston. He was stage manager of the Walnut St. Theatre in Philadelphia some years later, when I was attached to the company, and it was his especial delight to have a Sunday dinner-party with the young actors around him, and I was always an invited guest. He was full of fun, and kept us all in a roar of merriment. " Why?" he asked on one occasion, " why do some of these newspaper fellows sometimes say that I'm not a good actor? Ask Charlotte."—This was said with a chuckle, referring to Charlotte Cushman, who had been his predecessor in the stage management, and with whom his relations had been almost belligerent—" She knows ; she'll say it's because I'm a Blue-nose." He was born in Halifax, N. S. "Ask Walter, here ; he'll tell you what they think in Boston. He'll tell you that there I was the *pet* of the ladies—the pride of the *Irish*tocracy and the idol of the *pox vopuli.*" And then came out that merry laugh, whose influence no one could resist.

Mr. Blake died some years since, in Boston. He was suddenly stricken down, I think, while playing " Sir Peter Teazle," and soon passed away. Looking back over the changeful memories of the past, among the pleasantest I find those of my first stage manager and old friend, William Rufus Blake.

The poem spoken, the curtain drew up for the play, which was Mrs. Inchbald's comedy of " Wives as they were, and Maids as they are." Blake played " Bronzley," in his sparkling champagne-y manner. Mr. Charles Webb was the " Sir Wm. Dorrillon " of the cast. Mr. Webb was an actor of great ability; he had graduated from the " Mortonians," a society of juvenile amateurs in Philadelphia, of which Edwin Forrest was a member. In the dignified gentlemen of Reynolds and other authors whose plays were popular in the early part of the century, he appeared to great advantage, and equally so in depicting the " Tyrants " of the stage, but he had one failing which, strange to say, hardly lessened his dignity. Though sometimes a tipsy gentleman, he was never a tipsy *boor*, and he was never tipsy excepting from the waist downwards. All his inebriety seemed to settle in his extremities. The alcoholic indulgence weakened his pedal props, but seemed to have little effect upon his brain. The pugilistic demon of drink always hit him "below the belt," and his blows were emphatically staggering ones. It is but justice to say that his periods of indiscretion were not of frequent occurrence or long duration, and, like many others, he bitterly lamented his want of self-control.

"Sir George Evelyn" was played by Mr. Reed. I wonder if there are any old Bostonians who remember "Dan Reed"—or, rather, I wonder if any who ever saw him can have forgotten him. I think that is impossible. Certainly those who saw him play "Gesler" to the "William Tell" of Macready, in 1826, will remember how he fairly shared the honors of the night with the "star." J. Mills Brown was the "Oliver." Mr. Brown was a low-comedian, of infinite humor; his style quaint in the extreme, and his appearance that of a well-fed parson. On his lugubrious face a smile was never or rarely seen, but he made others laugh. Mrs. Blake was the "Miss Dorrillon;" Mrs. Charles Young, a very beautiful woman, the "Lady Mary Raffle," and Mrs. Pelby the "Lady Priory" of the cast.

An especial feature of that night was the orchestral performance. The leader, Mr. Ostinelli, was a brilliant violinist, identified with musical matters and universally respected. He had been long a resident of the city, so long, indeed, that he was continually talking of a return to his Italian home, for which he always intended to start "next summer." But the Signor was a much better musician than financier, and "next summer" always found him too impecunious to start. He had married a Boston lady, and was the father of a pretty girl some ten years old.

This young Miss afterwards became the famous *prima donna*, Elisa Biscaccianti, of world-wide fame. If one could have forecast the horoscope of little Eliza Ostinelli sixty years ago, what a revelation it would have been. The heighth of prosperity—the depth of want. Crowds of flatterers at one time, at another neglect and desertion. Diamonds to-day—squalor and poverty to-morrow. Singing *now* in the brilliant opera house—anon in the wretched dive. At one time plodding her weary way homeward to a miserable domicile, endeavoring to forget plaudits that were *painful*, in the remembrance of what had greeted her ears in brighter days; and soon thereafter, again listening to the ringing " Bravos " of the crowded theatre, from which she is drawn to her hotel in a chariot by her worshippers, who have detached the horses and taken their place. Truly, life is but a kaleidescope, and varies with every turn.

Mr. Ostinelli had gathered an orchestral force of great merit. Among its members was Mr. James Kendall, who, with his brother, Edward Kendall, ranked high as instrumental musicians. Edward Kendall's playing on the key-bugle, an instrument which has been superseded by the cornet, was almost marvelous. Doubtless, many of my readers can recall Ned Kendall's performance of " Wood Up," on the key-bugle. It rings

in my ears now. Both the Kendalls could play
on almost any instrument. James began as a
drummer boy in the war of 1812. His orchestral instrument in the "Tremont" was the clar-
ionette, and I here remember an occurrence which
affords a fair example of his character. I have
spoken of Miss Lydia Kelly as one of the popular stars of that era. She was a handsome woman, with a brilliant style, and was almost the
only actress who affected high comedy exclusively. She sang well, and in "Lady Teazle," "Beatrice" and "Letitia Hardy" always introduced
songs. Her temper was somewhat hasty, and
her manner imperious. While rehearsing "Bid
me discourse," with the full orchestra one morning, the accompaniments seemed to be all wrong,
and the song was tried over again and again
without improvement. Miss Kelly blamed the
orchestra, and the leader blamed the copyist.
Miss Kelly singled out Kendall as the chief delinquent, and he, in the coolest and most gentle-
manly manner, assured her that he was playing
the score exactly as it was written, and handed
the notes over the footlights for her inspection.
Stamping her foot and losing all self-control,
Miss Kelly kicked out angrily at Kendall, and,
barely missing his head, struck the notes from
his hand with the act. There was for a moment
the silence of amazement when Kendall, address-

ing the leader said: " Mr. Ostinelli, the lady for-
gets herself. I think, on reflection, she will apol-
ogize for what she has done "—or words to that
effect; I do not remember the precise terms.
There was another momentary pause, when the
lady, extending her hand, said: " Mr. Kendall
is right; I was hasty; I ask his pardon." The
cloud was instantly dispelled. The song was
tried again and the orchestral parts were all
right.

Mr. Kendall was a man of rugged nature, yet
kindly feelings; of simple tastes, with a rough
exterior, but a warm and generous heart. He
knew not how to " crook the pregnant hinges of
the knee," but had the honesty to speak the
truth before God and man, and the courage and
manliness in its championship to look either
friend or foeman full in the eye. His early
youth was passed in a continual struggle with
obstacles which not one lad in a thousand would
have surmounted; but his mature manhood was
rewarded by the respect of his fellow-men and
professional brethren, who recognized in him an
upright citizen—a true artist—an honest man!
Death had no terrors for James Kendall. Had
the great destroyer hovered o'er his lingering
couch and delayed the winging of the shaft, or
had wearisome disease preceded the inevitable
end, he would have had the patience to wait and

the courage to endure; but Death came to him
as he comes to the warrior on the battle-field, and
struck him down in harness. He had been a
resident of San Francisco for many years, and
was attached to the orchestra of the California
Theatre at the time of his decease, which
occurred in the Spring of 1875. He went to
the theatre as usual for the performance of his
duties, entered the music room, divested himself
of his hat and coat, and saying " Good evening,
gentlemen," to his companions, wheeled about
and fell to the floor a corpse. He spent the
Christmas Day prior to his death in a social
manner with the family of the writer, for we
were old friends. Our after-dinner conversation
drifted to the subject of Spiritualism. He had
been reading much upon the subject; was inclined to doubt, inclined to believe, but resolved
to investigate. The possibility of our deceased
friends returning in spirit after death, seemed to
him a gracious and consolatory idea, and he said
to me: "Walter, old fellow, we are both old, and
know not how soon the summons may come;
but if the doctrine is true—it *may* be, I almost
think it *is*—if I am called first, and am permitted to come to you, I will come!" He never
came.

One of the members of the company was a
little beetle-browed gentleman, of short stature

and very sallow complexion, named Frithey; he was a capital actor of short parts, but a part of any length was beyond his depth. Mr. Hyatt, from the " Bowery Theatre," joined the company shortly after the opening as *first* low comedian, Mr. Frithey holding place as *second*. When Hyatt's benefit came off, the announcement of Shakespeare's Richard III, with Hyatt and Frithey as the heroes of the fifth act, drew a merry crowd. They fought on horseback, and Hyatt announced in his programme that he would make his final exit, after a desperate conflict with Richmond, by a peculiar and novel method never before seen upon the stage. I don't think it had been seen *before*, though the gag, as it is called, has often been seen *since*. Hyatt simply made his exit through the bowels of the basket horse on which he sat, and disappeared in the bowels of the earth beneath.

On another benefit occasion, Hyatt announced a grand balloon ascension from the stage to the dome, by a young lady, who would dispense a package of lottery tickets. I think he caught the idea from hearing me recount the misadventure of my feline equestrienne in the juvenile theatre, but he changed my heroine's name, and called his feline aeronaut Mlle. Scratchini Pussiano. Mademoiselle went *up* in good order as announced, but instead of scattering the lottery tickets, in her fright broke away from her bonds and tumbled out of the balloon into the pit.

Little Frithey was exceedingly absent-minded, very slow in movement, and had a kind of fatality of being always too late, or behind time. There was a system of forfeits or fines for delinquency or carelessness at that time in vogue— it is not altogether abandoned now.

Some of the articles of this code of fines and forfeitures were unjust, and some were ridiculous. The strict *letter* of this old traditionary, " behind-the-scenes" law was rarely enforced, for the good sense of the management recognized the impolicy of its enforcement; but it seemed to be poor Frithey's ill luck to be continually stumbling over every forbidden thing. He would doze in the green-room and be too late for the stage ; he would wake up from his nap—he was an awful sleepy man—rush out in a hurry and be too soon ; he would enter at the wrong entrance, or from the wrong side, and make his exit in the extreme rear of the stage, when he should go off in front — not from any desire to be indifferent or willfully wrong, but from a dreamy unconsciousness that he was not right. He had been warned and fined, and the fine remitted several times, until the manager's patience had become exhausted.

I was in the office on a "salary day," when Mr. Frithey came in to receive his weekly wages, and Mr. Pelby, in a tone of indifference, addressed him with " Mr. Frithey, you have no money to receive to-day, you have forfeited your whole salary and three dollars over, thirteen dollars in all. I'll take the ten to-day and the balance next week. The prompter's forfeit book here has got eleven ' stage-waits' marked against you." Frithey uttered no word of complaint or remonstrance, and walked out as slowly as he had entered. It is but justice to say that the manager did not keep the money, but neither the remittance of the fine, or the warning given, or the levying of subsequent fines had much effect on the little, sleepy, absent-minded comedian.

The office of prompter was filled by a tall Hibernian, Mr. Henry Doyne. He was engaged as an actor, but consented to officiate as prompter until the management could negotiate with another party for the position. He was not an amiable man, his features were somewhat unpleasant, his manner brusque almost to rudeness ; he was my immediate principal, and soon I began to learn that the realm in the rear of the curtain was not altogether a " land of tranquil delights."

I hardly dared at that time to press my suit as an aspirant either to Mr. Pelby or Mr. Blake ; but Doyne knowing my ambition, laughed at me,

3

I could plainly see that. "And so, my boy," he
would say, "you want to act; well, I'll fix it for
you, don't bother Mr. Blake; I'll get him to cast
you for a good part — leave it all to me." I
think that the two or three month's experience of
the theatre had not been without effect, for I felt
more of the man within me, and realized more
and more each day—the fact which only hard experience can teach a stage-struck youth—that of
all professions that of the stage is emphatically
one for work; that work I wanted to begin. So
when Doyne one morning told me, as I prepared
the prompter's table for rehearsal, to go into the
green-room and look into the cast-case. I ran
well pleased, as directed, and saw—yes, absolutely
saw my name in the handwriting of the stage
manager, in the cast of a play. Yes, there it
was, in the list of names appended to the list of
characters that make up the "dramatis personæ"
of Shakespeare's "Catherine and Petruchio," to
be sure it was at the very bottom of the list—Mr.
Pelby's was at the top—and opposite *Petruchio*—
mine at the tail end opposite what? — *Nicholas*.
Now, I had read the "Taming of the Shrew,"
and seen it acted, but I didn't remember any
"*Nicholas*." Doyne was on the watch, and met
me with a grin. "Well, my boy," said he, "I
told you I'd fix it for you, and I've done it."
"What is the character," said I. "Oh! a foine

one, get the book and study it up." "Is it long,"
I asked. "Not very," he replied with another
grin. "I don't remember any such part," said
I. "Oh!" said Doyne, grinning again; "you
havn't much to say," its principally *business;*
"wait until rehearsal," with a still broader grin,
"you'll see." Rehearsal was called for the next
morning; in the interim I had re-read the play,
but could find no "Nicholas." The rehearsal
progressed as far as the scene in which Petruchio
brings home his shrewish bride, and to outshrew
her, administers his first lesson by whipping and
beating his affrighted servants around the stage
when they come at his angry command to bring
in his dinner and take off his boots; while the
scared wife stands trembling at the violence of a
temper worse than her own. Doyne here shouted
out to the property man to "bring the wash-bowl
for Mr. Leman," and Mr. Leman found out that
the important character which Mr. Doyne had
persuaded Mr. Blake to cast him for, was one of
the mob of menials which Petruchio whips around
the stage — not a word to say, but to come on
when shouted for by the angry Petruchio — with
a basin full of water, tumble over his master's
legs, breaking the basin with a sprawl, and run
off with a howl to avoid the angry thwacks and
blows which fall impartially on all around.
Doyne was right, there wasn't much to say,

there wasn't anything to say—it was all *business*, and *howling*, any amount of *that* was in order. The howling was to be done by Nicholas and his fellow victims, and the more Mr. Pelby whipped, and the more Mr. Leman and the other fellows howled, the more the heartless wretches in the pit and gallery would be sure to howl and laugh. Mr. Doyne had certainly kept his word; my "first appearance" was assured.   I never said a word to my friends outside, anticipating their surprise when they should see my name in the *posters*, but it wasn't there.   I consoled myself with the belief that it would certainly be in the smaller bills—the programmes for the evening— and there it was, away down at the *bottom*, to be sure, but it was there — "Nicholas, Mr. Leman." I played that part, and believe I played it well. I entered with alacrity, tumbled over Pelby's legs with agility, smashed the wash-bowl into fragments, and made my exit amid the noisy merriment of boxes, gallery and pit.   I ought to have been satisfied, for if applause is any criterion, my debut was a success.

CHAPTER III.

AMONG the celebrities whom I first knew in
my new sphere of life, was a gentleman
who had every element, physical and intellectual,
to place him in the very highest niche of theatric
fame, Augustus A. Addams. In stature he excelled Forrest, and was not unlike him in manner
and method. He died young, otherwise I think
Mr. Forrest would have found in him a dangerous rival. I also met for the first time an
actor whose popularity in America was second
to that of no one who had preceded him; who
during a long career as actor and manager never
lost his hold on the public, or did aught to wound
the feelings of any, even the most humble, of his
own profession. The man whom Mr. Murdoch
justly, I think, calls the " first romantic actor of

America." In form and feature, it is not exaggeration to say, that he was "express and admirable;" and excellent as he was in a certain line of characters—"David Duvigne," in "The Hazard of the Die;" "Walter," in the "Children in the Wood;" "Mazzaroni," in the "Brigand," and the like—when the spectator saw him in "Coriolanus," or "Benedick," he recognized his just claim to rank as a Shakespearean actor, no less than as the representative of a drama, which his peculiar talent had made all his own. When a mere boy, he became the protégé of Richard Brinsley Sheridan, and was engaged at Drury Lane Theatre; and at eighteen he acted "Laertes" to Elliston's "Hamlet" and played seconds to Edmund Kean in the whole range of that gentleman's characters—an evidence of his marked ability at the early age of twenty-two years.

I think Mr. Wallack's first visit to America was in 1817 or '18. He had crossed the ocean some three or four times when I first met him, and subsequently his trips ran up into the twenties. I remember one night in the green-room his taking off an old sou'-wester, which he wore in the character of "Michael" in the "Adopted Child" (what old play-goer that ever saw James Wallack play "Michael" can ever forget it?) and telling us how much he prized

it because it was given him by an Old Salt with
whom he had sailed six times over the sea.

Mr. Wallack was certainly as well known to
the whole American theatre-going public sixty
years ago as Cooper himself, and was a more
general favorite. He invariably opened as
" Rolla " and " Dick Dashall." In 1852, he
became the manager of Wallack's Theatre, in
New York city. During the first half of my
theatrical career, Mr. Wallack played repeatedly
in different cities of the Union, where I had the
pleasure to play with him. It was always a
pleasure for a young actor to play with James
W. Wallack, for with him he was sure of kindness, courtesy, encouragement, good advice,
approbation, if merited. He did not deem it
necessary, like some of his contemporaries, to
emphasize his stage directions with language
proscribed in the decalogue, and was always
mindful of the actor's feelings, whether his
salary rated high or low. Mr. Wallack's versatility was remarkable ; his range of characters
equalling that of John Hodgkinson, so well
known in the earlier years of the present century. Indeed, from what I have read of that
brilliant actor, I think that Hodgkinson and
James Wallack, Senior, were not unlike.

An incident *apropos* of Mr. Wallack's " Rolla,"
during that engagement may be noted : The

lighting department of the theatre was under the superintendence of an old Scotchman named Miller (it was before the era of gas). Miller lived in the basement of the theatre and had two or three boys, the eldest of whom used to assist his father in the lamp-room while the youngest ran about among the oil and dirt. The family ran wild. There was no mother to guide and guard, and the father had little control. On the evening of which I speak, the representative of "Alonzo's Child" had been taken sick during the performance, and a substitute had to be procured for the last act, where the child is very important. What was to be done? The time was short, and a child *must* be had for the last scene. Miller's youngest was thought of, and from beneath the stage he was unwillingly brought up and a dress hurried upon him. This youngest of the Miller tribe was an ill-looking boy of about two and a half years. He was small, even for that age, but could talk quite plainly. Alonzo's child has been captured by Pizarro, who intends to hold him as a hostage for his father. Rolla pleads in vain for his release, which being refused, he seizes the child, desperately strikes down the weapons of the guard, and, with the exclamation, "Who dares to follow, dies!" rushes over the bridge which spans a mountain torrent, saving the child at the sacrifice of his own life.

Mr. Wallack rescued the boy and rushed upon the bridge. When in the center, with the child held high with one hand, while, sword in hand, he turned for a moment to defy his pursuers, and the house rang with plaudits for the exciting and heroic picture, suddenly and moodily from the squeaking lips of the cherub he held aloft, came forth—" D–d–d—n your eyes; don't you let me fall!" Mr. Wallack got over the bridge, some-how, restored the precocious and interesting babe to the arms of its mother, and the curtain fell. Mr. W. declared himself so shocked at the awful profanity of the two-year-old ruffian that he came near letting him fall, and was with difficulty able to finish the performance.

That eventful first year of my theatrical life has for another of its memories, one whose name was as familiar as " household words " through-out all the land. Thomas Apthorpe Cooper was for a time the most distinguished actor on the American stage. It used to be a point of pride with an American to swear by Tom Cooper, as in later years he swore by Ned Forrest; and, without doubt, Mr. Cooper, in his prime, was a man to swear by. One critic tells us that " his face was expressive at his will of the deepest ter-ror or the most exalted complacency—the direst revenge or the softest pity. His form in anger was that of a demon; his smile in affability that of an angel." This is the language of hyperbole; but Mr. Cooper did not always sip from the honeyed cup. Many, even of his admirers, acknowledged that, while he exceeded in personal requisites every actor that had hitherto appeared on the American boards; while his voice could not be surpassed in sweetness and flexibility; his figure in beauty of proportions; his action in ease and grace, or his countenance in tragic expression; yet, in the niceties of reading and embodying the great characters of Shakespeare, he was not equal to some of his contemporaries.

I was but a boy when I first saw Thomas Cooper, two years before the time of which I write. He was but fifty years of age then, being born in 1776. I don't pretend to think that I had any critical judgment, but to me he appeared a god. I saw Macready afterwards, while still but a boy; *he* did not shake Cooper's throne. I never saw Cooke or Kean the elder. I have seen scores of tragedians in two generations since I passed the limit of boyhood, and among them — with *one* exception, of whom I shall by and by speak—I do not think any one impressed me more than when I first saw him— did Mr. Cooper. But Mr. Cooper had lived very fast, *was* living fast, and when he "turned the hill he found that 'twas rapid going down." For thirty years he had been Fortune's favored child,

the very " foremost plume o' the van," but Fortune is fickle, and his star had begun to wane,
while Forrest's was climbing up the sky. He
had just returned from England, where he had
been damn'd at Drury Lane. It is a question
whether the verdict there pronounced was just.
An Englishman born, by adoption he was an
American; all of his triumphs had been won in
America, and they had not forgotten that he
coaxed Cooke away, and was a supposed enemy
of Edmund Kean. In the practice of his profession he had received large sums of money,
and had spent them with reckless prodigality.
Broadway could show no more beautiful turn-out
than his, and taste and fashion had courted his
society in the zenith of his popularity; but the
evil hour was coming—had come; his sceptre
was rapidly passing away.

My humble position in the theatre forbade anything like familiarity with the great man, but as
a subordinate I had to call him from his room
during the performance (he never deigned to enter the green-room) to attend at rehearsal, and
do many things that gave me opportunity for
close observation, and I could see that he was a
dissatisfied and disappointed man. Mr. Cooper
was never much noted for suavity of deportment
in his intercourse with professional associates—
rather the reverse—but I saw no display of that

top-lofty temper which always frightened a large number of those who played with Tom Cooper, for his methods of stage direction had been entirely different from those of Mr. Wallack. But at that time he was certainly a subdued man, for no actor suffered immolation at his hands. A volume might be filled with anecdotes of Mr. Cooper. In his hey-day his reckless waste of money was proverbial. He would gallop a maggot, or cut a card, or make any, the most absurd wager for almost any amount. Standing one day in Broadway with an acquaintance, he observed a load of hay coming up the street. "I'll bet you," said Cooper, "the receipts of my benefit to-night, against an equal amount, that I can pull the longest wisp of hay from this load."— "Done," said the gentleman. The straws were pulled and Cooper lost. He said, with great nonchalance, "I've lost two hours' work." The short wisp of hay cost him $1,100. He had a numerous and interesting family of children. When young he would never allow them to cry. His method of cure was to dash a glass of water in their face; astonishment would cause them to stop. If they began again he'd dash another, and continue the dose until they stopped finally. It was certainly a stringent adaptation of the cold-water cure. One morning, by the manager's order, I accompanied Mr. Cooper to his hotel for a parcel to be taken to the theatre. It was a rainy day, and as we walked down School street the intermittent showers recommenced with violence. I raised my umbrella over Mr. Cooper's head, but he pushed it aside with, " Put it away, young man; put it down, sir. I never carried one of those things; I don't want it." I did as directed, and being ashamed to hold the umbrella over my own head while his was unprotected, I closed it up and we walked side by side slowly down the street in a pouring rain. Everbody knew Mr. Cooper, and wondered why that young man didn't hold the umbrella over his head. Mr. Cooper died in 1849.

Another of the notable memories of my first year, was the appearance of the " French Dancers," Mons. Barbierre, Madame Hutin, and Mlle. Celeste. This trio were the first artistes of the French Ballet who appeared in Boston, and a doubt was entertained whether the pronounced style popular in Paris would be approved. They had made a triumphant success in New York, to be sure, but Boston claimed to be, if not more virtuous, more circumspect than New York, and would the Boston ladies go to see them—would they take the risk of being shocked? that was the question. The house was crowded on the first night, and among the audience there was not more than fifteen or twenty of the softer sex; but the question was answered entirely to the satisfaction of the manager, and during the balance of the engagement the auditorium was packed, and the boxes were almost monopolized by ladies.

Monsieur Barbierre afterwards became a teacher of dancing, and settled in Memphis, Tennessee; Madame Hutin faded from public view; but Celeste achieved fame. She abandoned the ballet and shortly after married Mr. Henry Elliot, a New York gentleman of extravagant tastes, who evinced great shrewdness in managing her professional affairs, and spent her money faster than she could earn it.

Mr. E. collected together a number of hybrid dramas, the names of two or three I remember— I think I played in all of them, "The Fall of Derna," the "Wizard Skiff," the "Spirit Bride," etc., and made Celeste the central figure in each. No man better knew how to pull the wires, before or behind the curtain, and by adroit generalship and Celeste's dash and undoubted talent she became perhaps the most profitable star of her day. With the "French Spy" alone, I heard her say, she had made $100,000, and this long before its attractiveness had ceased.

But no amount of income could stand the drain of the bon-vivant who would sit in the green-room and recall with self-gratulation the names of scores of gentlemen with each of whom he had drank, at the least, "a thousand bottles of champagne." The lady and gentleman parted, and Madame went to London, where she soon achieved eminence. Celeste's acting in the "Green Bushes," the "Flowers of the Forest," and the "Wept of the Wish-ton-Wish," was the pure poetry of pantomime. I had the pleasure of playing with Celeste during her last visit to America. She died some years since, the precise date is not remembered.

As a specimen of the "sharp commentary" which the critics of half a century ago could occasionally indulge in, I append a part of a newspaper notice of one of Celeste's performances. It is headed: "Humbug and its *Premonitory.*" "Get up, Billy, and Chalk the Rope." "*Premonitory* is the *Humbug's* Avant Courier; as Crows, Vultures and Ravens hover over an Army before a Battle, so is *Premonitory* the Inevitable Precursor of an '*Engagement.*'"

❋   ❋   ❋   ❋   ❋   ❋   ❋

"A roll of drums, a flourish of trumpets enter *Humbug*, attended by interpreters. It swings round to this wing, then to that, points to the ground, points to the skies, or where the skies are represented by the flies, stamps, cocks its head like a listening rooster, puts its hand to its mouth, stamps again, puts both hands to its head, puts both hands to its sides, and then stops, and so does the music, which, all along, you are to recollect, is *appropriate*. Then while it takes breath, one of the interpreters explains that it meant something, and, astonished at the ingenious translation of what no one ever guessed meant anything, applause follows to the echo, enthusiastically started by the heavy cane of the premonitory — the interpreters smother a laugh. The music strikes up, and the gymnastics begin again. What's the use of talking? Melpomene talks, Thalia talks, the learned pig can't talk, Dandy Jack can't talk, then what's the use of talking? Talking is nonsense, as is proved by what Humbug's interpreters said, *vive la bagatelle!* Twenty to one on a match against common sense and private purses, to come off any time between the rising of the curtain and the shutting off of the gas." That is what I believe newspaper men call a " first-rate notice."

My immediate principal, Paddy Doyne, as he was called in the theatre, was relieved of the duties of prompter, and Mr. Hardy, an assistant in the paint-room, had been installed as his successor. I had been observant, and was rapidly picking up a knowledge of stage business, and the details connected with the representation of the drama — indeed both Doyne and Hardy often gave me the prompt-book, and trusted me to

" run the stage " for an evening, and the manager and stage manager seemed pleased and satisfied — but I was not satisfied. I still wanted to
act, and pretty soon I had another chance, and
here, as before, Doyne took the initiative. He
was very fond of playing Dr. O'Toole, in the
farce of the "Irish Tutor," and one day, taking me
patronizingly apart, be began — " Walter, my
boy, I am going to ask Mr. Blake to cast my
farce,"—he always called it *his* farce, for he said
no living man knew how to play Dr. O'Toole excepting himself—"and by the powers I've a great
mind to give ye a foine part in it, d'ye moind
what it is ? have ye ever seen it played ? get
the book, it isn't like ' Nicholas,' ye've a dale to
say, my boy, its a foine part, its the ' Beadle.' " I
got the book, and, smothered my disgust at the
low estimate of my ability ; and when the evening
came I played the part ; as Doyne said, it was a
spaking part, but I hadn't much to *spake*, merely
to ring a hand-bell and bawl out in a snuffling
voice, " I'll dance with Miss Tabitha Jenkins."
No, it wasn't much, but it certainly was an
advance beyond " Nicholas," and in a different
department of the drama. It might be said that
my first appearance was as a pantomimist ; my
second as a comedian. Yes, on the whole, the
Beadle like *Nicholas* was a success. Towards
the close of the season some musical organization

4

with which Mr. Ostinelli was connected, wanted
to make a visit to Maine.   Mr. Ostinelli's dream
of a return to his sunny Italy was still but a
dream, for the lack of lucre was a chronic complaint with him.   I met him one morning, with,
" Ah ! good day, Mr. Ostinelli.   I suppose you
leave for Italy as soon as the theatre closes ? "
" Well, no, Walter," he genially replied—the
Signor was always genial—"I think no.   I have
been in doubt if I go to Italy this summer or go
to Bangor.   Well, I think I go to Bangor " —
and he went.

The spectacular romantic drama of " Undine "
was brought out with great expense, and early in
the season " Pizarro " was got up in very grand
style.   Neither of these proved attractive.   With
respect to the first named, it was a disastrous failure.   One of the wags of the press suggested
that instead of " Undine, or the Spirit of the
Waters," it should have been announced as " Un-
done, or Spirit and Water."   The scenery for
these two pieces was painted by Henry Isherwood.
Mr. I. was a fine scenic artist, with a craze for
acting.   Nothing could be much worse than his
acting ; anything better than his scene painting
was rarely seen.   The painter's gallery of a
theatre is a great field for practical jokes.   Mr.
Hardy, who succeeded Mr. Doyne as prompter,
was much annoyed at the change, and would

have preferred remaining in the paint-room, and the fellows in the paint-room took a wicked delight in plaguing him. Every day at rehearsal, if the manager was momentarily absent, down would come a shower of old paint brushes, lumps of whiting and pieces of glue, labeled, " Hardy, ex-member of the Royal Academy, Stage Manager;" "Hardy, Painter to His Majesty, Prompter;" " Hardy, President of Academy of Design, Ballet Master." The fun was going on, very lively one morning when Mr. Pelby, hearing the racket, came quickly on the stage just in time to receive upon the crown of his handsome new hat, an enormous brush reeking with yellow ochre. The fun stopped at once, and the forfeit-book was balanced on salary day.

In the following year the theatre passed from the control of Mr. Pelby into the hands of a syndicate of gentlemen, of whom the two most active were Messrs. Dana and Mitchell. Mr. Francis W. Dana was a gentleman held in high estimation ; he was, I believe, the father of the well-known author of " Before the Mast." I graduated at the close of my first season with *honorable mention*, having been entrusted on three or four occasions with small speaking parts, and had passed muster with the public in the " Biondello" of the play in which I achieved my first great success, as " Nicholas." Mr. Dana accepted me "on sight," with an advance of wages, and I was enrolled as an actor of "general utility," at a salary of $8.00 per week. Mr. Dana engaged a strong company, and to give *eclat* to the opening, announced as acting manager for the first two months, Mr. J. B. Booth.

I feel diffidence in touching on the career of the great actor of whom so much has been written, and of whom so many statements have been made and anecdotes recorded which really belong to the dramatic apocrypha. Not to write the life of Booth, not to recount the incidents of his remarkable career, but to jot down a few of the items impressed upon my memory by personal and professional association at various times during some twenty years, is my simple purpose.

Mr. Booth's first appearance in Boston was in 1822, six years previous. From that time he had been at each season a visitor, and each successive season added to his popularity. To the duties of stage manager he brought, in addition to his great experience and learning, the most complete attention to every matter of detail and an industry that knew no limit. He studied the interest and reputation of the institution to which he was attached as entirely as if he had been the owner or lessee, instead of its temporary two-months' stage manager. (Granted that there was no reason why he should not have done so, yet how few men of far less name and fame on the American stage would have recognized the obligation.) From the night of the opening, the inquiry was on all lips, " When does Booth appear ? how soon is Booth to act ? " And during all the time he was each day in attendance at rehearsal, each night from the first music-call until the curtain fell upon the farce— the faithful sentinel behind the scenes. He opened in Richard, as was his custom. It was to me THE event, thus far, of my new life.

Mr. Booth's absolute identification with the character he represented, I think, can never have been exceeded by any actor of any era or clime. I remember a little incident on that opening night, slight in itself, and yet strikingly illustrative on this point. As the flats drew for one of the scenes of the fifth act, just as Mr. Booth was making his exit, a stage hand was inadvertently caught off-guard and exposed for a moment to the view of the audience. As Booth came off the stage, he looked at the prompter, with the utterance of six or seven words; they were not uttered with a tone of indifference, they were not hissed forth, they were neither snarled nor shouted out—but the six words, " How came that man in Bosworth field ?" were spoken with a deep intensity, and, accompanied by the lightning glance of eyes that flashed defiance—pity—despair—revenge or love, with equal power, they impressed upon the listener the actuality and presence—not of Booth—but of Richard, King of England.

In illustration of Mr. Booth's willingness to subordinate his own unquestioned position to oblige or serve a friend or employer, I will mention two incidents. On one occasion, at Baltimore, when in the height of his fame, he played the "second actor" to the "Hamlet" of Mr. Charles Kean; at his delivery of the soliloquy of "Thoughts black," etc., the house rose *en masse* and cheered him to the echo. And in the same spirit, when Mr. Martin, the representative of the small part of Almagro, in the play of "Pizarro," failed to make his appearance at the theatre in time, Mr. Booth ran up to the wardrobe, got Mr. Martin's dress, and was ready for the insignificant character at ten minutes' notice. This latter event passed under my own observation. I think if the rising of the curtain had depended on such a sacrifice of dignity on the part of Thomas A. Cooper or Edwin Forrest, it would never have gone up.

And yet Booth lost no jot of dignity by the act. He was a striking exemplification and proof that *acting* is an independent art and not a mere combination of oratory with scenic display. He was a born actor. He had a classical education, learned printing, and studied law. He had been a midshipman in the British Navy, and was gifted with great literary ability. None of his family had part or interest in the theatrical profession, but from an innate love of acting he resolved to be an actor, and at seventeen years of age left his home, and, against the wishes of his father, engaged with a provincial manager.

The highest descriptive powers often fail in giving an adequate idea of the wonders of nature. We read of the beauty and majesty of Yosemite; of the sublimity and grandeur of Niagara; and yet how futile and vain has been the attempt of the most skillful word-painter to show us the one or the other. We never *see* Yosemite until we stand within the mighty valley; we never see Niagara until we stand before the awful cataract. In attempting to describe the work of a great actor we are confronted with another obstacle. We are describing what no longer exists—the work has passed away, the memory only remains. My old friend, Mr. Murdoch, speaking of Mr. Booth, says that " his great charm in acting was the result of his imaginative powers and the soul-stirring sensations which his impassioned vocal effects produced when he was glowing with the fervor of the tragic muse." And Mr. Thomas R. Gould tells us that " his voice transcended music — that it brought airs from heaven and blasts from hell—it was the earthquake voice of victory, or full of tears and heartbreak; no one of all the orators of Greece and Rome, nor any one who has been fashioned after them in modern times, has probably ever portrayed the beauty, truth and power of the human voice as they were displayed in his best efforts by Booth." The three great actors of the age were Cooke, Kean and Booth. The first had passed away before my time; the second I never saw but once, and then only for a few moments, when he humbly pleaded in vain for forgiveness of an indignant public. Booth I personally knew for more than twenty years. In some respects they appear to have been singularly alike; it is not probable that either of them had any organic insanity, but there was frequently little difference between the excesses of their imagination and the freaks of the madman. Intellectually, Booth was the greatest of the three; he had the advantage of a good education and was a hard student through life. He spoke six or eight languages, and at the French Theatre, in New Orleans, had successfully played in the tragedies of Racine. He had wonderful conversational powers, and was a theologian as well as an actor; to him all forms of religion and all temples of devotion were sacred. He worshipped at many shrines. In passing a church he would reverently bow his head, and he read and admired the Koran. In the synagogue he would converse with the Rabbis and learned doctors, and join their worship in the Hebrew tongue. He read the Talmud, and many Fathers of the Roman church recount pleasant hours spent with him in theological discourse, and claimed him as of their persuasion, by his knowledge of the mysteries of their faith; yet no religion was too humble, and of all the places of worship he frequented, "that which he most loved," says his daughter, "was a floating church, or Sailors' Bethel." Mr. Booth had a wonderful individuality; no other actor resembled him; in his great moments there was something awful in his passion. He impressed the beholder as something supernatural; as a being from another world. In his composition, linked to grace, gentleness, beauty and electric swiftness, there was a towering and tempestuous passion, a supernatural energy that re-inspired even the muse of Shakespeare. Mr. Booth had a numerous family; with his eldest son, Junius Booth, Jr., I was on terms of intimate acquaintanceship for many years; he died a few years since. Mr. Edwin Booth I know, but not so well. Another son, the unhappy hero of one of the saddest tragedies ever acted on the great world's stage, I never knew. His name can have no place in these "memories."

CHAPTER IV.

THE assistant stage manager was Mr. Alexander M. Wilson, and the prompter was Mr. Collingbourne, whose very long name was subsequently abbreviated into Colinborn—the actors made it shorter, and always called him Colly. Mr. C. was a very good actor from the London minor theatres; he was full of anecdotes of Mr. O. Smith and Paul Bedford, an admirable pantomimist, and could fight a successful broadsword combat to the music of the overture to "Lodoiska," with a weapon in each hand and one between his teeth, and slay with perfect ease six or eight assailants. In Celeste's engagements he was invaluable. The first " old man " of the company was Mr. Jones from the Park Theatre. Mr. J. was of a very passionate temperament, and when angry at anything, or with anybody, would get beyond the power of utterance, and with hands behind his back, fillip up his coat-tails and dance and whistle. This habit had inoculated his stage method, and in the passionate old man, when he got to his dance and his phew! phew! phew! he would bring down the house. I believe that it was under his management in the western country that Mr. Forrest acted before he became famous.

Mr. Edward N. Thayer was the " Bob Handy" of the opening night. At that period he was an elegant comedian, and the most perfect and finished representative of the fops and butterflies of the old school then on the stage. His performance of " My Lord Duke " in Garrick's " High Life Below Stairs," was inimitable, and in the whole range of light comedy he was perfectly at home. Mr. Thayer was a great favorite in Philadelphia, and died some years since in that city at an advanced age.

There was a Mr. Hallam in the company. I think this gentleman was a grandson or great-grandson of Mr. Lewis Hallam, who, in the year 1752, opened the doors of the theatre in Williamsburgh—the *then* capital of Virginia—for the performance of the first play acted on the American Stage. He seemed to me a sort of link connecting the Eighteenth with the Nineteenth Century.

Mr. Bla*i*ke—known as Ben Blaike, or Blaike with the *i*—I remember played the " Postillion " on the opening night; his entrance in the comedy just preceded that of his master, Bob Handy, and the audience, thinking it was " Bob," gave him a rousing reception—in fact, he stole most of Thayer's thunder; he never got so much applause afterwards as he did that night—by *mistake*. Mr. Ben Bla*i*ke was another combat fighter, and was always hunting for new " melo-drams," as he called them. He came into the green-room one morning with a package as big as a tea-box, and thrusting it upon Mrs. Duff with a request that she would take them home and read them, answered to her question of " What are they, Mr. Blaike ?"—" Eleven new melo-drams, with all the music !" Mrs. Duff suggested that he had better submit them first to the manager for perusal. I think they died unseen.

Away down in the programme of that first night was printed, " Peter—Mr. Scott." Like many men who have "achieved greatness," John R. Scott began at the very foot of the dramatic ladder, and by perseverance rose to its highest rounds. He was for many years a prime favorite in New York, under the management of the late Thomas S. Hamblin, and in England played "Sir Giles Overreach" and other tragic characters with success. I knew him long and well; and of all who ever knew John R. Scott, "none knew him but to love him."

I have now to recall a name that gleams out brightly through the lengthening shadows of the past. Mrs. Mary Duff had been long before the public, having made her first appearance in America sixteen years prior to the time of which I write, as "Juliet" to the "Romeo" of her husband. It was admitted that a more lovely Juliet had not been seen, but a lack of power and conception was too evident, and she gave but little promise of assuming a position that eventually placed her in the front rank as a tragedienne.

Mr. and Mrs. Duff were prime favorites, and she re-appeared at this time with undiminished power. Booth and Mrs. Duff made a combination of supreme excellence, such as I had never before seen and have never since looked upon. I especially remember their performance in Shiel's tragedy of the "*Apostate*"; it was a concentration of talent on which every surviving lover of the drama still dwells with many a lingering reminiscence of the bye-gone glories of histrionic excellence. Never can I forget that closing scene of the fourth act—the electric eyes of Booth, blazing with hellish malignity, his arms twined around the despairing "Florinda," whose lovely and expressive face, as well as the tones of a voice "made all of music," bespoke an agony beyond all power of description—the picture is burnt into my memory.   I quote a portion of the dialogue :

PESCARA.

Thou shalt see him
In maddening agony ; thou shalt behold him,
And vainly think thou couldst have saved him, too—

FLORINDA.

How ; save him !   Can I save him ?

PESCARA.

Be my wife !

FLORINDA.

Your wife !   Oh, no ; it is too horrible.

PESCARA.

I'll hunt for life, in every trembling limb
And chase it down ! the driving steel shall plunge—
Nay, do not stop your ears—for his shrill screams
Shall pierce the solid deafness of the tomb !

FLORINDA.

They're in my brain already !   Oh, Hemeya,
Let me not hear thy cries—let—let me fly
And 'scape from it.   Oh, for some depth of Earth
Where I may plunge, to hear that scream no more.
Unhand me ! let me fly !—'tis in my heart—
My eyes—my brain—

PESCARA.

Look there! look there! he dies! see where he dies!
The wheel goes round—see, the red froth of blood!
His hair stands up and drips with agony.
On thee, on thee he calls, and bids thee save him.
Look there!

FLORINDA.

Spare—spare him! Villains—murderers!
Oh, spare him!
Hemeya! lo, they wrench his heart away!
They drink his gushing blood!—oh, God! oh, God!

When Florinda fell into Pescara's arms—the tension of a shuddering silence that had absorbed the audience burst into a roar like Niagara. Mrs. Duff played in a piece called the "Bohemian Mother," in which her remarkable power over an audience made itself felt by the utterance of one *shriek;* I forget the plot of the play, but I believe the interest of the spectator was led up to the point where the wretched mother thinks that she has taken the life of her illegitimate child. That one shriek was of itself a drama, and touched the human heart like the "*Was he alive?*" of Mrs. Siddons, or the "*Do it! nor leave the task to me*" of Fanny Kemble. Mrs. Duff's sister was the first wife of the poet Moore, and there is a tradition that his song commencing, "Mary, I believe thee true," was addressed to Mrs. Duff.

What pleasant "memory" is this that comes up from the long ago? It is that of my friend, my contemporary, my manager; a good actor, a successful dramatist, an eminent physician—Mr. J. S. Jones, better known as Dr. J. S. Jones. Mr. Jones began at the very bottom of the profession, and for the first eight or ten years we were on terms of the closest intimacy. He was a prolific author, and some of his dramas still hold possession of the stage. From the commencement of his theatrical life, the study of surgery had quite as much attraction for him as the study of the drama, and at the close of his managerial career he became an eminent physician and surgeon of Boston, his native city.

I shall have further occasion to speak of Doctor Jones, but am tempted here to refer to a circumstance causing the Doctor and myself a profound chagrin at the time and ridiculously laughable. We neither of us possessed any skill worth speaking of as swordsmen, but, like most young actors of those days, were well pleased to be cast for a part which called for a *combat.* There was considerable emulation between us as to which could "fight a combat" the best, and our knuckles were often sore from the trials between us to test the point. At length some now forgotten melo-drama was played in which we were pitted against each other. I was a smuggler and he a soldier. Anxious to acquit ourselves well, we arranged a long and telling fight, and rehearsed it over and over again; it was not to be an indiscriminate melee—a mixed-up scrimmage—oh, no; we had both of us been often in *that* kind of a stage fight; but this was another thing; we were to have the stage all to ourselves, for the first time—and lo! the issue! From over anxiety, and want of self-possession which grew into absolute fright, during the whole of that "desperate combat" our weapons never once came in contact. Jones would make a thrust at one part of my anatomy, which I would defend by guarding another. In our vain efforts to deal the effective blows which we had practiced so long, my sword would miss his, and run round after it, describing a circle, in a fruit-less effort to "catch up"—and then his gleaming blade would come at mine in the same ridiculous fashion. When I struck at his head, he would guard his legs—and I adopted the same tac-tics; the more we missed the more anxious we were to hit, and the less able to do so. Jones was inclined to laugh when our mishaps began (he was of an easy turn of temper), but when the contemptuous laughter of the audience was blended with a sibilant sound he looked graver—and I never felt more serious in my life. We slashed away, mixing *premes* and

5

flemishes and *double-flemishes* in the air, the
audience meantime convulsed with mirth, and
the orchestra enjoying the fun, Ostinelli sitting
up high on the leader's chair and laughing till
the tears ran from his eyes. An inglorious
retreat terminated the fray in which we had
succeeded in hitting each other often enough.
Jones came out of the fight with a swelling on
his forehead as big as a walnut, and my wrist
got a slash that prevented the use of my hand
for a week.

Ashamed of the ridiculous exhibition we had
made, we both resolved to avoid *future* failure,
and went into training with *Colly*, and subsequently with Mr. W. H. Smith, who was an
admirable master-of-fence, and fought no more
combats in the air.

I am reminded here of another stage combat
of a remarkable character, at a later period, when
I was a member of the "National" company.
The melo-drama of the "Secret Mine" was produced, and an equestrian company had been
engaged to assist in the representation. I played
the leader of a band of Spahis, or soldiers, or
something of the kind, and the opening of the
scene discovered us "*en bivouac*" awaiting the
foe; our opponents—the mounted men of the
circus—were to charge on us through the pos-
tern, and after a "desperate combat of horse and

foot," as the play-bills had it, were to be driven from the stage. The whole arrangement seemed smooth at rehearsal—but at night it was a failure. The stage had been strewed with saw-dust and tan, and all the lights being turned off, was excessively dark. On rushed the cavalry with a loud blare of trumpets, and each man arose to the encounter. I singled out the leader and "went for him." The stage was exceedingly crowded, and what with the semi-obscurity of the scene and my own near-sightedness I mistook the horse for the man, and hit him a staggering blow on the head. My opponent was on guard, and puzzled at my action, reined his horse back; I was equally puzzled, and still thinking the horse was the man, said to him *soto-voce:* "What's the matter—have you forgotten the fight? Don't you remember? it's head blows and then two 'eights'"—and suiting the action to the word I hit him another lick. The horse gave a snort of protest against this unprovoked assault, and the indignant circus-rider put the spurs to his sides, and nearly galloped over me in his angry exit. That was the first and only time I ever fought a combat with a horse.

Thomas Archer was an actor who combined all the requirements for eminence; but they were, unfortunately, blighted and withered by want of self-control. With a grand physique and a voice remarkably powerful and sonorous, he had received a stage-training that fitted him to meet all the requirements of "*leading man*" in a first-class theatre, and for the short time he was before the public, was a prime favorite; but the demon of indulgence wrecked the fair fame and name of the poor actor. He lost position—reputation—everything—and ended his career in the lowest theatre in the lowest slums of London.

The opening address of the second season of the Tremont Theatre was written by the accomplished poetess Mrs. Ware, and spoken by Mr. Archer.

On Mr. Booth's retirement from the stage management Mr. Cowell succeeded him. "Old Joe Cowell," so called to distinguish him from his son, young Joe, who succeeded so well in imitating his father's manner and voice, especially in the character of "Crack" in the "Turnpike Gate"—one of Mr. Cowell's specialties—that the one might well be taken for the other. I remember Mr. Cowell's affability, and the interest he felt in my professional progress with much pleasure; and it was a pleasant reminder of the old days to receive from his grand-daughter, the accomplished Miss Sydney Cowell, nearly sixty years after, her portrait, backed with the legend,

"'To my dear grandfather's old friend, Walter Leman."

A theatre had been built in Salem, Massachusetts, and a detachment of the Boston Company was occasionally sent down for an evening's performance. It was before the era of railroads, and the transit was made in Concord coaches over the old Newburyport turnpike. These excursions were a pleasant change to the actors, and everybody liked to "go down to Salem" for a night. The progress of a company of actors in those days was rather a novelty—there were no "combinations" sloshing around as now; and, whether true or not, it was reported that the old women who lived on the road, when they saw the "Tremont" company approaching, used to call out in great trepidation: "Sally, take in the clothes—the actors are coming!"

I remember a strange alarm that was started on that Salem road on one occasion, though not by the actors. The robbery of Major John Bray by a noted highwayman named Mike Martin, caused great excitement throughout New England sixty years ago. Martin had been guilty of numerous crimes, and was said to be leagued with another notorious outlaw, under the cognomen of "Captain Thunderbolt"—Martin himself being known as "Captain Lightfoot." A dime novel kind of pamphlet had been published recounting the exploits of these knights of the road, and all the wonder-mongers were talking about Captain Thunderbolt and Captain Lightfoot. We had gone down to act in Salem that evening with Mr. Booth, when at dusk a horseman, in great alarm, rode up to the hotel and reported that he had been waylaid by a highwayman, some two miles out of town, who presented a shot-gun and demanded "money or blood"—that he escaped by the speed of his horse, and heard the robber's missiles whistle by his ears in his flight. It was "unanimously resolved" that the daring robber could be no other than "Michael Martin," and in hot haste a posse of ten or fifteen bold spirits started out on horseback (followed by the man who escaped) to scour the country and catch the miscreant. As they approached the scene of the alleged crime, in the semi-obscurity of a misty moonlight night, the man who ran away cried out: "There he is—there he is! Look out, he's got his gun leveled—he's going to shoot—look out!" But the leader of the posse dashed up to the spot, regardless of the warning, and, instead of "Mike Martin," found—a roadside *pump!* and for his gun, the wooden handle sticking out at an angle of forty-five degrees.

I remember another circumstance on that occasion, trivial in itself, yet tending to illustrate the many-sidedness of Mr. Booth's character. Two young men of the company got engaged in a friendly impromptu sparring bout, after rehearsal, and we all became (the ladies of the company included) interested spectators. Mr. Booth looked on pleasantly for a while, and when the bout ended, put himself in position, illustrating in *action* and by intelligent comment the art of self-defence.

Another Salem incident I recall to memory, in which "Cora's child" again comes to the front. The little one had got the toothache, and to appease its crying, the mother gave it sugar-plums. (Sugar-plums for the toothache!) Of course, this made the matter worse, and just as Wilson, the "Rolla" of the night, was about to appeal to Pizarro's magnanimity with—

> " And wilt thou harm that child ?
> By Heaven, 'tis smiling in thy face"—

a loud howl convinced him that an alteration of the text was necessary, and, equal to the emergency, he asked—

> "And wilt thou harm that child ?
> By Heaven, 'tis *blubbering* in thy face."

That little girl was afterwards Mrs. Anne Sefton, and later Mrs. James Wallack, Jr.

As Salem *has the floor*, I will add one more trifle. Henry Horn and Mrs. Austin, the famous vocalists, had played a grand engagement in Boston, and were sent to Salem for one night. The play was "Guy Mannering." Horn was disgusted at the meagre house which greeted him, and when as the great "Moonshee" he was hailed by "Dominie Sampson" with "Saalam alaikum!" Horn threw an angry glance around the empty benches, and replied with emphasis, "Salem—I *don't* like 'em!"

Mr. John Gilbert was my contemporary in the early days of which I write. I think he made his first appearance in 1828, playing "Jaffier" in "Venice Preserved," and subsequently "Sir Edward Mortimer." His efforts in tragedy were applauded. In the course of his career I believe he has played almost everything; but he is noted more particularly for excellence in the delineation of *old men*. Mr. Gilbert has been long attached to Wallack's Theatre, where he is a great favorite. The mention of Mr. Gilbert's name reminds me of the fact that of all the members of the stock company attached to the Tremont Theatre in 1828–9, he and myself are the only survivors; and of the stars who appeared during the season only Clara Fisher (Mrs. Maeder) and Miss Lane (Mrs. John Drew) are living. Of all who saw the curtain rise on the opening night of the previous year, excepting myself, not one survives; the rest—managers, actors, musicians—have all been borne to the bosom of our common mother.

> "If it be now, 'tis not to come; if it be not to come, it will be now; if it be not now, yet it will come; the readiness is all."

It was during this season that I was brought into professional intercourse with Miss Clara Fisher. Her first engagement at the "Tremont" was a remarkable success; indeed, wherever she appeared she created a furore. She played male characters with spirit; her singing was fascinating, and she acted her songs while she sang them. With what archness of manner, with what buoyancy of spirits, with what taste in costume, did she capture the young men (the old boys of to-day) who thronged to see her sixty years ago. The mere mention of her name will resuscitate in the breast of every surviving Old-boy reminiscences of her versatility and ability.

In the succeeding Summer I was playing under the management of Mr. George Barrett, at Providence, Rhode Island, where Miss Fisher appeared for a few nights; and afterwards at Newport. I recall the pleasant sails down Narraganset Bay, the merry company on the steamer's deck, and Clara Fisher in the centre, engaged in *Cutting up the Ox*. With what roars of laughter we used to play that game. I dare swear that she remembers it. Miss Fisher became afterwards Mrs. J. G. Maeder, and has reached a venerable age, respected by all.

Miss Louisa Lane, who was announced as an "infant prodigy," I first knew at the time of which I write. Fifty years afterwards I played in San Francisco with the accomplished actress, Mrs. John Drew, once the little girl known as Louisa Lane.

Mr. and Mrs. George Barrett! Pleasant "memories" come back to me as I recall those names. For years I played with both. "Gentleman George," as he was called, made his *entree* on the stage of the old Boston Theatre, as the *child* in Reynold's comedy of "Laugh when you Can," in 1799. He was a general favorite. Mrs. George Barrett was for years more than a favorite—she was the petted idol of the Boston public; of rare excellence in her art, it would be hard to say what she played best, she played everything so well. She possessed great personal beauty, which the touch of time seemed powerless to mar, and when I last acted with her, as late as 1853, she was as lovely in form and feature as when I first saw her thirty years before. Like Cleopatra, it was as if—

> "Age could not wither her,
> Or custom stale her infinite variety."

She died some years later, and retained her rare beauty and grace to the last.

Another " memory" of one gone to the " far realm," like most of those I knew in those days, and with him his companion—both my friends and associates for years.

William Henry Sedley was a Welshman by birth. On adopting the stage as his profession, the name of *Smith* was added, and he was always known as W. H. Smith. His wife was Miss Sarah Lapsley Riddle; her sister, Miss Eliza Riddle, with whom, many years later I acted in the South, was, I think, the mother of the well-known writer—Miss Kate Field. The pair became great favorites with the public; Mr. Smith as leading man at the " Tremont," and afterwards at the " Warren Theatre; " the handsome and dashing " Harry Smith," and his pretty wife as a soubrette and ingenué. She was a very petite figure, and at her first appearance caused great merriment—when, as " Albina," in the " Will," she had to say to her father—" Here, stand behind me, I'll hide you from their sight." Mr. Webb, who played " Mandeville," was a man of large stature and proportions ; it was like a frog hiding an ox. After the lapse of nearly half a century, I met Mr. Smith on the Pacific Coast as stage manager of the California Theatre, in San Francisco, and occasionally varying his duties by the performance of some comedy old man.

Edwin Forrest ranks among the notably great " memories " of the time. I met him first within

a year after I had come in contact with Cooper.
He was the very antipode of Cooper in his deportment and bearing at that period of his life.
Any one who was civil could speak familiarly to
Forrest; it took a bold man to speak familiarly
to Cooper; but there was a wonderful change in
Forrest with the progress of time. He was looked
upon as the great American star—the noblest
representative of our national drama. He had
struggled bravely through all the obstacles that
impeded his early career, and was recognized as
the legitimate successor of Cooper. Mr. Forrest's
decease is of so recent a date, and the details of
his public and private life are so well known
through the exhaustive " Life," compiled by Mr.
James Rees—as also through Mr. J. E. Murdoch's
interesting work, " The Stage," as well as through
the judicial reports of the unhappy litigation that
embittered his days and transformed the once
rough but *pleasant* gentleman into a moody, dis-
contented man—that I have but little to say that
has the merit of being novel respecting him. I
played with Mr. Forrest at various times, and in
various places, during the earlier portion of my
theatrical career, oftentimes as his second, and
found no difficulty (as indeed did no one who was
attentive to his or her duties,) in acting with him.
He was a man who most certainly had strong
likes and dislikes, but up to the time when the

skeleton of suspicion intruded upon his hearth-
stone, he was popular with the members of his
profession.   I met him for the last time professionally—prior to my removal to the Pacific
Coast—at the Walnut St. Theatre, in Philadelphia, in 1847.   After the lapse of seventeen
years, I met him again in San Francisco, and lo,
the change ; the man was transformed ; whether
from ill health, or the fatigue of the voyage, or
chronic brooding on the unhappy termination or
rather the unhappy continuation of his domestic
suit-at-law, or from all these causes combined, he
succeeded in making every one in the theatre as
miserable as himself, and utterly failed to interest
or attract the public.   In Mr. Rees' " Life of
Forrest "—a work of 524 pages—Forrest's tour to
California is dismissed with *two lines.*   I had the
pleasure of meeting Mr. Forrest again, two years
after, at the Boston Theatre, and candor com-
pels me to say that Mr. Hamblin's prediction
made to Mr. J. E. Murdoch, with respect to
Forrest many years previous, seemed to be literally fulfilled.   Mr. Hamblin used the words :
" Forrest is not now conscious of it, but he will
yet realize the fact that constant growling at
people will cause him in time to growl at himself.   He is building around himself, as I may
say, a wall which every year is increasing in
height, so that after awhile no one will be able to

get a peep at him, and he will then feel, when it is too late, that he has shut the world out, and cut himself off from all social intercourse, save with the petting and the petted few to whom he extends an ' Open Sesame ' to his varying moods of bitterness and mirth."

I think the saddest commentary on Mr. Forrest's unhappy temperament is afforded by the practical failure of his life-dream, the " Forrest Home for Actors." Procrastination and the affixing of conditions quite inconsistent with the habits and feelings of those who were to be prospectively its inmates, have so hampered and circumscribed the charity, that a poor dozen or less of superanuated artists are maintained by the bounty that was meant to be unlimited. But whatever may be said of Edwin Forrest as a man, it may not be denied that as an actor he was among the foremost that our time has seen. As Spartacus and Coriolanus, as Lear and Othello, as Virginius and Richelieu, he will be remembered by the thousands who glory in his triumphs and uphold his fame.

I draw once more the curtain of the years and discover—whom ? A son of Momus, who, like many another of his profession, originally labored under the mistake that he was intended for a tragedian.

Henry James Finn was a native of Cape Breton. He was brought when a child to New York, and when about twenty years old, enlisted as an assistant to the property man of the Park Theatre, and thought himself amply paid for his services, if permitted to appear on the stage to say " the carriage waits," or in some other minor capacity. He had been lawyer, painter, schoolmaster, editor, and eventually melo-dramatic tragedian of the Surrey Theatre. Those who saw him in " Lord Ogleby," " Monsieur Jacques," " Dr. Pangloss," " Bob Logic," " Beau Shatterly " and " Mawworm," could hardly associate the son of Momus with " Marc Anthony," and " Iago," and " Pythias," which he played as second to Cooper. I well remember the first night of Macready's engagement, when he was the " Icilius " to the great man's " Virginius," and played the part well (that was a notable night. Dan Reed, of whom I have already spoken, played " Dentatus ; " the Hon. Daniel Webster entered the box attended by a crowd of prominent gentlemen, and was received with repeated cheers. I remember, too, the marked applause which Mr. Webster gave to Reed's " Dentatus "), but this is a digression. Mr. Finn was for several seasons a member of the "Tremont" Company. He was a desirable guest on all festive occasions, and kept the table in a roar, but his features ordinarily

were sober and sedate. He met with a tragic
death, being a passenger on board the steamer
" Lexington," destroyed by fire on Long Island
Sound, on the night of the 13th of January, 1840.

CHAPTER V.

MISS ROCK was an actress of distinguished
ability. She came out from England with
Mr. Finn for the Federal St. Theatre, and returned after a sojourn of some two years, playing as a star at the "Tremont," and subsequently, I believe, in New York. She appeared to
great advantage in genteel comedy, was a fine
singer, and performer on the harp. On the production of the "Tempest," she was the "Ariel"
of the cast.

6

That revival of the " Tempest " calls up another name, familiar as household words, that of Mr. Comer.   *Tom* Comer, as everbody called him, was engaged by Mr. Dana as Musical Director, and for many long years was a great favorite of the public.   The management, I remember, was in great doubt respecting a proper " Caliban " for the " Tempest," when Mr. Comer suggested Mr. Colingbourne.   The selection vindicated his judgment.   In his performance of " Caliban," our little friend Colly proved himself a Shakespearian actor, although he had graduated from the " Cobourg Theatre," where Shakespeare was not very often seen.

Madame Feron, the famous *prima donna*, I knew at this time.   She played a brilliant engagement, opening in the " Barber of Seville." When quite a child she sang in London when the famous Catalani was queen of the opera, and was jocularly called the little cat, to distinguish her from the great singer who had the refined appellation of the great one.   Madame Feron had sang in all the European capitals, and was acknowledged a great vocalist.   She was a very elegant woman, somewhat inclined to *enbonpoint*, and of great simplicity and affability of manner. In speaking, one day, of the grandeur of the lyric stage in Italy, she told me that she once played at " La Scala," in Milan, in an opera in which was a grand processional pageant, with *seventy horses* on the stage.

At this time, also, commenced my acquaintanceship with another famous comedian, who, like so many more, would persist in thinking he was a tragedian, James H. Hackett. He made his first appearance in conjunction with Mr. J. Barnes, in the "Comedy of Errors." The men were no more alike than Messrs. Robson and Crane, with whom the public of to-day are familiar, in the representation of the "Two Dromios." But Hackett's imitation of Barnes' manner, and, above all, of his remarkable voice, made the illusion even more complete than in the case of the latter gentlemen. The representation crowded the house for many nights. Mr. Hackett always claimed to be, and certainly thought that he was, a tragedian; the public never recognized his claim. I remember well, when at a subsequent period he played "Richard the Third," he was heartily laughed at. But he was an admirable imitator of the heroes of tragedy, and Kean, Cooke and others lived again in his imitations. His performance of "Falstaff" was noted, and his fame as a representative of the peculiarities of the Yankee character was wide-spread. Mr. Hackett was an esteemed gentleman, and during life filled a large space in the public eye.

I was re-engaged as a member of the company for the following season, having reached the position of "Walking Gentleman." Mr. Wilson was Mr. Dana's representative, and Mr. W. H. Smith was the stage manager.

In February Mr. Forrest produced his prize tragedy of "Metamora." John Augustus Stone, the author of "Metamora," was a man of singular temperament. He had made some attempts at play-writing previous to the production of the remarkable drama that certainly made a great deal of money for Mr. Forrest, if it did not enhance his fame. The play underwent much manipulation at the hand of the tragedian before its representation, and his wonderful and powerful acting carried the piece through. Mr. Forrest was very tender on the topic of "Metamora," and very ready to resent any depreciation of Mr. Stone's ability as a dramatist; but, without doubt, his estimate of the piece coincided with the opinion of the intelligent portion of the public. Mr. Stone was an actor, as well as a play-wright. I subsequently acted with him in two or three "Yankee" plays, or plays in which the "Yankee" was the prominent part. He committed suicide by drowning some years later—I forget the exact date—when partially insane.

Another bright "memory" of my old days, is the production of the opera of "Masaniello"—

mainly because it brings with it the name of *William Barrymore.* This gentleman was the son of the original representative of "Pizarro," at Drury Lane, and his whole life had been identified with the theatre. He was a most admirable stage director, and his wife, Mrs. Barrymore, was undoubtedly the finest pantomimist and most graceful dancer that had been seen—in that style of dancing which is attractive from *grace* alone. Her performance of "Fenella," the dumb girl, was one of the most beautiful and touching appeals to the sympathy of an audience ever seen within a theatre. Mrs. B.'s dumb show made you *feel* what she said, and, unlike many who gesticulate to music, she needed no interpreter.

Musically, the production of Masaniello was a great event—Mrs. Austin and Miss Hughes were in it, and the hero of the piece was John Sinclair, another of my great memories of the past. Mr. S. was a Scotsman, and had been a soldier; his voice was of wonderful sweetness and power, and it was not unusual for the audience to recall him for six or eight repetitions of his popular ballads; but Mr. Sinclair was an abject slave to his beautiful voice; he couldn't take a walk, he couldn't dine out, he couldn't attend an evening party for fear of that exquisitely tuned organ being disarranged. Poor Mrs. Sinclair used to attend him assiduously every night, bobbing from wing to wing with a box of lozenges or troches or a bottle of physic, or a tumbler of something or other to keep that treacherous servant up to concert-pitch; and sometimes she received anything but thanks, for Sinclair was a very nervous and irritable man.

I remember a most absurd occurrence during the representation of " Midas ; " Mr. S. was the " Apollo," and " Jupiter " was acted by Mr. Rice. This gentleman had a powerful voice, a pronounced manner, an excellent set of teeth, and a habit of accompanying any energetic action with the ejaculation—" whiz ! " The business of the scene requires Jupiter to banish Apollo, with an accompanying flash of his thunderboldt ; at the proper time, Rice with an emphatic " whiz ! " although it was not set down in his part, launched his flaming bolt at Sinclair, unfortunately the pepper-box cover of the tin cylinder came off with the act, and the whole charge of powdered rosin was spread over Sinclair's white satin tunic; the picture was an impressive one ; poor Sinclair standing aghast, ejaculated, " God Almighty ! " which was not set down in *his* part—and holding out the skirts of his ruined dress with the forefinger and thumb of each hand, gave an appealing glance to the audience, as much as to say—see what a pickle I'm in ; and Rice, who seemed to enjoy the joke, stood defiant and triumphant, shaking the empty thunderboldt—his form dilated, his head erect, and his handsome teeth grinning from ear to ear.

Mr. Kilner—Old Tom Kilner, joined the company during the season. I think that there are many living yet in Boston who *remember* this grand *Old Man* for cheeriness of manner, for rich and unctuous humor, for a laugh of such joviality that it admitted no parallel, Kilner must ever be remembered by those who knew him. I think that William Rufus Blake was more like Kilner than any actor, but Mr. Blake was hardly his equal. Kilner's acting in the passionate and hearty old men was delightful; his " Captain Copp " and " Col. Hardy," in Poole's comedy of " Paul Pry," and characters of the like nature, left nothing to be desired.

There was some changes in the company the next season—Mr. Russell represented Mr. Dana, and Mr. George Barrett became stage manager. In November an engagement was made with Mr. Charles Kean, and that gentleman, then but little more than twenty years of age, made his first appearance as Richard III, and met with an enthusiastic welcome. He was noted for a *peculiarity* in his manner of delivery, and a certain holding back, as it were, of his powers, for especial passages of his author—which told those who had played with the elder Kean, that the boy had the trick of the father. It would be

superfluous to dwell on the career of Charles
Kean, it is well known. I saw him after the
lapse of more than a third of a century, on the
Pacific Coast. He was delighted to meet the
" boy " that he had known in Boston so many
years before. Among my " memories " of this
period, I recall the opening of a theatre in what
was then known as Flagg Alley, near the " Bite
Hotel," the names do not suggest a high-toned
locality, but there was some high-toned acting by
two dwarfs, respectively thirty-nine and twenty-
five years old, and thirty-six and thirty-two inches in height; that is not a very great tragedy
altitude, but I have known full grown actors,
indeed, there are some before the public now,
whose dramatic measurement in popular opinion
does not exceed thirty-six inches, and yet in
their own eyes they are giants.

About this time, I became acquainted with one
of the most remarkable exemplars of precocious
dramatic talent known to the history of the stage,
Master Joseph Burke, who was known as the
" Irish Roscius." This wonderful boy created
a furore second only to that produced by the famous Master Betty, a quarter of a century before.
During his engagement the fashionable and literary world of the city crowded the theatre, and
the other social gatherings, appropriate to the
gay season, were quite neglected. Unlike his

predecessor, Master Betty, Master Burke did not
confine his juvenile efforts to " tragedy " alone.
His varied repertoire included " Shylock," " Dr.
Pangloss," " Sir Abel Handy," " Richard III,"
" Terry O'Rourke," " Dennis Brulgruddery,"
" Hamlet," " Dr. Ollapod," " Romeo," and " Young
Norval," and several farces in which he played
dual parts. The list bespeaks the versatility of
his talents. The rush for seats was so great that
the management resorted to the auction process
in their disposal. I remember the young gentleman's *debut*—his acting of " Young Norval,"
and the professional a-plomb with which he tap-
ped his violin in front of the stage, and led the
orchestra in the overture to " Guy Mannering."
As a remarkable lad, Master Burke lives in the
memory of those who saw him, but, like Master
Betty, as he grew to manhood he graduated to
forgetfulness ; remarkable precocious talent is
rarely prognostic of *after* success. Master Betty
drifted to obscurity when he ceased to be a boy,
and within a short time Master Burke played to
empty benches. If I may be allowed to express
the opinion of one, only twenty years of age, and
unfitted at that time to speak as a critic, I should
say that Master Burke's comic personations were
far better than his efforts in tragedy, and that of
his serious parts, " Young Norval " and " Romeo "
were the best. Great social attention was paid

to him, and if he was the artist in the theatre, he was the boy out of it, and coasted his sled on the common with a boy's zest.

An anecdote is told of Dr. Burke, his father, which illustrates the character of the plain-spoken Irishman. During his professional tour, Master Burke was fulfilling an engagement in a city which chanced to be visited at the same time by a clergyman who had a great reputation as a revivalist. This gentleman was noted for his " Boanerges " voice, and his habit of introducing into his exhortations and prayers, tropes and similes and metaphors quite inconsistent with the gravity of his subject. The popularity of the boy operated to the disadvantage of the preacher, and the attendance at his meetings was correspondingly decreased. Dr. Burke, impelled by curiosity, attended the revival service one evening, and found the reverend gentleman " laboring " in great excitement, with a not over-crowded congregation. The service combined alternately exhortation and prayer, with vocal music, and when the reverend speaker arose to pray, the greater portion of his invocation was in behalf of " Master Burke." " Oh, Lord !" he shouted; oh, Lord! have pity on this poor little baby sinner; oh, Lord! send down into his little heart Thy grace with the power of a shower of fifty-sixes." (" Fifty-sixes " were the standard weights for weighing heavy merchandise in the old-fashioned beam-scales of that day.) "Oh, Lord! prod his poor little soul with the sharp ox-goad of repentance! Oh, Lord! cinch his little soul tight with the cinch of salvation, and take the cinch-buckle up two holes more! Oh, Lord! shake his little soul over h—l, *but don't let him fall in !*"

These extraordinary adjurations moved the risibles of a portion of the congregation, but the Doctor, recognizing the sacredness of the place, preserved a becoming gravity until the preacher, wiping the great beads of perspiration from his face and sliding his coat-sleeves half-way up to his elbows, started in on his exhortation, moved, apparently, not by the spirit of mercy, but of wrath; descending to personality in his comments on the character and motives of the father of the boy, declaring him to be an extravagant old voluptuary, living on the wages of sin, because he was too vicious to lead a sober life, and too idle and lazy to work. The Doctor kept his temper under this unbecoming personal attack, and on the following morning waited on the preacher, and informing him who he was, and that he had been present at his meeting on the evening previous, added, that while he recognized and admitted the reverend gentleman's right to pray for his son, although he questioned

the efficacy of his method, he positively protested against being made the mark of public pulpit
slander himself, and assured the gentleman that
a repetition of the attack would be met by personal chastisement; to which the other replied,
with an air of sanctimonious humility—" I am
but a weak vessel, and if it be the Lord's will to
send me to the bottom, down I go; but while I
float I will fight Satan, and in the cause of the
Lord, I should look upon a horse-whipping as a
crown of glory."—" Would you ?" replied the
Doctor; "I shall attend your meeting to-night,
and, by the powers! if last night's programme is
repeated, while you are coming out of the church
you'd better prepare for the coronation! " The
programme was not repeated.

Mr. T. D. Rice, known to the world as " Jim
Crow Rice," first appeared in Boston, in 1832,
at the " Warren Theatre;" his prototype in the
famous song and dance, which led the way to
fame and fortune, was an old slave employed as an
hostler in a stable in Memphis or Nashville, and
Rice's imitation of this old darkey, known to all
the citizens, was an instantaneous success. The
peculiarity of the song, so utterly unlike anything that had preceded it, caught the public
fancy in every town in the Union, and brought
forth a host of imitators, North and South.

Prior to Mr. Rice's advent, our dusky "man and brother" had small representation in the acted drama. In tragedy "Zanga" and "Othello," were almost alone, and these were Moors and not negroes. In the comic drama I can recall only "Mungo" in the "Padlock;" "Sambo," in one of Reynold's comedies, the name of which is forgotten, and two or three more; but Rice's success started the burnt-cork drama into a fitful existence which is even now hardly closed. Most of the professors of the new negro drama, drifted into minstrelsy; but few of them possessed a tithe of Rice's talent; they were minstrels, not actors; he was an actor, and a rare good one; his playing in some of the ethiopianized farces of the day was the very quintessence of humor, and in some musical pieces written for him, notably in a grandiose burlesque of the opera of "Fra Diavolo," entitled "Bone-squash Diavolo," his bravura singing of "Smile my fortune," and the largamente style in which he rendered—"Oh, I'm sorry that I sold myself to de debil," were superb. Mr. Rice visited England, and was a great success in London. He married a Miss Gladstone, a member of the theatrical family of that name, but not herself attached to the stage.

I played many times with Mr. Rice in my early Boston days. He was a genial, well-informed gentleman, with a most affable temper, which made him a charming companion. His generosity and liberality were not conducive to the accumulation of great wealth. His latter days were clouded with ill health, and fortune did not smile upon him towards life's close ; but he was ever and always a *man*, a true man, and his memory is fragrant with those who knew him in life, for the true gentleman he was.

The evening of November 3, 1831, is remembered by me as being the first appearance of a gentleman whose advent, it was feared, would be attended with serious riots. Mr. Anderson, the vocalist, and his lady, formerly Miss Bartolozzi, who played "Henry Bertram" and "Julia Mannering," in "Guy Mannering." Mr. Anderson had been guilty of some indiscreet expressions with respect to America and Americans. There were two parties in the house, but the friends of Anderson were in the majority, and things went on in a chaotic manner until the piece was nearly over, when the malcontents were re-inforced by the crowd which burst in from the street. "Fire ! Fire !" shouted the mob, as some of them leaped the orchestra railing, and Signor Ostinelli and his fellow musicians made a precipitate retreat. It looked very serious for a time, and poor Anderson was frightened out of his wits. We squeezed him out of the green-room window, between the wall and a massive stationary lattice, which could not be removed, on to a shed, and he retreated to his hotel; some of the rioters were arrested. Anderson appeared subsequently for one or two nights, but was treated with public neglect.

Frederick S. Hill—old Bostonians remember him—was a Boston boy, newspaper man, actor, newspaper man again, literateur, critic, and essayist, and for many years writer and manager for Mr. Pelby, of the Warren Theatre. He is one of my memories of 1832. He made his *debut* as "Romeo."

A pretty, new theatre had been erected in the city of Portland, Maine, and in the summer of 1831 it was opened by Mr. Alexander M. Wilson. I was a member of his company; Mr. Archer was the leading man, and became, as in Boston, a great favorite. Mr. Forrest was engaged, and opened as "Damon," and as Mr. Wilson, the manager, desired to play "Pythias," Mr. Archer was persuaded to take the subordinate part of "Dionysius." Up to this time, Mr. A. had been able to keep his demon under control, with one or two slight lapses, but, alas! on that fatal first night of Forrest, he had yielded to the tempter, and came to the theatre utterly demoralized. In the important senate-scene which occurs early in the play, when called upon to assume regal power, he staggered to the chair, sat oscillating upon it, and blundered out an incoherent mass of non-sense instead of the text of the author, and final-ly, instead of advancing down the stage with soldierly mien and addressing Forrest, as he should have done, with—

> " We now,
> Assuming our own right,
> Command from this, that *was* the senate house,
> Those rash, tumultuous men, who still would tempt
> The city's peace with wild vociferation
> And vain contentious rivalry !   Begone !"

he reeled down to where Forrest stood, fell on his knees before him, and with stammering, un-certain utterance, said: "Oh, Damon, go off! We don't want you here—get out of this Senate House—do go off—go away—go away!" Forrest looked at him with an expression that cannot be described, but uttered not a word.   Knowing Mr. Forrest as we did, it was a matter of wonder among the actors that he did not burst into one of his explosions of wrath.   Archer staggered up the stage, and " Philistius " and the rest got through the remainder of the scene as best they could.   I do not think that Mr. Forrest ever for-gave him.   In a professional life of more than half a century, that was one of the most pitiable scenes I ever witnessed on the stage.

But that was not the only mishap that Mr. Forrest met with in that short engagement.   It was the last night but one, and the prize tragedy

of " Metamora " was announced for the first and
only time. There was a band of Penobscot Indians on a basket-making tour encamped in the
outskirts of the city, and it occurred to Mr. Wilson that the appearance of these red men in an
Indian play would be an additional attraction,
and he proposed the matter to Mr. Forrest.
Forrest looked on it with disfavor, remarking
that such untrained help generally marred the
performance instead of improving it, but he
finally gave a reluctant consent to the scheme ;
and so it was announced that the management
had at great expense engaged a band of Penobscot warriors to assist in the performance, and
that they would appear as attendants on Metamora, and dance in their native costume the war
dance of their tribe.

Indian nomenclature is always a puzzle, but
the names of those red men were more than
usually puzzling ; they were all printed in the
play-bill in type as large as Forrest's ; I can
recall but two of them, "Jo Sawkikks" and "Saul
Ninepence." The night came, and the house
was crammed. They had been told what to do
at rehearsal, but seemed to have but a vague
idea of what little was expected of them apart
from the war-dance ; the only response to everything said being either silence or "Ugh !" In
the fourth act, after being addressed by Meta-

7·

mora in a long war-harangue, they were to circle round the stage, with their weapons brandished, (while Metamora stood in the centre,) and go finally off, leaving him alone.

When the scene was reached at night, before Mr. Forrest had uttered three lines, they started their war-dance in earnest, breaking in on his speech with a most unearthly yell, and circling round the stage with a series of antics ten times more violent than in their morning practice, absolutely refusing to go off. They had been especially told not to touch Mr. Forrest, but whether they disregarded the order wilfully, or whether in the excitement the latent savage had become aroused within them, I do not know. They went for the great chief, tomahawk in hand, going through the scalping movement and brandishing their weapons before his face, and pulling him about in the most indiscriminate manner. Forrest shook them off with fury, and shouted, " Go off!" but they paid no attention, and started into another mad dance; Forrest yelled louder, "Go off!" but still they kept it up, yelling louder and dancing wilder than ever. In vain Forrest shouted "Go off!" in vain the prompter bawled "Come off!" in vain he endeavored to signal them to get up the stage, until Forrest in wrath howled out in a tone loud enough to be heard above the din, " Drop the curtain!" and the curtain came down with a *thud*, nearly crushing two of the red men and leaving half their number outside.

When the curtain touched the stage, Forrest eaten up with anger, shouted to the prompter, " Where's that *other* Indian ?   Where's Wilson ? Send him here !"

Mr. Wilson was of a spare, muscular frame, with an exceedingly swarthy complexion, and his face might warrant the supposition that there was a strain of Indian blood in his veins. Wilson came upon the stage—he had been engaged with the prompter in the vain effort to get rid of his recruits, and was in an ill-temper himself. "So, Wilson !" said Forrest; "a pretty show you've made of my play, by God ! I told you how 'twould be, but you were full of your d——d *Jo. Sawmills* and *Paul Tuppences !* You had better close this theatre, and go off on the war-path with your tribe, and take Archer along with you !" And so saying, he strode off to his dressing-room. It was evident that he had not forgiven poor Archer. As he openly avowed himself, Mr. Forrest was indeed " *a good hater.*"

Mr. and Mrs. J. Barnes came to Portland for a few nights. Old Jack Barnes used to say that he traveled as an antidote to his wife; that she always set the people to crying, while it was his business to send them home with a laugh, and certainly he never failed to do that. I believe that Mr. and Mrs. J. Barnes were a very happy couple, but they didn't always pull *exactly* together in the matrimonial team. What married couples do? One morning, old Jack came to the theatre with a cloud on his brow, and was met by Mr. Wilson with, "Hello Jack, good morning! How are you? How's your wife? Ain't she coming to rehearsal?" "I don't know," moodily replied Barnes. "Don't know; havn't you seen her this morning?" "Yes," said Barnes. "And didn't she tell you?" queried Wilson. "No," growled Jack. "We're hostile— we don't *speak*, we *correspond*." This answer given with the peculiar tone, and ludicrous expression of the mouth, the corner of which Barnes would draw down till the opening in his face resembled a pothook, created general laughter; in the midst of which Mrs. Barnes came upon the stage, and smilingly approached her husband; the cloud on his face vanished at once, and he met her in the same cordial manner. Every one could see that Jack and his wife were not *hostile*.

Mr. Alexander M. Wilson, of whom I have frequently spoken, was a good actor. He played tragedy with judgment, and was an admirable personator of Frenchmen. He was the "Jean Jacques Frisac" of the spectacle of "Paris and

London," which had a phenomenal run for those days; and his performance of " Mons. Morbleau," was praised by those who had seen Matthews in the character. I never met Mr. Wilson after the close of that pleasant summer season, fifty-five years ago.

Among my remembrances of the following year, the production of the " Brigand," is foremost. The performance of the hero, " Allesandro Massaroni," by Mr. Wallack, was a superb illustration of the romantic drama, his singing of " Love's Ritornella " popularized the air; and it was played on every piano, and whistled by every boy in the city. Another great event was the appearance of the world-famous " Ravel Family," the hero of the organization was " Gabriel." For a third of a century he was almost continuously before the public, and in all the mysteries and wonders of French pantomime he was a perfect master of his art. He had no " rival in his day," and I think no superior in ours.

I call up another pleasant " memory " of one whose name is familiar in every quarter of the globe where the English language is spoken— the author of " Home, Sweet Home." In the month of April, a complimentary testimonial was tendered to John Howard Payne, who had just returned to the city of his early triumphs after an absence of twenty years. How freshly come back to me the events of that pleasant night, the address of welcome, from the pen of Park Benjamin, spoken by Mrs. Barrett, closing with these lines—

" A change of scene—the nearest and the last,
We need no spirit to reveal the past ;
For, lo ! 'tis present, and before you now,
The warrior-child with sword and plumed brow.
The student, bending o'er the written page ;
The actor, proudly marching on the stage ;
The author, bringing forms to life and light,
Which here reflected you may see to-night,
At length has come—Heaven grant no more to roam—
To his own native land, his ' Home, Sweet Home.' "

The performance consisted entirely of selections from the various plays of which Mr. Payne was the author. At the close of the address, the orchestra struck up " Home, Sweet Home," and amid loud cheering Mr. Payne came forward, almost powerless to speak ; but he rallied, and made a most graceful and feeling speech.

CHAPTER VI.

THAT season made me acquainted with two actors, whose names are stamped ineffaceably on the pages of Stage history on both sides of the Atlantic—Charles Kemble and his accomplished daughter.

Mr. Kemble opened in " Hamlet," and on the following night Miss Frances Anne Kemble appeared as " Bianca" in Milman's tragedy of " Fazio." Mr. Kemble did not much startle the public with his " Hamlet" or " Beverly," but when they saw him in " Mercutio" and " Benedick," " Don Felix" and " Young Mirabel," their admiration was unbounded. He was at that time more than sixty years of age, but his high-comedy personations were infused with such a perfect finish and airy grace that all acknowledged his excellence. He had the rare judgment of knowing exactly where to stop in the most highly-colored scenes, and never crossed the line of demarcation between the delicate and the gross. This was evinced especially in his playing of the tipsy scene of "Don Felix" in the comedy of the "Wonder," where he has hurriedly to assume female attire; he kept the audience in wild mirth, and yet there was nothing in his fine management of the *almost dangerous* scene to call up the shadow of a blush on the most modest cheek. The same may be said of his "Young Mirabel" in the "Inconstant."

Miss Fanny Kemble flashed into popular favor at once, and appeared in many of the roles which were made famous by her aunt, Mrs. Siddons. The engagement was brilliant, almost beyond example. "All the world," to use a popular phrase, came from far and near to see the "Kembles." Mr. Kemble's deportment in the theatre was exceedingly courteous, and conversation used to flow freely and pleasantly in the green-room. The subject of politics came under discussion one day, and in speaking of an election which had just been decided, he laughingly remarked:

" And now, Mr. Leman, as you've just decided this thing, you'll go to work within six months to *un*-decide it again. What's the reason that in America you are never willing to let things remain *fixed*, as you call it? Just as soon as you get them *fixed* all right you begin to make a change, and do it all over again. Why are you never satisfied?" To which I replied: " I think, Mr. Kemble, that on the whole, our people are *satisfied*—satisfied in the conviction, that if *dis*-satisfied it is within their power to abate the dissatisfaction." He paused thoughtfully for a moment, and then said, " Well, I don't know, perhaps they are right."

I remember at another time the just indignation he expressed at the attack of a certain Lieutenant Randolph (I think that was the name) on the person of President Jackson — the circumstance chanced to be alluded to as we stood behind the scenes—and Mr. K. vehemently exclaimed, " The scoundrel! If I had been present when he offered such an indignity to that noble old man I would have brained him."

During the engagement of the Kembles, a young native of Boston—who, ten years later, met with a painful death, at the early age of thirty-three years—came prominently before the public. Charles H. Eaton was my personal friend and a man of brilliant promise. During his short career he achieved a wonderful reputation in the highest walks of tragedy, and had he lived would have won a permanent place in the temple of histrionic fame.

About this date a little theatre had been erected in Lowell, and Mr. Barrett was invited to open it for a short season. There had been considerable opposition among the townspeople, and an application for a license to play was refused by the authorities; it was an awkward dilemma— the house was ready, the company engaged, the play advertised, and under a guarantee of some prominent gentlemen of the town, to see him financially unscathed, Mr. Barrett resolved to raise the curtain.

There was no interruption of the performance, as was feared; but the next day George Barrett and George Andrews were summoned to appear before Justice ———, and answer to the charge of high crimes and misdemeanors, in acting without a license, at the Justice's Court in the town and county aforesaid. When the case was called, the little room was crowded, for the people had taken sides, and much feeling was being evinced. The defendant's counsel moved an adjournment to a more convenient and larger room, which the magistrate granted, against the wish of the prosecution; and the afternoon session of the Court was held in the Town Hall. By this time the whole town knew what was going on, and the hall was full of spectators.

The first witness called by the prosecution was "Mr. Frank Kenny." Kenny was a middle-aged man with thin legs, a somewhat protuberant abdomen, a rubicund nose and very bright eyes. He was an actor of "little business," as it was termed, and being a fine penman, improved his moderate salary by copying for the theatre. He had imperturbable good humor, and was much addicted to singing snatches of doggerel songs—the chorus of one, which appeared to be his favorite, running something in this wise—

" Shoul, shoul! shoul, go-rool!
Cut straw—banyan! Jump Jim Crow," etc., etc.

On taking the witness stand, the first question by the prosecuting attorney was—" Mr. Kenny, were you in the theatre on the night of the day mentioned in the complaint?" *Kenny*—" I was, sir." *Attorney*—" Where was you standing?" *Kenny*—" I wasn't standing anywhere, I was sitting down." *Attorney*—" Where?" *Kenny*—" In the U. E. O. P." *Attorney*—" What does the U. E. O. P. mean?" *Kenny*—" Upper entrance, opposite prompt." *Attorney*—" Opposite what?" *Kenny*—" Opposite the P. S." *Attorney*—" Oh then, P. S. means, I suppose—" *Kenny*—" Sometimes L. H. and sometimes R. H"

Attorney—" And those initials mean, I suppose, right hand and left hand." *Kenny*—" Yes." " And which side were you on, Mr. Kenny ? " asked the counsel. " I was on the right hand side," replied Kenny. " Oh then," said the attorney, " the right hand side is always the prompt side." " No, it ain't," answered Kenny ; " sometimes the left hand is the prompt side." " Well, well," retorted the attorney, becoming nettled, " either the left hand side or the right hand side is always the prompt side; ain't it ? " " No, it ain't, " said Kenny. " In the French theatre in New Orleans, they've cut a hole in the stage, and prompt from the middle."

The counsel, much annoyed, appealed to the Court ; the Court didn't seem to think that the witness was in contempt, but told him to confine himself to simple answers, and the examination proceeded. *Counsel*—" Did you see Mr. Barrett on the stage on the night in question ? " *Kenny*— " I did not." *Counsel*—" Did you see Mr. Andrews ?" *Kenny*—" I saw a man that *might* have been Mr. Andrews." *Counsel*—" Might have been ? Did you see his face ? " *Kenny*— " He was looking the other way." *Counsel*— " Well, was he like him in person ? was he of the size of Mr. Andrews ? What is Mr. Andrews' size ? " *Kenny*—" He's of different sizes." *Counsel*—" Different sizes ? " *Kenny*—" Yes ;

when he plays ' Falstaff,' he's fat ; when he plays ' Goliah Spiderlimb,' he's lean." *Counsel— very angry—*" Come, come, Mr. Witness, don't prevaricate ; you have already testified that you saw a man who looked like Mr. Andrews in the play that night." *Kenny—*" No, I didn't ;" you didn't ask me *that* question, it was *before* the play ; I went away before the play began." *Counsel—*" Oh, you went away to avoid giving testimony in this case, I suppose ? " *Kenny—* " No, I didn't ; I went home to practice my song." *Counsel—*" Your song, what song ? " *Kenny—* " Shoul, go-rool ; " did you never hear it ? this is the chorus—

" Shoul ! Shoul ! Shoul go-rool !
    Shoul a poppa, poppa, roppa, loppa, poppa, kool,
    Cut straw, banyan ! Jump Jim Crow,
    The Lawyer leaves Court, a courting to go ! "

The Court and spectators exploded in a roar of laughter at this doggerel, and Mr. Frank Kenny was excused from any further examination.

The prosecution proved their case, and after two or three performances the fine was paid and the theatre closed.

My next manager was Thomas Barry, Esq. This gentleman, for a long time connected with the Park Theatre, organized a strong company, of which my old friend Wm. Rufus Blake was a member.

Tyrone Power—more often called Paddy Power —was one of the first stars introduced to the public by the new manager. In the performance of the Irish gentleman Mr. Power was eminently happy; and his *low* Irishmen, though not so boisterous as those of most of his successors, were full of a rich humor and buoyant with merriment. What an eye he had, and how he used it. Until we got accustomed to Mr. Power's manner, there was a degree of embarrassment in acting with him, arising from his habit of repeating *sotto-voce* the speech of the other party to the dialogue; it rather annoyed one to have a running accompaniment of his own words in a minor key. Mr. Power owned that at times he was quite unaware of doing it. Mr. Power was hardly what could be called *fair* with respect to his professional associates, and would hurry *up* or hurry *over* anybody or anything to make his point; at times this might be deemed excusable, but sometimes it was felt to be a hardship by those who acted with him. In the opinion of wise judges, Mr. Power was the finest representative of Irish character ever seen on the American Stage. Mr. Power was a passenger on board the steamship "President," lost at sea.

This year introduced to the public two singers who at once eclipsed, if they did not extinguish, all other musical celebrities yet seen in America —the "Woods." They appeared in an English version of Rossini's "*Ceuerentola.*" Mrs. Wood reached the highest perfection that anyone had dared to imagine, and her husband astonished all by the fluency of his execution and the sweet and mellow tones of his voice. Every opera in which they appeared won them new triumphs. Two years later they re-appeared, when Bellini's opera of "La Sonnambula" was produced. It literally took the town "by storm." Mrs. Wood's singing in "Amina" made the character difficult, almost impossible, for her successors. They came again in 1836, and once again in 1840. The gentleman's voice had improved in the interval of time, the lady's had fallen off in certainty and volume; but those who heard them at *that* time will tell the listener that nothing like the duets of Mr. and Mrs. Wood have ever been heard in America.

Mr. Wood had a hasty and petulant temper that kept him in a state of chronic warfare with the press, and a sharp Yorkshire idea of the value of money. He got his deposit out of the United States bank just in time, and by a clever device, got rid of his stock in the same institution just in time, and on his return to England became a farmer, settling near York.

Mrs. Wood was the Miss Paton, whose portrait as " Mandane," in Dr. Arne's opera of "Artaxerxes," may be seen in the old books. She then became the wife of Lord William Lennox, and a separation taking place, was espoused by Mr. Wood.   Mrs. Wood was very amiable in deportment ; indeed, she had an excessive familiarity of manner at times, that somewhat detracted from her personal dignity, and was as fond of flattery and praise as an over-indulged child ; talking during the performance, when not on the stage, indiscriminately, with everybody, and showing her jewels to all who would look at them.   As thus: " See ; ain't it pretty—this diamond necklace ; it was given to me by the Duchess of Devonshire ; it cost three thousand pounds."   Or, " Sir Something Somebody gave me this brooch ; I think it's charming ; don't you ? "   She always had a cluster of "ballet-girls " and " stage-hands " around her, behind the scenes.   Certainly, this peculiar trait of character in Mrs. Wood was pleasanter than the imperious, " don't-touch-me " manner of some of the queens of the lyric and tragic stage ; but she wasn't altogether dignified.   On her return to England, Mrs. Wood entered a convent, and a few years after re-appeared on the stage, in

Dublin; I do not know anything of her subsequent career.

I have mentioned that my first stage manager, Mr. Blake, was attached to the company, and recall a funny scene in which he figured, with Mr. Still. This gentleman had been engaged as "Musical Walking Gentleman." He had been quite a singer in his day, but his day had gone by; he was a man very slow in his movements, with a rather stolid expression; had not an amiable temper, and objected to playing any part that had not a song in it. He had been cast for "Willoughby," in the comedy of the "Dramatist," which is a very ungracious part, but a song was introduced to mollify his feelings. Blake was the "Floriville" of the play, a part which he played with delightful spirit and abandon. In one scene of the comedy, "Floriville" circumvents "Willoughby" in some dishonorable advances and a duel is the result. Mr. Still had forgotten his rapier, and when challenged felt for his sword, and not finding it, said to Blake, "What am I to do? I've forgotten my sword," and drawing towards the side of the stage, called out in a subdued tone to the property-man, "Bring me a sword." Blake pressed his challenge, rather enjoying Still's annoyance, and Still kept edging towards the side-scene, repeating, "Bring me a sword," when suddenly, from

8

the wing, there was thrust forth, in view of the audience, the basket-handle of a fighting-sword. At the sight, Still was himself again, and, exclaiming, " Ah! lucky circumstance; some one has left a sword sticking in a tree," he threw himself into position and cried out, with a shout, " Come on !"

When off the stage, Blake commiserated with poor Still, and said in a tone of mock sympathy, " My boy, I was *so* sorry for you; I didn't know what you would do. I thought *you'd sing a song*."

In 1834 I had the pleasure of making the acquaintance of James Sheridan Knowles. Mr. Knowles opened as "Master Walter," and played the heroes of his own pieces with earnestness and spirit. His figure was not of the heroic mould, and his tragedy had a touch of the brogue. His reception was a very warm one; it was not a usual thing in that day for authors to appear in their own dramas. Macklin and Colley Cibber had passed away, and Boucicault had not yet come, and I think the attractiveness of Mr. Knowles was increased by his dual character of author and actor. As a dramatist, Knowles stands in the front rank; as an actor, if not great, he was pleasing; as a man he was as warm and genial as the summer sun. I cannot reconcile the idea of James Sheridan Knowles, as I

knew him, ever becoming a controversial clergyman ; and yet *that* is what he *did* become at a
subsequent period, abandoning all his old walks
of literature, and enlisting in the ranks of the
Baptist church.

In the following year a clergyman of Philadelphia preached a sermon severely condemna-
tory of the stage. This discourse called forth
a spirited protest from Knowles. The article is
too long for insertion here, but I copy a few lines
to show its spirit :

> " Unmerciful ! whose office teacheth mercy !
>   Why damnest thou the actor's craft ? Is he
>   To starve because thou think'st thyself elected
>   To preach the meek and lowly Saviour's peace ?
>
>   *   *   *   *   *   *
>
>   Would by his art thou more had'st profited,
>   Thou ample, comfortable piece of flesh !
>
>   *   *   *   *   *   *
>
>   Act not the damner of another's creed,
>   Nor call the Arian—Universalist—
>   Socinian—Unitarian—Catholic—
>   An Infidel ! Judge not, lest ye be judged ! "

This from James Sheridan Knowles ! and yet
I read subsequently, in the English papers, of
his preaching controversial sermons, and defying
any Catholic to meet him in open debate ; it
seemed to me incredible.   Fifty-three years after
that brief but pleasant acquaintanceship with
Knowles, I was walking in the beautiful ceme-

tery of the necropolis, in the city of Glasgow, Scotland, and came upon a simple, massive granite monument, bearing the inscription, "JAMES SHERIDAN KNOWLES." The preacher was dumb; the actor was silenced; the service and the play were over; the curtain had fallen.

The centennial anniversary of the birth of Washington, in Boston, as elsewhere, was appropriately remembered. The theatre was decked with flags and streamers, and the delivery of a prize-poem was a part of the evening's programme. There was a scatter-brained lady attached to the theatre, by the name of Hamilton. She was gifted with wonderful loquacity, and had the faculty of talking for an hour or more without saying anything. Mr. Barry, the manager, though an estimable man, had, not unfrequently, a chilly and far-away manner that appeared anything but pleasant, even to those who knew him best; and was always in the habit of expressing by a short, spasmodic laugh—something between the grunt which a pugilist would utter if hit below the belt, and the sharp bark of a dog—his opinion of anything not in accord with his taste or judgment, or that he deemed unworthy of belief.

We were all assembled in the green-room in the morning of that centennial, February 22d, and were discussing the day and the celebration, when Miss Hamilton burst into the room, shawl off her shoulders, and bonnet-strings flying, with —" I say, folks; who is this old Washington they're making such a fuss about ? " Everybody looked at her in silent amazement, and Mr. Barry, slowly scanning her figure from head to foot, exploded that demoniac, monosyllabic laugh, which everyone knew said, just as plainly as if he had uttered the words—" Miss Hamilton, you're a blooming idiot." The lady returned to England the year following. She was a harmless soul, without a balance-wheel. I don't believe that she ever knew, to the day of her death, who or what George Washington was.

The winter of 1834–35 also made me acquainted with one of the great ones of the mimic world, the favorite alike, of England and America— Charles Matthews. How much has been written of Charles Matthews, how much might still be written, yet not the half be told. With what painful interest we read his devoted wife's story of that last four months of his professional life in America, which terminated but three short months before his mortal life closed. When Mr. Matthews played that final engagement, he was a nervous invalid; the climate disagreed with him; the physicians of New York, Philadelphia and Boston all refused to prescribe for him, and recommended his return to his native air; the

winter was one of intense severity, the mercury
would be, one day, twelve degrees below, and the
next, twenty-five degrees above zero; and he
acted all the while in a positive state of mental
and physical discomfort; for a few hours he would
make the most gigantic efforts to throw off his
depression and physical suffering, and when on
the stage, the audience never knew that they
were extracting amusement from a sufferer; and
how he acted—I can remember, but I cannot describe. Among my "memories," there is one—
pleasant, yet sad; delightful, yet sorrowful;
joyous, yet sombre—it is the memory of the
wonderful mimic and comedian, Charles Matthews. During that short and remarkable engagement, Mr. Matthews played " *Caleb Pipkin,*"
in Buckstones' drama of the " May Queen." It
is absolutely impossible to give the reader any
idea of the versatile humor he displayed in this
part, which not only convulsed his audience, but
set us into uncontrollable laughter on the stage.
After the first performance of the piece, bets
were current among the company that they
would be able to *resist* or *yield* to the mirth-pro-
voking power of the comedian, as the case might
be; but no man who had the temerity to back
himself ever won. Matthews would get us into
a roar of laughter in spite of ourselves, and
when successively we would go upon the stage,

that *look* of his, and the utterance of four words—
" we've found old Boyer "—would banish all
gravity—despite our desperate efforts not to
laugh ; would excite the wildest mirth of the audience, and stage and boxes were all as one; but not
a smile on Matthews' face, not one ; but a something, a combination of facial expressions, absolutely irresistible and quite impossible to describe.

In his " at homes," or monologue entertainments, Matthews would sit behind a table, and
for the space of an hour or an hour and a half,
or more, keep a crowded house in hilarious
mirth. I remember one imitation of an old
Scotsman, who claimed for his countrymen absolute supremacy in science, painting, poetry, everything. His friend gave but a reluctant assent to
his claims, but the Scotsman declared it was sus-
ceptible of proof. " Look," said he, " at the record of history ; was not Wallace a Scot—and
Bruce, and Argyle, and Knox, and Christopher
North, and Home, and Hume—were they not all
Scots ? Indeed, ye'll not venture to contend for
a moment that Scotsmen have not been the very
foremost men o' all the world, or to deny that every man of brilliant parts in history has been a
Scotsman."—" Good G—d !" exclaimed the other ; " I suppose you'll tell me next that Shakespeare was a Scotsman."—To which the old gen-

tleman answered, " Indeed, he had talent enough
to warrant the supposition."

The manner of Mr. Matthews in giving this
little bit of character delineation; his imitation
of the old Scotsman's sense of national vanity,
and his self-esteem were delightful.

Another intensely amusing personification of
Mr. Matthews', was that of an old-time itinerant
showman, who haunted the English fairs and
represented dramas and tragedies without any
company, playing all the parts himself, in a sort
of second-hand style; an instance of which he
gave in recounting his management of Homes'
tragedy of " Douglas."

For the part of " Young Norval," he had a
lank, red-headed, bandy-legged, awkward boy, ill-
dressed, with hose too long and kilt too short,
brought on from the side-scene, and immediately
started in, with a confidential glance at the
audience, thus :

> " This (young gentleman's) name is Norval,
> On the Grampian hills
> This (young gentleman's) father fed his flocks ;
> A frugal swain
> Whose constant care was to increase his store
> And keep his only son (this young gentleman) at home,
> For (this young gentleman) had heard of battles
> And (this young gentleman) longed to follow to the field
> Some warlike lord; and heaven soon granted
> What (this young gentleman's sire) denied.
> This moon, which rose last night, round—
> (As this young gentleman's shield ought to have been)"—

When Matthews got thus far, and looked at the great *square* shield which the "noble Norval" held awkwardly aloft, and then to the audience, before introducing the "ought to have been," the mirth was irresistible—the whole audience was in a roar.

Mr. Matthews returned to England and died within six months.

In the following April, Boston witnessed the first musical efforts of a lady who afterwards became the acknowledged queen of tragedy, with no rival near her throne—Miss Charlotte Cushman. She was a native of Boston, but for some years previous had been a resident of the adjoining town of Charlestown. I remember her well as a girl, and a vocalist in the choir of the Bulfinch street church. Miss Cushman appeared as the "Countess," in the opera of the "Marriage of Figaro." In the year following, she appeared as "Lady Macbeth," and surprised the public, who had hitherto known her only as a singer. Miss Cushman had a fondness for male parts, and played at this time, "Fortunato Falcone," "Henry," in "Speed the Plough," and "Patrick," in the "Poor Soldier." She might, perhaps, have become a great singer, had she not ruined a naturally fine voice by overtaxing it; and it may truly be said that she became a great tragedienne by the force of circumstances. Miss Cushman's voice always retained a coarse and harsh tone, the probable result of her over-strained vocal efforts.   Breaking down as an opera-singer, in New Orleans, she became the pupil of Mr. Barton, an actor of the Macready school, and made an instantaneous success as " Lady Macbeth," a part to which she had devoted the most careful study.   Subsequently she supported Macready ; his influence assisted materially in her rapid rise to fame and fortune, and her constant professional association with him, no doubt, led to a certain mannerism and tone that made her appear a female copy of that gentleman, pure and simple. There was little of feminine softness in anything Miss Cushman did upon the stage, but there was a perfect mine of depth and power.   She loved society and fame and money, and she had them all.

I knew at this time, another lady, the heroine of a famous run-away affair with the violinist, Paganini.   He had preceded her to Paris, where she was to join him, in accordance with the arranged plan ; but on reaching Boulogne, she found not Paganini, but papa.

Miss Watson was a "pretty little singer," nothing more.

John Reeve, who, like John Dunn, was known as the " Rascal Jack," I also well remember.   It used to be said of the late William E. Burton, that he was an imitator of Reeve; but he declared that Reeve copied him. I think the two comedians were naturally very much alike, and certainly, in point of personal beauty, neither had the advantage of the other. John Reeve, as "Cupid," was a funny sight.

Another memory of the past time, the old Drury Lane veteran, Dowton, a great actor. I can see him now, "in the mind's eye," the very absolute realization of "Sir Robert Bramble," "Old Dornton," "Sir George Thunder," and a half-dozen more of the old fellows of comedy that delighted the public. Mr. Dowton was at that time seventy-one years old, and, as a capable critic declared, "His representations of choleric humanity were carried to the summit of perfection."

At this time it was my privilege to form the acquaintance and friendship of one whose name is bright in the remembrance of all who ever knew him on either side of the Atlantic; the polished and perfect comedian, the grand and impressive tragedian, the graceful and finished elocutionist, the successful· and practical farmer, the candid, honest and upright man—James E. Murdoch. He was a member of the "Tremont" company during two seasons, and in 1840–41 was stage manager of the "National Theatre," in Boston. It would be superfluous to attempt in detail, any record of Mr. Murdoch's brilliant career, in these "Memories." The history of that career is stamped ineffaceably upon the annals of the American stage, and no words of mine can add to its lustre. I never had the pleasure of meeting Mr. Murdoch but once after his departure from Boston, nearly fifty years ago. He still lives in an honorable old age, with the undisputed claim to rank, not only as a great American actor, but as a true lover of his country and his country's flag; a patriot with a great American soul, who, when the storm of rebellion swept the land, devoted his time and talents to alleviate the agony of the dying soldier, and—

"Dry the widow and the orphan's tear,
    Of those who perished in their country's cause."

Mr. Balls, a comedian from Covent Garden Theatre, appeared at this time. There was much discussion among the critics as to the relative merits of this gentleman and Mr. Geo. Barrett; I recall a couplet of the day, which said—

" Throw the chaplet of fame—
    And e'en let it rest as it falls.
    Should it light on the forehead of Barrett,
        Or rest on the forehead of Balls."

CHAPTER VII.

JOSEPHINE CLIFTON is another of my "memories." Miss Clifton was a magnificent woman, and challenged admiration in many characters that Fanny Kemble had made all her own; she has been long dead. The Keeleys, too — that little couple, bright and merry—I remember with pleasure; and Fanny Jarman, and Ellen Tree, that bright particular star of the dramatic firmament, whose praises in prose and poetry were sung fifty years ago on both sides of the Atlantic, of whom John Quincy Adams wrote—

"Nature to thee her fairest gifts imparts—
She bids thee fascinate, to win all hearts—
The wife, the Queen, the wayward child we see,
And fair perfection, all abide in thee."

Miss Tree afterwards became the wife of Charles Kean, and I had the pleasure of recalling the old days, when after many long years, I met her with her husband on the shores of the Pacific.

The liability to conflagration in any building devoted to theatrical uses is so great, that it has been said the average life of a theatre cannot exceed a period of more than fifteen years; in my time I remember many narrow escapes, especially one that occurred during the engagement of the "Woods." While crossing the rear of the stage my attention was attracted by a glimmer overhead, which I took to be the reflection from a fragment of tin-foil upon the "border;" but I was instantly startled by the thick falling of sparks of fire, and hastening in great fright to report what I had seen, a rush was made for the paint-room, where a large stove filled with anthracite coal had ignited the floor beneath, which was bursting into flame; carpenters and stage-hands and all who were able came to the rescue, but it was a difficult and dangerous work to extract the red-hot fuel from the furnace in time to prevent the whole mass from breaking through the charred floor and falling upon the stage beneath; had not the discovery been made, in a few minutes the theatre would inevitably have been in flames. The house was filled from the gallery to the orchestra, and the possibility of an impending tragedy was a fearful contemplation. There was, of course, intense excitement behind the curtain, but Mr. Barry ordered the performance to proceed, while we all worked zealously, but silently; and the audience was not aware of the danger, although those nearest the stage had a suspicion of something wrong behind the scenes. It was a sincere cause of thankfulness that the night did not afford a parallel to the horrors of Richmond and Brooklyn.

Another instance of the possible danger which (even with the exercise of the utmost carefulness) surrounds the employés of a theatre, and which was attended with loss of life, I will here mention. It occurred two years later in the same theatre, during an engagement of Mr. Charles Kean. The play was " Pizarro," and the house—it being Thanksgiving night—was very full; Mr. Kean had just made his entrance in the second act, and hardly began to speak, when a loud rattling noise was heard, and from above, on the left-hand side of the stage, a counter-weight to the act drop, a massive bar of iron, some six feet long, weighted with heavy iron rings, parted from the rope by which it was suspended, and bursting through the floor of the " flies"—the side gallery of the stage—fell prone on the head of Mr. Stimpson, an attache of the theatre, who stood beneath; he fell dead to the floor instantly. I stood within four feet of him and was spattered with his blood. The awful noise stopped the action of the play and startled the house. Mr. Kean turned and saw the bolt fall; white with horror, he hastened from the stage, and the curtain was dropped. It was an awful scene; every drop of blood seemed to gush from the victim's body, and the steps leading to the music-room were dripping with gore. The audience were informed of the sad casualty, and the crowded holiday throng left the theatre in silence and in sadness.

I was witness to another fatal accident of the same nature many years later, when I was a member of Messrs. Ludlow and Smith's company in St. Louis. A lady of the company was struck dead during the performance, by the heavy barrel of a suspended scene which fell from above; and while her lifeless body lay in the green-room, the *star* of the night shocked the feelings of the ladies and gentlemen of the company by his wish to " go on with the play." His unfeeling proposition was met with an indignant No! In this world of ours *there are men and there are men*. All the money in the Bank of England wouldn't have tempted Charles Kean to make such a proposition; but the other gentleman, rather than lose two or three hundred dollars, upon the ground that "the people in front didn't know how bad it was," would have gone on with the play—and the lady lying stark and dead behind the scenes! The gentleman has been deceased these many years; his name shall have no place in these "memories."

Everybody in our generation has heard of Yankee Hackett, but few, I think, have heard of Yankee Hill. The evanescent nature of the actor's fame is exemplified in the forgetfulness which has fallen upon the little man with twinkling eyes, and sly, still humor, who as Yankee Hill used to make his auditors laugh very heartily half a century ago. Mr. Hill's Yankees were the very reverse of Mr. Hackett's, but they were true to nature—not of the boisterous type, but rather the quiet, noiseless, cunning Down-easter, who whittled and talked a good deal, but never very loud. I remember him well; he was a pleasant little man, and played successfully in all the Atlantic cities. Like so many more that I have known, "he is dead and gone."

Another mighty shadow of the past rises to my mental vision, worthy to rank among the foremost. As a purely classic actor, Mr. Vandenhoff (the elder) has not been excelled, perhaps not equalled, by any of his contemporaries. He played in the season of 1837–8, opening in "Coriolanus." Since the time of Fennell and

Cooper, Addison's tragedy of "Cato" had found, I think, no representation on the American stage; it was revived by Mr. Vandenhoff. I remember his impressive performance in "John of Procida," and also the charm of his "Richelieu" and "Othello"—indeed, nothing was wanted in any of his personations to satisfy the most critical judgment and acute perception. Mr. Vandenhoff did not prove very attractive, strange to say; but the highest genius and talent is sometimes doomed to neglect. He was a grand actor.

I played about this time with a Lowell lady, Miss Hildreth. She appeared as "Marianna" in Knowles' play of "The Wife." She retired within two years, and became subsequently, I think, the wife of General Benjamin F. Butler.

In May, 1838, a lovely girl, only seventeen years of age, appeared as "Alice," in a drama called "Ernest Maltravers." Miss Missouri was by birth a sister of Josephine Clifton. The history of this talented and beautiful creature is of itself a tragedy. She became the victim of selfishness, slander and cupidity, and died soon after, mad—"a lovely rose, cut off before her time." Time has not banished her matchless face and form from my remembrance.

The first performance of Bulwer's play, the "Lady of Lyons," took place at the National

Theatre at this time, the hero being represented by the notorious George Jones, better known as the "Count Joannes." I knew Jones well; he was the son of a police officer of Boston, born, I think, upon the sea. His advent upon the stage at the old Federal St. Theatre occurred some two years before the opening of the "Tremont," to which he was attached for the period of one season. Mr. Jones was always remarkable for his self-esteem, which was evinced even at that early date, by an occurrence which I well remember. On an opening night he had to make his first entrance upon the stage with Mrs. Finn; the lady, being a popular favorite, was greeted with loud applause, which Mr. Jones assumed as being all for himself, and, leaving the lady up the stage, advanced to the footlights with obsequious bows and smiles; a chilling suspension of the applause convinced him of his mistake. Mr. Jones costumed the part of "Claude Melnotte" in a most remarkable manner, wearing, as the "Prince of Como," an Italian doublet, with long, hanging sleeves, reaching almost to his feet; he looked like a bat. His subsequent extraordinary career is well known. Mr. Forrest represented "Claude," at the "Tremont;" the "Pauline" was Mrs. George Barrett; no lovelier "Pauline" was ever seen.

At this time I first saw Mlle. Augusta. She was a beautiful woman, and a beautiful dancer; indeed, up to that date, probably the best the American public had seen. Ellsler had not yet come.

Mr. and Mrs. Sloman I also knew for the first time. Like Mr. and Mrs. J. Barnes, they treated their patrons to a mingled banquet of smiles and tears—tragedy and farce.

Towards the close of the season, the fortunes of the drama became almost desperate; beyond even the power of the no-haired-horse, or the great tragedian, Shales, to revive.

Shales was a young man of somewhat feeble intellect, completely stage-struck, and impressed with the idea that he was born to be a great actor. The wags of the city got hold of him, and assured him that in the character of " Richard III " he would make a phenomenal impression; and indulged in oyster suppers at his expense, while they rehearsed him in a stable-loft. A benefit was announced for Mr. Shales, and the house was filled with a crowd prepared for fun. Never was a more enthusiastic reception given to a debutant; than the debutant never was a more ridiculous figure seen; reading, pronunciation, carriage, gesticulation, were the height of absurdity. Screams of laughter and ironical applause, missiles of various kinds, and paper bags of flour did not seem to destroy his self-possession; and towards the end, when a great hoop, entwined with cabbages and turnips and other "garden truck," was thrown to him, amidst tremendous shouts of applause, he received it with smiles as the curtain fell. Immediately loud calls for "Shales! Shales!" were heard, and he re-appeared to receive another ovation. From the proscenium-box a large salver, on which was a gorgeous service of plate—made of tin—was offered for his acceptance. Every article of the tea-set was of the most exaggerated size and shape; the teapot had a spout a foot long. He took the gift, and standing apparently undecided what to do, a wag in front shouted out: "Take it home to your mother, Mr. Shales; tell her to give a tea-party and we'll all come," and he bore his present off in triumph, amidst a tornado of flour-balls, and a hurricane of applause. From the green-room, the triumphal wreath found its way to the paint-room of the theatre, and thence to the pump, which at that time stood at the head of State street, where, on the following day, it was exhibited to the gaze of admiring crowds, and then sent to New York for the gratification of the friends of native talent. The plate was boxed up and sent out to a suburban hotel where Mr. Shales' admirers intended to assemble for "a good time;" but the landlord, thinking the joke had gone far enough, dropped the box and contents into the river. If Mr. Shales lacked shrewdness, certainly his father and mother were shrewd individuals, for they bagged over $1,100 by their eminent son's performance of "Richard III."

I recall another first appearance, of somewhat the same character, which took place during my early days. A member of the company, to improve his chances on his benefit night, availed himself of the ridiculous notoriety of an individual, whom, I dare say, many old Bostonians remember, and it was announced that Mr. Emmons would, on that occasion, make his first appearance in a grand patriotic national drama, written by himself. Mr. Emmon's honorable occupation was the manufacture of spruce and ginger beer, from which he had obtained the soubriquet of "Pop Emmons." He was an older man than Shales, but not much, if any, wiser. His weakness was the forum rather than the stage, and he improved the opportunity to get before the public on holidays and any days that offered the chance of gathering a crowd.

On a certain Fourth of July morning, the papers informed their readers that the "distinguished orator, Mr. Emmons, would deliver an oration on horseback, at eleven o'clock, upon the Common, to which the public was courteously invited." The "public" wouldn't have missed such a chance for fun if it had *not* been invited, and at the appointed hour, Mr. Emmons, manuscript in hand, his "head-quarters in the saddle," on a lean and ill-conditioned horse, passed through the gates into the center of a large and admiring crowd. Gracefully acknowledging the plaudits, he started in on his oration, but had only uttered a few sentences when a mischievous gamin in the throng amused himself and his gang by thrusting a pin into the haunches of his horse. Emmons turned round with an expostulation and a mild rebuke to the youngster, and started in again with his speech. In a minute or two, another jab of the pin made the horse dance and the crowd laugh; again Emmons protested, and again resumed his oration. This was repeated several times, to the anger of Emmons and the great merriment of the crowd, until, finally, just as Emmons rose in his stirrups, and with wild gesticulations, began to apostrophize the bangled-tar spanner, or the bar-tangled banner, or something of the kind, one urchin, more wicked than his fellows, gave the horse a prodigious prod, and the animal, thinking, if his rider did not, that "patience was no longer a virtue," bucked viciously and tumbled the orator heels over head upon the grass. Satisfied with this successful commencement of the National Holiday, the patriotic young vagabonds adjourned to the frog-pond to stone the frogs, and see the balloon go up, while Emmons gathered himself up and went away lamenting the ingratitude of republics.

Mr. Emmons' first appearance on the stage was as successful as Mr. Shales, *and in the same way;* but the gentleman who resorted to the unwise expedient to improve his exchequer received no pecuniary advantage.

One more stage absurdity, though not of the same character, I am reminded of. A Mr. Sumner L. Fairfield, who I believe had some reputation as a writer sixty years ago, made his first appearance at the old Boston Theatre—I forget what he played—but it was not a pronounced success. Through the influence of his friends he was engaged as a regular member of the company, and was advertised to appear on his second night as the " *Uncle*," in " George Barnwell." The audience were a little inclined to laugh at his acting, when, to be serious would have been more grateful to his feelings, but he got on passably well, and was shot " in regulation style," by " George." Unfortunately he fell too far down the stage, and was left outside the curtain, in full view of the audience. There was a titter of suppressed mirth in the house, which was increased after the lapse of a moment by his bobbing up his head, as if to see if anyone was coming to carry off his dead body. No one came, and presently he bobbed up his head a second time—as Falstaff does on the field of Shrewsbury—and bobbed it down again. The house was now in a roar of laughter; a moment more, and for the third time, seeing no one coming to his relief, he got up, looked dazedly at the audience and walked off. The* situation would have been an admirable one for Finn or Burton, but for a tragic novice it was too much. Mr. Fairfield dissappeared from public view.

In 1839–40, the theatre was opened under the management of my early friend and associate, Mr. J. S. Jones, and in January two benefits were given to the families of Mr. Henry J. Finn and Mr. Charles Eberle, who, with some three hundred others were lost by the burning of the steamer "Lexington," on Long Island Sound. These benefits apart from their charitable purpose were notable for the artistic array of volunteers. Mr. Tasistro, who was once connected with the "London Atheneum," and was subsequently, I believe, a government clerk in Washington, appeared, but won no laurels as an actor. I remember at this time Mr. Dan Marble, in his line of Yankee characters, he was quite unlike Hackett or Hill, but he was excessively funny, and he will be remembered by old theatre-goers for his "Sam Patch," and "Game Cock of the

Wilderness;" these two monstrosities of plays were worse than bad, but Marble's acting in them was more than good.

Place aux dames! Fanny Ellsler, the finest danseuse that ever crossed the Atlantic—the peer of Taglioni—the superior of Cherito—arrived in New York in the summer of 1840; and I saw her on the stage for the first time in September. The newspaper writers and critics of that day were so dazzled by her success, her talent and her personal charms, that the utmost power of language was exhausted in their praises of the "divine Fanny."

In the "Beauties of the Opera and Ballet," she was described as "tall, beautifully formed, with limbs like those of the hunting Diana, a small and classical head, a pure, fair skin that required no artificial whiteness, beaming eyes, finely-curved lips, and glossy hair of bright chestnut hue, braided over a forehead formed to wear with grace and dignity the diadem of a queen or the floral wreath of a nymph."

I do not think that there is much exaggeration in this description. I certainly remember Fanny Ellsler as one of the most beautiful women I ever have seen. She carried America by storm; from Baltimore to Boston the mania spread; all the ladies wore Ellsler cuffs, all the gentlemen wore Ellsler boots, all the bakers baked Ellsler bread.

Her queendom was undisputed. She was to the ballet what Malibran was and Patti is to the opera. When she floated on the air in "La Sylphide," or jingled her golden-heeled boots in "La Cracovienne," or beat her castanets and swept the circle of the stage in "La Cachucha," she was the personification of grace, the absolute "poetry of motion."

Fanny Ellsler was accompanied by Monsieur Sylvain. This gentleman was a clever dancer; gossip said that Hibernia, not Gaul, gave him birth, and *Sylvain* certainly sounds a little like Sullivan. During Miss Ellsler's visit she contributed her benefit money on one night towards the completion of the Bunker Hill Monument. She returned to Europe with an ample fortune, and died, I think, some two years since.

Fanny Ellsler's contribution to the Bunker Hill Monument fund was the cause of much squibbing and joking at the expense of Bostonians. I remember one "cartoon" representing the completed column with Fanny perched on the apex "*en pirouette;*" and the press all over the country had many good-naturedly malicious flings at the lax patriotism that permitted a ballet dancer to finish the work which had been so long delayed. I do not think, however, that the "*amour propre*" of Boston was very much frayed by those comments. Boston is not the

only locality where such work has met with delay.
During the many years that the Washington
Monument lingered to completion, a gift of six
hundred dollars would not probably have been
refused by the building committee, even if offered
by an opera dancer.

The construction of the Bunker Hill Monument was to me a boyhood matter of great interest.
I used to dig dandelions and fly kites in my
younger days on the grassy slopes of Bunker
Hill, and was very proud when on one occasion,
a party of tourists boosted me up on the pedestal
of the old masonic shaft, which stood near where
the present monument stands, to read the inscription commemorative of Warren and his fellow
patriots.

I was at school in Bradford when the corner-
stone of the monument was laid, and came home
for the occasion.   That was a great day.   In the
procession there were some twelve or fifteen survivors of the battle, and the old fellows held
up their powder-horns and cartridge-boxes, and
waved their hats from the barouches to the excited crowd.   Webster—" Black Dan," as his
admirers loved to call him—and Lafayette, I saw
for the first time.   When the foundation had
reached the surface, the first two courses above
ground were by some error mislaid, and had to
be taken up and relaid in accordance with the
architect's plan.

Some years ago a tablet was placed a short distance from the base of the column, to indicate the exact spot upon which Warren received his death wound. An English gentleman, visiting America, called upon his friend, a Boston merchant, who had received many courtesies at his hands, during a visit to the mother-land. The Boston gentleman anxious to do the handsome thing for his English friend, took him around to see all the lions of Boston and vicinity—reserving Bunker Hill for the last. When they reached the sacred spot, to illustrate the history of the day, he began with—" Here you see is Charlestown—across the river you will observe is Copp's Hill, from the base of which the British force embarked; yonder, below the navy yard, is the point where they disembarked; up this steep, to the left hand, General Pigott advanced with his grenadiers, towards the redoubt—just where we stand—in which Prescott and the Continentals awaited the attack." The English gentleman was greatly interested, and the Bostonian, moving slowly towards the stone tablet, and pointing to the inscription, said impressively — " Here Warren fell!" The Britisher looked at the stone, and then to the top of the monument, and repeated, " here Warren fell! Did he? Was he hurt?" The Yankee amazed at the question replied, "*Hurt?* great God, sir, he was *killed!*"

The Englishman took the cigar from his mouth, gave another glance at the stone, and again at the top of the column, and with cool imperturbability replied, " Killed; was he ?   How high do you say it is, two hundred and two feet?   Well I should think he would have been."

Among our centennial anniversaries, that of Bunker Hill was not forgotten, and as the writer is a Bunker Hill boy, he may be pardoned for inserting here the following verses which were offered as his contribution to the festivities of the Bunker Hill Association of San Francisco, as one of his " *memories* "—

THE FIGHT OF BUNKER HILL.

In the story of the days of our sires,
One chapter rekindles all the fires
  That live in the breasts of the free ;
'Tis the story of the fight
On Bunker's grassy height,
  Where Mystic rolls his tide to the sea.

In the year seventy-five, on the morn
Of the seventeenth of June, with the dawn
  Hope comes to the crushed of the earth ;
And the shining page unfolds
Where a thousand gallant souls
  Pledge their all for the land of their birth.

With shovel, pick and spade, through the night
They have toiled side by side till the light
  Of the sun in the morning blazes out ;
Then, the mattock cast aside,
They stand ready to abide
  Weal or woe—life or death in the redoubt.

Across the river deep, by the steep
Of the hill where their forefathers sleep,
  The king's men are gathering for the fray ;
And, adown the placid stream,
The frigates lie agleam
  In panoply of war, on the bay.

Now the drums beat to arms, with alarms
Of bugle-blast and trumpet-call, and throngs
  Of Boston's pallid women gaze in fear,
From out " the belfry arch
Of the tower of the church "
  Whence the signal blazed forth to Paul Revere.

The artillery thunders out, and the sky
Is lurid with the flames that on high
  From the rebels' burning roof-trees ascend ;
And the hurtling shot and shell,
With the energy of hell,
  In the loud and awful diapason blend.

Anon the crowded boats are ferried o'er,
And three thousand trained veterans leap ashore,
  The order of the king to fulfill ;
And from the strand where they land,
The scarlet-coated band,
  With Pigott in the van, mount the hill.

In the Continental host not a word—
Not the echo of a whisper can be heard,
    Till within a hundred paces come the foe ;
Then, from Prescott, in the redoubt,
The word to "Fire!" rings out,
    And down the hill the shattered columns go.

They rally once again, mid their slain,
The prestige of their prowess to retain,
    And their gory steps retrace to win the prize ;
When old Putnam, full of ire,
Cries out—"Soldiers, hold your fire
    Until you see the whites of their eyes!"

The yeomen, with their spirits all aflame,
Pick their flints, and with sure and steady aim,
    From their muskets send the quick and certain doom;
And the foemen melt away .
In the wild and stormy fray
    Of that day, to the grave and the tomb.

A hotter blast of death ne'er before
The veterans of the line ever bore,
    But their unquestioned valor all in vain,
'Gainst men who fate defy,
And boys that dare to die,
    And the grenadiers go down the hill again.

Clinton views the bloody strife from afar,
And with freshly-gathered hosts hastens o'er
    To redeem the flying field from the rout ;
While, no powder left to burn,
The Continentals turn
    And withdraw, inch by inch, from the redoubt.

Of the means to battle longer bereft,
No craven spirits they—for they left
  With muskets clubb'd, fighting as they go ;
And with patriotic pride,
Every one of them that died,
  Died with face and with breast to the foe.

And this is the tale of Bunker's fight
For the right, 'gainst Briton's might ;
  The story that our fathers tell
Of the morn and afternoon
Of that sweltering day in June
  When Warren and his comrades fell.

And this story of the days of our sires,
We will tell to our children, and the fires
  Of freedom unextinguished shall be,
While Warren and his braves
Rest in their holy graves,
  And Mystic rolls his tide to the sea.

CHAPTER VIII.

IN 1841, I had the pleasure of hearing another
great celebrity of the musical world—John Braham. He was nearly seventy years old, and had
been acknowledged, in his prime, as " England's
greatest tenor." His success on the stage was
indifferent, but in the concert-room he still proved
attractive; as an *actor* public judgment was
unanimous in pronouncing him exceptionally
bad; but in the " Bay of Biscay," " Scot's Wha
Hae," the " Death of Nelson," and other such
songs—he vindicated his claim of supreme excellence. Twelve years subsequent to the time of

which I write, Mr. Braham sang in London to admiring crowds—he was then more than eighty years old. For some seven or .eight years, Mr. and Mrs. Seguin—they were always known as the " Seguins "—were greatly popular. I recall the gentleman's acting and singing, in the operas of " Fra Diavolo " and the " Bohemian Girl," very vividly. Mr. Seguin turned low-comedian before his decease—and why ?

Another fine actor of the period was Mr. William Creswick ; this gentleman has recently played to large and admiring audiences in the Australian cities, and won fame and profit, notwithstanding he has passed the boundary of three score and ten years.

In the season of 1838, I rejoined my old manager, Mr. Pelby, and was a member of the " National " Company. After an absence of several years, Mr. Thomas Cooper made his reappearance, with his daughter. He came to take leave of Boston, and doubtless thought that sympathy for the father would be aroused by kindly feeling for the child ; the young lady had no marked ability, but was accepted for her father's sake. The spell once wielded by the magician was broken by time and indulgence, and the engagement of ten nights produced an average nightly receipt of $130. In other days Mr. Cooper had frequently played to $1,200.

This was also my first introduction to a young Miss, who afterwards held high rank as an actress. Jean Margaret Davenport was at that time about fourteen years old; she evinced great ability as "a juvenile prodigy," which title she was known by in the "bills," and is one of the few examples in dramatic annals of the precocious bud bearing sturdy fruit. As Mrs. Lander, she was well known in after years, and was generally popular. Her father was a shrewd and politic manager, and guarded his daughter's interests with parental fidelity. He was said to be the original of Dicken's "Vincent Crummles." He has been dead many years. Mrs. Lander retired from the stage about fifteen years ago.

Here too, I first knew the comedian—Silsbee. This famous actor, achieved a great reputation in England, as a personator of Yankee peculiarities. I met him often professionally in after years. He died in San Francisco about a quarter of a century ago, and was buried in the Yerba Buena cemetery. Municipal improvements some three years latter necessitating the removal of the cemetery, the body of the deceased actor was found undecayed, and perfect in form and feature as when placed in the ground.

I became acquainted with a lady at this period, who subsequently won a reputation co-extensive with the boundaries of the land that gave her birth. Miss Julia Dean was, when I first saw her, tall, exquisitely graceful, with the complexion of the lily, and features of perfect loveliness; she came from good dramatic stock, being the grand-daughter of Samuel Drake, one of the pioneers of the drama west of the Alleghenies, and was a native of Louisville Kentucky. For many years, at intervals, I had the pleasure of playing with this beautiful, brilliant, and in some respects unfortunate lady, not only in the East and South, but also on the Pacific slope; and among my cherished memories retain the name of Julia Dean Hayne. I shall have further occasion to speak of her.

The National Theatre was for a short time under the stage management of Mr. J. G. Cart-litch. "Old" Cartlitch, as he was called, had blossomed from the minor theatres of London some forty or fifty years antecedent to his appearance in Boston; he was the original "Mazeppa," and had never forgotten it, and didn't let anyone else forget it; he was the concentrated essence of bucket-topped boots, smuggler's belts, big buckles, fighting swords and pizzicato music; he had never played anything in all his life except *to music,* and never meant to if he could help it. The theatre at that time was essentially a melo-dramatic house, yet nevertheless the legitimate was not seldom presented, and as Mr. Cartlitch was hardly "at home" in the old comedies, or, for the matter of that, in the new ones, Mr. J. B. Wright, the prompter, and afterwards the manager, generally came to his relief. I remember that the exigencies of the theatre compelled him once to cast himself for "Young Malfort" in the "Soldier's Daughter," and while at rehearsal awaiting his cue to enter, and not taking it up, answered, on Mr. Wright's saying, "That's your cue, Mr. Cartlitch," "Well, where's the music? I can't come on without music; Mr. Holloway, please play three bars from the hurry in "Mazeppa." Mr. Cartlitch had another peculiarity: in making out his programmes he would always give every piece a double title; it was the "Rendezvous; OR, The Cock'd Hat and Simon"— it was "Lucretia Borgia; OR, The Seven Coffins and Seven Cups of Poison"—it was "Bill Jones; OR, The Bloody Black Brig of Bermuda." When on one occasion the comedy of "The Will" was to be cast, Mr. Cartlitch was greatly puzzled for his second title; but looking the play over and finding that Sir Solomon Cynic conceals himself among some straw in a closet, in one scene, he was relieved of his embarrassment, and the posters announced in big letters: The Elegant Comedy of "The Will; OR, The Old Man in the Straw!" Mr. Pelby, who was a man of taste and judgment, surprised at this remarkable announcement, put his interdict on Mr. Cartlitch's double titles.

The short but necessary word "*or*" in connecting Mr. Cartlitch's double titles, reminds me of an occasion in which it became a matter of debate and dispute between Mr. Barrymore, the capable stage director of the Tremont Theatre, and a gentleman of the name of Rasimi, who was a member of the ballet corps, and occasionally trusted with a line or two to speak. Rasimi, after reconnoitering the cottage of a supposed criminal, whom in his capacity of constable he was to apprehend, was to approach the house and knock upon the door, exclaiming as he did it, " Open the door instantly, or ——," leaving the occupant to understand what might be expected if his demand was not complied with.

Mr. Rasimi entered, made his reconnoissance, knocked on the door, and made his demand, bringing out the last word with a full stop, and with the force of a catapult, "Open the door instantly, OR !"

Mr. Barrymore corrected him, and desired another trial, but with the same result—" Open the door instantly, OR ! !"

And Mr. Barrymore impatiently exclaimed: " Good God ! Mr. Rasimi, don't you understand the meaning of the words ? They're simple enough—it's a threat of what you'll do if the door ain't opened. You mustn't speak it in that way—it's a break."

To which Rasimi angrily retorted: "Do you think I'm a d——d fool? Of course I know what it means; I know it's a *break*—didn't we rehearse it? Of course it's a *break*—he opens the window and breaks a jug over my head!"

Mr. Barrymore gave it up—the Rasimi reading prevailed.

I recall with great pleasure the three years in which I was a member of the "National" company. The associations were pleasant, and friendships life enduring were formed. Mr. Pelby was a gentleman of rather hasty temper, but just in his dealings. In his position as actor and manager animosities would inevitably arise, but he was always open to conviction, and was ever willing to right a wrong or overlook a fault, if not too flagrant. In this connection I recall a little incident. I was rehearsing a very obnoxious, disagreeable part in some melo-drama the name of which is forgotten; the last speech before making my final exit ended with what Rasimi didn't understand—a break; it ran something like this—

"My prospects in life blasted, every fair hope crushed, and by you, my bitter foes; may vengeance reach you. I shower on your heads the curses of a ruined man! And now I—I—" (Exit, guarded.)

Annoyed and in ill-temper at being compelled to play a part against which I had protested in vain—I was, without doubt, careless whether I was right or wrong—and wilfully terminated my speech, as Rasimi ignorantly terminated his, thus—" I shower on your heads the curses of a ruined man, and now I exit guarded." Mr. Wright, the prompter, half laughing said, " You'll not say that at night, Mr. Leman;" to which I replied, " I don't know, perhaps I will;" and Wright answered, "I hope not, the old man will be in the pound, and if you say it there'll be trouble." The " old man " was the manager, and the " pound," as we had christened it, was a box adjoining the orchestra, communicating by a door with the box office, in which Mr. Pelby used nightly to sit and scrutinize the performance; anything wrong did not escape him, and anything right he was always willing to acknowledge and compliment, and he was a pretty able critic. Well, night came, and sure enough the " old man " was in the " pound;" but I had nursed my dissatisfaction all day, and when I came to the exit speech, I gave it with peculiar energy, looking directly at Mr. Pelby, as I shouted out— " And now I exit guarded." I saw him rise from his seat as I made my exit, and he met me in the wing with—" well, Walter, you've had your joke, but when you go to the office on salary day, I think you'll *exit forfeited.*" He spoke the truth; my joke cost me ten dollars—or it would have cost me that sum—had not the manager, with a little friendly advice, remitted the fine.

In the summer of 1838, a portion of the company rusticated in the then pleasant village, now city, of Waltham. The Massasoit House, a handsome hotel, had just been erected, and by invitation of, and with the assistance of some young gentlemen amateurs, a short series of performances was given in the hall of the hotel. This pleasant summer divertisement introduced me to three gentlemen, all of whom became my life-long friends; two of the three have been prominent in various positions of honor and trust, and the third, many years since achieved a national reputation. I will speak first of him. General Nathaniel P. Banks, was at the time a machinist, in the employment of the Waltham Cotton Manufacturing Company, an ambitious youth, without influence, fortune or powerful friends, but possessing a spirit of stern determination and great fixedness of purpose. I think that if he had adopted the stage as his profession he would have reached an eminent position; he was the *star* of our amateur friends, and his performance of " Damon " packed the hall. Subsequently he played " Claude Melnotte " at the " National," for his friend Haynes' benefit, and played it well, too. Beginning life as " Bobbin-

·boy," he became "Amateur Actor," "Editor," "Inspector of Customs," "Town Representative," "State Senator," "Speaker of Massachusetts' House of Representatives," "Governor of Massachusetts," "Member of U. S. House of Representatives," "Speaker of that Body," "Railroad Manager," "Major-General of Volunteers," and again "Member of Congress ;" such a record speaks for itself, and demands no comment. Gen'l Banks, when I first knew him, possessed a well-built figure, an expressive eye and a nimble foot, and at the Central House balls, which we used to enjoy so much, could lead down the middle and cast-off, in "Money Musk" and "Hull's Victory," with as much activity and more grace than any dancer in the room. I have seen General Banks but three times within the last thirty years. I believe that he is now a resident of Boston. He is one of my pleasant memories—long may he live!

The second of this trio of old friends, is the Hon. Gideon Haynes. Like Banks, he was, and still is, a perfect specimen of physical humanity, and could wrestle with any competitor of his weight, coming out the victor in four trials out of five. He had a decided inclination for the stage, and became a member of the "National" company, and also of the "Tremont;" but a restive spirit drove him to other fields. He be-

came prominent in politics, and was for many
years Warden of the Massachusetts State Prison,
which office he filled with the highest credit, introducing wise reforms, and leaving the institution in the most prosperous condition. Perhaps
the best epitome of my old friend's career and
character will be found in the annexed extract
from a letter received from him in response to an
invitation to attend my golden wedding. If it
meets his eye, I know " Gid " will forgive me for
making his letter an " open " one.

     *   *   *   " Is it possible that fifty years have
passed since that event? A glance into the mirror reminds
me that time rolls on, but, although approaching the seven-
ties, I am, in feelings, as youthful as when we were knocking
about in the old ' Tremont.' How few of those we knew in
the old days are left—how many have passed ' over the river.'

  " My life has been rather an eventful one—merchant, machinist, actor, senator, warden of state prison for fourteen years,
crossed the Atlantic eight times, spent ten years in Brazil,
kept boarding houses and hotels, had two wives and seventeen
children. The twenty-ninth of last August was the thirty-
ninth anniversary of my first marriage, and the fifth of November the twenty-fifth of my second; and here I am to-day,
as fresh as a daisy and as happy as a prince, and would like
nothing better than to lead Mrs. L. down a contra-dance of
twenty-five couples, as we used to do in ' ye ancient times.'

  " My four eldest daughters and one son have married happily, and are all settled near me, with lots of grandchildren."

    *   *   *   *   *   *   *

I think that letter proclaims the kind of man
my old friend, Gid. Haynes, is; God bless him.
I greet him with an " all hail!"

The third of the trio of old friends, the last and best beloved, is now no more. The Hon. Nathan Porter was some six or eight years my junior. He adopted the stage as a profession, and made rapid advancement, but the fascinations of political life won him from his first love, and he left the stage, studied law, and entered on an active public career. He took high rank as a debater in the Senate of his native State, and at the bar was known as a forcible and logical pleader. In 1853, he removed to California, was chosen District Attorney for the city and county of San Francisco, and Right Worshipful Grand Representative of the I. O. O. F. of California. He had just entered on his legislative career, as a member of the State Senate, from Alameda County, when death cut short his useful and honorable life, at the age of sixty-one years. He was borne to the tomb with sincere manifestations of public and private regard; and, among many others, I, as an old friend, had the privilege of laying my chaplet of remembrance upon his bier. I trust I may be pardoned for introducing here a brief extract from what I then said, for all life long Nathan Porter was my best, my dearest friend; his name and fame are among my dearest " Memories."

   *   *   *   " I should be doing an injustice to Nathan Porter to place my humble tribute to his memory upon the

ground of personal friendship alone ; in him there was a cath-
olicity of humanity that went out beyond friends and kindred
and home ; it embraced the members of the profession which
he honored by his character and adorned by his talents ; it
went out to the members of that grand association who in
him found the truest exemplar of their motto : "Friendship,
Love and Truth ;" it went out to mankind and to the world.
He had not only the largest charity for the frailties of humanity, but he had planted within him a most unalterable determination to maintain the right and condemn the wrong,
whether the wrong rode in silk and purple, or grovelled in
wretchedness and rags—the slave of no dogma, his religion
was his blameless life. As son—brother—husband—father—
friend and man there is no blot on his stainless escutcheon ;
the blandishments and temptations of official station, that too
often dim the brightest shield, never placed a smirch upon the
blazonry of his. As between right and wrong, his honest
voice never gave forth an uncertain sound ; in the path of
duty he could be seduced by no sop and conquered by no
valor. In short, to sum his character in little, his life was
gentle, and in him the elements blended so graciously, that
nature stood up and said to all the world : "Here is a man !"

In those days, as in ours, it was an act of
courtesy, as well as a matter of good policy, for
the management to invite notable strangers to
the theatre. Among the many distinguished
individuals who attended the performance as
public guests, I recall General Jackson, and can
see him as he stood up in the box, very tall, and
as straight as an arrow, holding the broad-
brimmed white beaver hat, one side of which was
permanently turned up by the constant clutch
of his hand, while he bowed bareheaded to the

thousands, who welcomed him with continual cheers.

Davy Crockett was another invited guest; he was a man of medium size, clean shaved, clad in black, and looked more like a clergyman than a fighter. He was very curious to see everything in the "play-house," and wanted an introduction to all the actors and all the ladies. His wish was gratified, and from the green-room he went to the *flies*, the paint-room, under the stage, and everywhere, and evinced all the interest in what he saw that a child exhibits with a new doll; and he excited an equal interest which would have been painfully increased could we have known that within two years he would lie a stark and bloody corpse, with fifty gaping wounds, surrounded by a holocaust of slain foes in the memorable Alamo.

Still another visitor I remember, but unlike Andrew Jackson, not the idol of the people. Aaron Burr came to the theatre uninvited, perhaps to seek a momentary forgetfulness of himself, and of what he might have been to the people he sought to betray. Mr. Burr came very quietly to Boston, where he remained some two or three days, lodging at the Tremont House; no notice other than a mere line or two in the papers was taken of his arrival, and one evening, in company with two gentlemen, he took seats in the theatre;

it was soon buzzed round that Aaron Burr was in front, and he became the object of curious, but not offensive observation. As he entered, the curtain was just going up on the "*Falls of Clyde.*" In this little drama, Edward Enfield, the brother of the heroine, Ellen, taunts the young Laird Kenmure, upon false grounds of suspicion, into a duel, and after Kenmure's pistol has missed, returns the fire and slays him; it seemed a fatality that of all pieces in the drama, Mr. Burr should have come, for the last visit that probably he ever made to a theatre, to witness a scene so forcibly recalling his fatal duel with Hamilton. Every eye in the house was turned upon him, as " Kenmure " fell, and I think there was not a man or woman in the audience that did not, at that moment, pity Aaron Burr. Within a short time he rose, and with his friends left the theatre; he was not present more than twenty minutes altogether. He died about two years after on Staten Island, over eighty years old.

Among the engagements of those early years, Mr. Frederick Brown was for a time at the "Tremont," I forget the exact date. Mr. Brown had been an actor of prominence, and was a popular London favorite. He is the hero of the amusing pantomime story recorded in Mr. Murdoch's work, " The Stage." The equestrian drama of the " Cataract of the Ganges," was revived with

great splendor, Mr. Brown playing "Mokarra."
In this character he wore a long, full robe of
white, reaching to his feet, and made his entrance
in a chariot from beneath the stage, drawn by six
horses.   Dismounting from the chariot and advancing down the crowded stage amidst the glare
of innumerable torches, instantaneously, as quick
as thought, his whole dress, from his feet to his
head, was in a blaze.   There was a momentary
thrill of horror, which was relieved almost as
quickly as it was aroused, for the flame was
merely the ignition of the furzy cotton surface
of his costume, and went out as quickly as it is
kindled.   It was rather a startling incident, and
brought out a great peal of applause when Mr.
Brown, unhurt, went on with his part.

I remember an amusing incident which happened in those early days, when a young gentleman in a subordinate position, completely turned
the laugh on the stage manager, Mr. George
Barrett.   It was in Sheridan's farce of the
"Critic," which is, in point of fact, the Duke of
Buckingham's "Rehearsal," with another name.

Mr. Barrett was very fond of playing "Puff,"
the author, and great license was admitted in the
language and business of the *play within the
play*, which forms the comic element of the piece,
the ladies and gentlemen cast to the several
parts in "Mr. Puff's" play having *carte-blanche*

11

to make any rejoinder or reply not violating the
rules of propriety or good taste. The young
actor was playing the " Beefeater," and has to
withdraw from the scene with—

> " I never can endure a rival's bliss,
> But, soft—I am observed !''

He spoke his lines and went off, when Mr.
Barrett called him back with—" You mustn't
make your exit that way ; you mustn't bolt off,
you must *steal* off. Please try it again." Again
it was tried, and again he was called back by
Mr. Barrett. " I told you not to bolt off; you
mustn't go off so abruptly ; you must *steal* off.
Can't you do it thus ? You look as if you knew
how to steal." There was a laugh here at the
expense of the " Beefeater," which he turned upon Barrett, by retorting, " I haven't had so much
practice in stealing as you have, Mr. Barrett; I
haven't been manager for twenty years."

There was a little man, named Knaggs, in the
theatre for several seasons. He was a kind of
dried-up man ; and if he had any heroics to utter,
always set the audience to laughing. Under Mr.
Barrymore's management, the spectacle play of
" Napoleon " was produced. It was full of battles and tableaux and marches, and one of the
grand scenes which Mr. Barrymore particularly
prided himself on, was the pageant burial of

Marshal Lannes. Everybody was in the piece, and some of the company had to double. At the last moment, a man was wanted to lead the burial cortege and speak the speech to the soldiers, recounting the virtues of the hero Lannes. Knaggs was enlisted, and was in the middle of his speech of six lines—which was quite as much as he could carry—when he stopped abruptly and exclaimed—"But, Mr. Barrymore, I'm burying myself!"—and so he was; he had played "Marshal Lannes" in the previous act, and no one chanced to remember it. Barrymore scratched his head, puzzled what to do, but every man in the company was busy with something to do, and he said, finally—"Never mind, Knaggs; bury yourself; they'll never find it out, and if they do it's no matter."

Knaggs used to make some funny mistakes. On one occasion, when everybody was full of the United States Bank, and the removal of the deposits, the comedy of the "Hypocrite" was performed. Mr. Knaggs played the officer who enters in the last scene to arrest Dr. Cantwell. The text reads thus:—"Is your name Cantwell?" to which the Doctor replies, "Yes," and is told that "I have my Lord Chief-Justice's warrant against you." "For what?" asks the Doctor, and is answered, "For a cheat and impostor." Knaggs was all right with the first question, but his second part read—" Then I have my Lord Chief Justice *Taney* against you." "What!" cried the doctor, and Knaggs repeated the assertion more positively than at first. It was evident that General Jackson and the Supreme Court had got into his brain.

But greater men than Mr. Knaggs often make mistakes. A list of misreadings and transpositions of words, perpetrated on the stage through inadvertence, momentary abstraction and other causes, would fill a volume. In the fourth act of the "Gamester," there is a scene between "Mrs. Beverley" and "Stukely," in which, for the basest purposes, "Stukely" vilifies the character of her husband, without at first mentioning the name of the man he slanders; "Mrs. Beverley" at length demands to know, imperatively exclaiming:

" How injured? and who has injured me?"

And "Stukely" replies: "My friend—your husband."

On the first night that Miss Fanny Kemble played "Mrs. Beverley," the "Stukely" of the evening answered her inquiry of "Who has injured me?" by emphatically replying, "Your friend—my husband!" It was a very elegant audience that filled the theatre, but to suppress the laugh was impossible.

I once heard a young lady on the stage declare that she "had been roaming in the flower-garden among a wilderness of red and white *noses.*" And an actor once assured me, in confirmation of the truth of what he had heard, that " There is not the *sloughtest dite*, my lord."

In the summer of 1841, I was playing for a short season in Providence, where a new theatre had been opened by Mr. W. H. Russell. One of the first engagements was that of Mrs. Seymour, who was announced as from " Covent Garden" and "Drury Lane." The lady may have been in Covent Garden and Drury Lane— in the *boxes;* but I hardly think she had acted there, in any other than a very subordinate position. She was an exceedingly beautiful woman, married to a wealthy gentleman much older than herself, who took great delight in her acting, and was willing to pay for it. Most of the younger members of the company, and of the elder ones too, were fascinated by the personal charms of Mrs. S.; indeed, she was a woman to excite admiration anywhere.

I played " Romeo" to this lady's "Juliet." The play in those days used generally to end with the revival of Juliet from the narcotic, and her dual death with Romeo; at the rehearsal I had brought the lady from the tomb, and we were discussing the arrangement for a "double fall" upon the stage, entwined in each other's arms—which is a very pretty piece of stage business, if properly executed—and had rehearsed it in *one* way and then in *another*, Mrs. S. being very desirous that it should be effective at night, and saying, "Is this way the best—or the other? What do you think, Mr. Leman? how do you feel?"

Among others, George Locke — afterwards Yankee Locke—was standing in the wing; he was then a novice. After rehearsal he accosted me with: "Do you know how I envied you— and she asked you 'how you felt.' By Jove! I don't know how *you* felt, but if I had been in your place, and that beautiful woman had asked me how *I* felt—my feelings would have been too big for utterance."

CHAPTER IX.

I SPENT the summer of 1842, in the city of
Montreal; the manager of the theatre was Mr.
Latham, and his stage manager was Mr. Tuthill.
I think old New Yorkers must remember "Paddy
Tuthill"—never a more genial soul lived—he
was not a very good actor, but had the common
weakness to think himself one; but he was a good
dresser, off as well as upon the stage, and the
possession of a considerable income enabled him
to indulge a fancy for over-dressing, to the extent

sometimes of two and three different suits in one day—a velvet coat in the morning, flannel suit at noon, and dress coat in the evening. I first became acquainted with Mr. William Wheatley in Montreal; an acquaintance which grew into friendship in after years. I shall have further occasion to speak of him. Miss Melton, a very popular vocalist of that period, Hackett and T. D. Rice (Jim Crow), were also with the company for a few nights; but my especial memory of that summer is Mr. Charles Dickens. Three or four performances were given by the "Garrison Amateurs"—aided by the ladies of the company—and I saw Mr. Dickens in two characters "Alfred Highflyer" and "Snobbington." Very many years after I heard Mr. Dickens on the lecture platform, and he appeared to more advantage there when old, than when young, on the stage. I know that at the time, I thought him rather *flippant* than *lively;* he delivered his dialogue so rapidly that it was almost impossible to follow him. I trust I shall not be thought invidious in speaking thus of the amateur performance, even of so great a man as Dickens. I speak not as a critic, but simply as an observer.

In 1843, I was engaged by Mr. Thomas S. Hamblin, for the Bowery Theatre, New York, where, in the month of August, I reported for service, and opened as "Banquo," Mr. John R.

Scott being the "Macbeth." It took but little time for me to know that I was misplaced, and stating frankly to Mr. Hamblin that I wished a release, he courteously granted it; and I immediately joined Mr. E. A. Marshal, with whom I had been in correspondence. I remained at the "Bowery" Theatre but two weeks; proceeding immediately to Philadelphia, I was enrolled by Mr. Marshal as a member of the "Walnut St." company—the "Chestnut St." Theatre being at the same time under his control. My old friend William Rufus Blake was stage manager, and the acting manager was Miss Charlotte Cushman. The company was a strong one, including among the ladies—Miss Susan Cushman, Miss Alexina Fisher, Mrs. Thayer, Mrs. Blake, Mrs. Wm. Jones and Mrs. Mossop, and among the gentlemen—W. R. Blake, J. M. Field, better known as "Straws"—the father of Miss Kate Field—Henkins, Hadaway, E. L. Davenport, and others. In October, Mr. W. H. Macready, made his first appearance at the Chestnut St. Theatre as "Hamlet." This was the first time I had been brought into professional association with this famous actor—born, one might say, almost in the theatre. His father being a well-known provincial manager, he had every opportunity for studying his art and its professors, and he stood confessedly at the head of his school of acting, which was founded rather on the Kemble theory, than on the system of Garrick, or Mossop, or Kean. I had seen Mr. Macready nearly twenty years before, when I was but a boy, and the remembrance of that first night, when as " Virginius " he stirred my senses, and awoke my admiration, which was blended with a kind of stage-fright at acting with one who had the character among the profession of being so particular and methodic that a breath mis-breathed would put him off his balance, and a syllable mis-placed would stop the action of the whole machine. This feeling was more or less prevalent with all the members of the company. Miss Charlotte Cushman played the "Queen" to Macready's "Hamlet," and he was so well pleased with the lady, that he chose her as his female support in his subsequent engagements, and thus made the way to her London career feasible and plain.

Mr. Blake, knowing Mr. Macready's peculiarities, was especially anxious that all should go right while Mr. Macready was with us, and indeed all went very well, even to the satisfaction on the whole of Mr. Macready himself, although there were one or two little accidents during that memorable engagement, that to Kean, or Booth, or even Forrest, would have been as nothing, but came very near upsetting Mr. Macready. One of these I have a right to mention, as I was the innocent delinquent. It occurred towards the close of the engagement, when "Hamlet" was repeated. But first I will allude to the experience of my friend Mr. William Wheatley, who played the supporting seconds to the star.

It happened almost every night that on the fall of the curtain, Mr. Macready would send his dresser to the stage manager with a desire that Mr. So-and-So, whoever it might chance to be, should be sent to Mr. Macready's dressing-room, and, with more or less of fear and trembling, the actors would go to hear what Mr. Macready had to say; and from the expression on their faces when they emerged, the inference was drawn that Macready's remarks had not been over complimentary.

Mr. Blake, as I have said, was extremely anxious that everyone should do all in his or her power to please the exacting star, and before the rising of the curtain would come into the green-room and say: "Now, gentlemen and ladies, let us all take care to have everything go right with Mac.; be very particular that everything is done exactly as it was rehearsed"—and when the actors came forth from Macready's room, would meet them with a satiric smile on his handsome face, and ask what "Mac" had said, assuring them that, "of course, Mr. Macready had only sent for them to compliment their performance."

Mr. Wheatley generally escaped these inter-
views, but on one evening Blake came running
into the green-room with: "Wheatley, Mac wants
you—it's *your* turn now;" and Wheatley went
as desired, to the great man's room; he remained
there an unusually long time, and on coming
out, Blake, who had all the time been on the
watch, wanted to know what kept him so long,
and what Mac had been saying to him. From
Mr. Wheatley's constrained manner and un-
pleased look, it was quite apparent that the
interview had not been altogether satisfactory;
but he got away from Blake as quickly as possible by saying, with an enforced tone of cheerful-
ness, that "*he had a delicious half-hour*" with
Mr. Macready. Blake gave a chuckle, which
bespoke his misdoubt of Wheatley's report; and
on the following evening, the "Hamlet" night,
when dressed for "Polonius," came into the
green-room, and in his inimitable manner, looking at Wheatley, wondered who would have the
delicious half-hour with Mac to-night.

I played the "King of Denmark," and between
the last two acts had taken off my sword, and
forgetfully had left it in my dressing-room. Just
as the last scene was being drawn, Miss Cushman said to me, "Mr. Leman, where's your
sword? Your sword — you've forgotten your
sword. Here, somebody bring Mr. Leman a

sword!" And the property man had barely
time to place in my hands a fencing-foil as the
scene opened. The play progressed to its close
—Hamlet disarmed and slew the King, and the
curtain fell. I went to my room and was beginning to disrobe, when Blake came trotting to the
door, and with his wicked grin, said "Walter,
Mac wants you; you've escaped a good while,
but it's your turn for a delicious half-hour now,"
and following me out, to my extreme annoyance,
added, "Egad! I'll go, too; I'm stage manager,
and I'll hear what he says;" and we went together to Mr. Macready's room. On the way, I
asked myself, "did I by any possibility drop a
word—did I misplace or give a wrong cue?" I
could recall no such error.

I entered, with Blake behind me, and asked
Mr. Macready's pleasure. He was sitting on the
sofa, and after a gasp he began—" Mr. Leman, I
—I have always found you—found you exceedingly careful, and — and very attentive; but
where did you get—where, sir, did you con—trive
to get"—here he gave a great gasp—" that awful tool, that skewer, that—that—a—a kitchen
spit, to draw it on me for a regal weapon, whipping
it out from beneath your robe like a ramrod; oh,
sir!"—with another gasp—"it so affected my
nerves that—" Here I said, " Mr. Macready, will
you allow me to explain"—and he broke in, hold-

ing up his hands in horror—" My dear sir, it
can't be explained "—with another gasp—" it ad-
mits of no explanation.   Have you got the tool
about you?   You knocked me up in my dying
speech ; I—I was completely unnerved."   Here
he paused long enough for me to say that as it
was a momentary thing, the *quality* of the
weapon could be of little consequence ; that being
so far from the audience, and so quickly passing
in action, the sword was, in fact, hardly seen.
Here he rose up aghast.   " My dear Mr. Leman,
hold, enough ! enough ! no more !   When, in
your futile explanations, you tell me 'tis of no
consequence, because the audience could not see
its quality, you shock my sensibilities ; you—
you—" and he fell with another gasp upon the
sofa.   I was still anxious to excuse the mishap,
and was about to speak again, when Blake, who
had been enjoying the scene with ill-suppressed
mirth, whispered, " Come along, Walter," and we
were leaving, when Mr. Macready, having partially
recovered from his emotions, spoke again.   "Mr.
—eh—Mr.—Mr. Blake !"   Blake had enjoyed
my rebuke, and I thought I'd enjoy his ; so, when
he paused I did the same.   " Mr.—Mr. Blake—
sir ; I regret to say it, sir, but *you* nearly destroyed my best scene !   I was paralyzed at the
impropriety which you committed !   I was
shocked in the play-scene to see what you did !

You laid—yes, sir, you absolutely laid your hand upon the king's chair; upon—the—king's—chair! If the play is repeated, I hope—I—do—hope, Mr. Blake, that such a flagrant—flagrant outrage on regal dignity will not be committed." Mr. Blake didn't think, after seeing the fruitlessness of my attempted explanation, that it was worth his while to offer any, and we left the presence.

In after years he made a very laughable story of that interview, and confessed that his friend Leman, didn't have all of the delicious half-hour to himself. In reality, I do not think that, apart from Mr. Macready, anyone in the house noticed that Mr. Blake chanced to put his hand on the back of the king's chair, or knew that the king drew a foil instead of a sword. It was a ridiculous fuss about nothing.

Many stories were in vogue during Mr. Macready's professional visits to America, of annoyances to which he was subjected, in one of which, Mr. Decius Rice, the "Jupiter" who spoiled Sinclair's satin dress, figured. Mr. Rice's business, in the last scene of "Werner," was to catch Mr. Macready as he fell, and support him while he uttered his dying speech. At rehearsal, Mr. Macready said—" You will hold me, thus, while I am speaking, and do not lay me down upon the stage until you have mentally counted twenty.

You will please understand, sir; and be particular, no matter what I do, whether I speak slowly or otherwise, you are not to lay me down until you count twenty; thus, one, two, three "—indicating the rapidity with which the mental numeration was to be made. At night, Rice got Macready into his iron grip, and either because the actor had been too rapid in his speech, or Rice had been too slow in his counting, he had only reached to about *ten*, when Macready said to him, *sotto voce*, " Lay me down, sir." Rice responded, " Oh, no, sir," and continued slowly, " eleven, twelve, thirteen." Macready, in a fume, repeated, " Eh—good G—d, sir; lay me down !" Rice again replied, " Oh, no, I don't; you told me to count twenty, and I mean to do it," and slowly went on to " eighteen, nineteen, twenty," and then laid the tragedian down coolly upon the stage. When the curtain fell, Macready was speechless with anger, but "Jupiter" rather enjoyed the joke.

Another story was current of Mr. Macready's experience with a company whom he chanced to play with, in which discipline was the exception, and negligence the rule. Mr. Macready had depended on the *supporting* gentleman who traveled with him, to see that the rehearsals were properly gone through with ; but in consequence of neglect and inattention, departed on one occasion from his ordinary rule, and came to the theatre in person for rehearsal, which progressed a little way, when Mr. —— was missing. Macready was told by the prompter that Mr. —— had gone out, and requested him to read his part. Macready horrified at such a violation of discipline and dramatic propriety, stopped the rehearsal for fifteen minutes, when Mr. —— returned with a jaunty air, and to Mr. Macready's angry comments excused himself by saying that he only "went out to get his *hat ironed*." Macready looked at him in amazement, gave a suppressed groan, and the rehearsal was resumed; when, in a few moments more, another gentleman, Mr. ——, was missing; again the rehearsal was suspended. Mr. Macready impatiently dancing the "Mouchoir," which met with Mr. Forrest's disapprobation in Hamlet, and the manager almost equally angry. After a stop of a quarter of an hour the delinquent returned, *his* excuse for causing the delay was, that he went out for a "snifter." With a despairing groan, Mr. Macready addressing the manager, said : " Mr. —— I do not, sir, understand the—the customs of America; but I—I—really this neglect is very—eh, very extraordinary. One gentleman tells me, after being guilty of gross neglect, that he went out to get his 'hat ironed,' and another gentleman offers as an excuse—that he only went out for a

' snifter.'   As I said I—I—eh—I am not familiar
with American customs or phrases, and—I—I—
don't know what a ' snifter' is—but I—eh, if I
might ask a favor, I would request the gentlemen
who iron hats and dispense ' snifters,' to suspend
business during rehearsal."

In September, the company was transferred to
the Walnut St. Theatre ; where, in the series of
old comedies with which the season commenced,
I remember the names of Miss Cushman and
her sister Miss Susan Cushman, Mr. Edward
Davenport and Mr. Spear.   Mr. Davenport I had
known since the early days of the Tremont, to
which he was attached for one season.   He became a prime favorite in Philadelphia,   went
thence to New York, and eventually to England,
attaining high artistic rank, and at his death,
which took place some years since, was lamented,
not only as a man and gentleman, but also, as
one of the foremost actors on the American stage.
George G. Spear, I had also long known; he was
another Boston boy, a graduate of Mr. Pelby's,
and a participant in our Waltham summer theatricals, and also in our Waltham winter balls, at
the Central House in that pretty village—now
city—which still stands, or did a year ago, as in
the days of yore.   I remember, very well, on one
occasion, how we started from the theatre, at the
close of the performance, in a " one-horse shay "—

the common driving vehicle of the time to go to the ball—it was but an hour and a half from the city, and a light snow-storm coming on. Old Spear—he was never called anything else but Old Spear—who would insist on driving, although he knew nothing about it, got the lines crossed, turned the horse round, and swore he was "all right," against my assertion that he was "all wrong," until the lights on East Cambridge bridge convinced him that he was going back to Boston, and not to Waltham. Mr. Spear was for some years attached to the "Walnut," and afterwards went to California in the early days. He is now an inmate of the "Forrest Home."

Miss Charlotte Cushman withdrew from the theatre, I think, before the close of the season—there was always a something—which if not belligerency was at least *armed* neutrality between Miss Cushman and Mr. Blake. Pre-eminent as the lady was, even at that time, in tragic power, she was not so happy in comedy; and she played all the best of it; indeed, she played the best of *everything* in the female line. In all the comedy scenes between the lady and gentleman, Blake had the "call" with the audience. Miss Cushman possessed a large amount of personal ambition, and never missed a chance to obtain or wield a social sway. Her sister had become a member of a certain female organization presumably in furtherance of this object, and Blake would come into the green-room and make ludicrous inquiries about the prospects of the " organization for promoting the entrance of actresses into the upper ten sphere," and ask about the income and prospects of " the female sacred button-hole society." Miss Cushman would give Blake a very meaning look at such times. I think that it would have been almost impossible for them to dwell in professional unity, and no doubt the separation was agreeable to both.

Mr. Peter Richings succeeded Mr. Blake in the position of stage manager. There is probably no actor better known, traditionally, than Mr. Richings ; indeed, theatre-goers of this generation cannot have forgotten the tall, finely-built, dignified, scholarly gentleman, who when young was for years a New York favorite, and at a later period starred through the length and breadth of the land with his accomplished daughter, the fine singer, and perhaps the most thorough musician of her day, Miss Caroline Richings. Mr. Richings was a versatile actor, and noted as one of the best dressers on the stage. I knew him for a long time, and met him in after years on the Pacific Slope—ever and always a perfect gentleman.

I first knew Mr. George Jamison in Philadelphia. This gentleman, whose name was afterwards so unhappily associated with the domestic infelicities of Mr. Forrest, possessed most wonderful and versatile mimic powers; with little effort and ordinary application, he could have rivalled Matthews. His first appearance on the stage was in a protean character, or rather charters, in his native city, New York. I believe the occasion was the benefit of Mr. Charles Eaton, of whom I have already spoken. Mr. Jamison visited England subsequently, and I played with him at a later day in New Orleans. I think I never knew a more perfect "chameleon," if the term may be applied in a dramatic sense, than Mr. Jamison; he was an impressive actor of tragedy, and could play "Brutus," "Macbeth," "Jeremiah Clip," and "Old Pete" in the "Octoroon" equally well. Mr. Jamison lost his life by being run down on the Hudson River Railroad, in 1868.

Another gentleman, whom I first knew in Philadelphia, and knew for many years after on both sides of the Continent, is Mr. Joseph Smith —"Smithy," as he is called, or more often, "Little Smithey." Mr. Smith always *had* and *has*, I presume, to this day, an absolute immunity from defilement by contact with any dirt, dust, soil, or any substance whatever; indeed, it would never adhere to him. In after years, when we traveled the mountain roads of California in company, while I would dismount from the stage coach black and begrimmed with dust, Smithey would step down looking neat as a bridegroom. I have always thought he possessed some charm to preserve his personally neat appearance. His organ of *Order* is also fully developed, and where "Smithey" is, one is sure to find neatness and order combined. And it is a pleasure to testify to the purity of Mr. Smith's moral character as being equally unspotted. He was a pleasing actor, especially in Fops and Exquisites. He is now an inmate of the "Forrest Home."

Another of the notable men of what may be termed the first era of the American stage, I at this time became acquainted with—Mr. Wm. B. Wood. He was almost the only one of the "old guard" left to remind the Philadelphia theatre-goers of the past. Though not a very old man (he was but sixty-four) he was physically somewhat feeble, and had practically retired from the stage some seasons before. In company with Mr. Warren, he had for many years been the manager of the Chestnut Street Theatre, which Philadelphians always called "Old Drury," and his first appearance as an actor dated as far back as 1798. The warmest admirers of Mr. Wood never claimed that he was a genius, but he had ap-

plication and perseverance, and all old Philadelphians spoke with respect of Mr. Wood. He
professed light comedy when in his prime, and
was fond of the society of the green-room, where
he could talk of the past, tell stories of the past,
and recount his triumphs in the past. I greatly
enjoyed " Billy Wood," as he was always called,
though I think he was a little inclined to under-
rate his contemporaries, and overrate Billy Wood,
and he had a habit of qualifying all he said, with
a " but." As, " Mrs. Merry was a very fine actress, but——" and " Conway played ' Jaffier ' remarkably well, but——." He took his farewell
of the stage while I was in Philadelphia, and
was honored by the patronage of the best citizens—vice-president Dallas among them.

Mr. James Wallack, Jr., I had the pleasure of
becoming acquainted with in Philadelphia at this
time, and his friendship is one of my pleasant
" memories." Mr. Wallack was a very fine act-
or, so well known to a great portion of the public of to-day, praise on my part would be presumptuous. He was for two or three seasons a
stock-star of the " Walnut " company, and his
acting of " Melantius," in the " Bridal," the
" King of the Commons," and like characters,
was superb. I had the pleasure of meeting him
after a lapse of years, in California. His wife,
a very fine actress, was the little " Cora's Child,"

who " blubbered in ' Pizarro's ' face," in Salem, so many years before.

While a member of the "Walnut Street Company," I frequently played in Baltimore, it being found advantageous to intermit the season at Philadelphia, by visiting the Maryland metropolis with an attractive star or an attractive play, and these visits recall my remembrance of Mr. Blake in three characters, the performance of which stamped him as a master of the mimic art —"Grandfather Whitehead," "Jeoffrey Dale," and "Jesse Rural."

In the fall of 1845, a "Patriotic Drama" was announced, under the title of the "Battle of Germantown," by Walter M. Leman. This, my first attempt at dramatic composition, was prompted by the persuasion of Mr. Spear, who had read a nouvelette with the same title, by a Mr. Lippard, and wanted to play the Yankee who figures in the story. The piece was well received, played many nights, and has since been repeated in New York and other cities. No merit is claimed for it other than that of being a passable medium of expression for the exuberant patriotism of Americans on an American holiday.

At the disastrous period of the Revolution, made memorable by the sufferings of Valley Forge, and the subsequent conflicts of Brandywine and Germantown, great service was rendered to the American cause by a band of organized volunteer yeomanry from the eastern counties of Pennsylvania. This partisan band of " Mounted Rifles," for such they really were, was called the "Black Rangers." The following song being the feature of the piece, I will insert it as my only " memory" of the forgotten " Battle of Germantown."

THE RANGER'S MIDNIGHT SONG.

Beneath yon moon, at night's high noon,
　　Grasp we each brother's hand,
And stake our all to stand or fall
　　By our dear native land.
Our arms are ready for the strife—
　　Our powder, it is dry.
Our flints are picked, our aim is true—
　　To the white of the foeman's eye.
Up, Rangers, up—mount, Rangers, mount !
　　Our steeds, our steeds are here;
The hour has come, and the tap o' the drum
　　Proclaims the foeman near.

The Ranger's band with steady hand
　　Will grasp the rifle true ;
There's no retreat in the Ranger's feet
　　When the enemy's in view.
Our girls have filled our cartridges
　　And cast our leaden balls—
There's kisses for him who returns alive,
　　And tears for him who falls.
Then Rangers draw your saddle.girths !
　　Your neighing chargers rear
And champ the bit at the tap of the drum
　　That speaks the foeman near.

Our cause is just—in God 's our trust ;
  The hireling slaves we'll foil ;
Our pine-tree banner ne'er shall trail
. In the dust of freedom's soil.
Our trumpet's throat brays out the note
  Of death to Albion's sons,
While on we ride, through the battle's tide,
  'Mid the flashing of the guns ;
Each Ranger's foot in the stirrup put,
  With your sabres gleaming clear
In the light of the moon—for the tap o' the drum
  Proclaims the foeman near.

In December of the same year, a one-act sketch, with the title of "Freedom's Last Martyr," was thrown together in haste, and announced for representation as from the pen of the author of "The Battle of Germantown." This little drama, based on the historic incident of the death of Colonel Ledyard, at the surrender of Fort Griswold during the Revolutionary War, was well received and played many times, but has faded into oblivion.

In May of the next year, on reception of the startling intelligence of the outbreak of hostilities on the Mexican border, at the request of Mr. Blake, I wrote the "Campaign of the Rio Grande." This piece was in two acts, and owed its success rather to the patriotic sentiment of the public than to any real dramatic merit in its composition; it was played many nights, and occasionally revived during the season ; but, like its predecessors, it "died and made no sign."

My fourth and more pretentious effort as a playwright was produced in January of the following year, under the title of the "Prairie Bird." It was a dramatization of the Hon. George Augustus Murray's popular novel with the same title, and met with pronounced success. It ran a week, and was occasionally represented during the season's continuance. It had the advantage of an admirable cast. Mr. James Wallack, Jr., Mr. Wheatley, Mr. Chapman and Mrs. James Wallack being in the distribution. The "Prairie Bird" has been successfully played in Boston and also in California; but in all probability its career is run, and it will be heard of no more. With that conviction, its author may be pardoned for recording it among his "Memries."

There was a bright-eyed, brown cheeked little girl, running about my house in those early Philadelphia days, who called me "Father." In the month of August, of the following year, she came trotting home from school one day and told how a play-mate of hers was "working a sampler," and how she was working upon it such pretty lines that some one had written on her birthday; and she did wish that somebody would write some lines for *her* birthday when she was ten years old. In the parlor of that little girl, now a middle-aged woman, hangs a "sampler" faded with years, but carefully preserved, and in its web embroidered—

FROM MY FATHER,

ON

MY TENTH BIRTHDAY.

First fair boon from Heaven sent
Laughter—loving Ellie—lent
To thy parents from above;
Earliest pledge of fondest love,
Thoughtless, happy, hasty child.
Frank, impetuous, wayward, wild,
Rude in health; in 'haviour bold;
Ellie—thou art ten years old!

As thou standest by my side
In thy girlhood's joyous pride,
Hopes and fears alternate sway—
Ellie, on thy natal day.
What is past we know full well,
What's to come—ah! who can tell?
May thy character unfold
Brighter as thou growest old.

When a babe thy mother's breast
Lulled thy infant form to rest;
Every grief and every care
Found a sympathizer there;
Till her sun of life shall set
Ellie—thee she'll ne'er forget;
Ellie, let it not be told
She's forgotten when she's old.

Ellie—guard thy every step
In the path of virtue keep ;
From her ways if thou shouldst part,
Ah ! 'twould break thy father's heart ;
Rather in an early tomb
Would he lay thee in thy bloom ;
Virtue's better far than gold,
Ellie—in the young or old.

As thy barque puts gaily forth
Freighted with the joys of youth
To avoid the rocks of care—
Look to God, the guiding star.
If truth dwell while thou art young,
In thy heart and on thy tongue,
Ellie, then shalt thou behold
Peace and happiness when old.

CHAPTER X.

IN July, 1848, I penned a dramatic sketch, in
one act, which was played under the title of
the "Volunteer's Departure and Return." Illustrated by a series of tableaux, portraying the
varied scenes in the life of a volunteer, commencing with his departure from the happy fireside,

continued through the perils of the camp and the battle-field, and ending with his return to

"Home, Sweet Home."

The return of the Pennsylvania Regiment of Volunteer Troops from the Mexican war suggested this trifle. It answered the purpose for which it was written.

In August the regular season opened, when the comedy of the "Millionaire" was presented as the initial performance. I had commenced writing this play during the closing days of the previous season, but four of its five acts were completed during the interregnum of some five weeks that preceded its production. It was favorably received by the public, and, on the whole, generously spoken of by the press; indeed, I am convinced that it received all the praise it merited, and perhaps more. That it was faulty in construction, I know; in my endeavor to observe the *unities* I sacrificed *effect*, and committed the common error of the inexperienced dramatist by over-burdening my play with too much dialogue and too little action. It ran one week to remunerative houses, and the author's friends were present in force on his benefit night. The Comedy had the advantage of an admirable cast, including Messrs. Richings, Wheatley and Chapman, and Mesdames Alexina

Fisher, Blake, Thayer and Mossop, and was introduced by a happy prologue written by my friend, James S. Wallace, Esq., and spoken by Miss Alexina Fisher.

Among all my "memories," what pleasanter one can I recall than that of Alexina Fisher? Playing as I did with her for several consecutive seasons, and being on terms of intimate friendship, I had ample means of knowing her as she really was—a genial, pleasant, kind-hearted little woman; a most versatile, accomplished and fascinating actress.

She was always so prime a favorite with the Philadelphia public that the play hardly seemed a play unless Alexina Fisher was in it; and she held her throne against all rivals to the last of her career.

She was the heroine of all my crude dramas, and was always as true as steel to that professional *esprit de corps*, which is never more grateful to an actor than when he turns author. In after years, as Mrs. Alexina Fisher–Baker, she met with brilliant success in California. I have not seen her for many a year; like myself, she is no longer young. Should this book ever meet her-eye, she will understand me when I say that I greet her across a continent, "with pleasure— with pleasure."

On the evening of a complimentary benefit to Mr. E. A. Marshal, the manager, I recited an occassional address, in which I had introduced by name, the ladies and gentlemen of the company as willing contributors to the festival in honor of their liberal employer.   I append a few lines :—

   * * * * * * *

" But soft ! methinks I hear the public say,
 ' The ladies, Mr. Leman, where are they?
 You have not named them yet ; oh, fie, for shame !
 What, leave the ladies last—you are to blame !'
 Your pardon, gentle sirs, I mean no ill—
 Pray you observe, I'm following the ' bill.'
 The ladies, then————"

   * * * * * * *

" And Alexina Fisher, just the thing
 As you all know—she's laughing at the wing ;
 Little, but big enough to lead the van,
 See her in boy's clothes—' every inch a man ! '
 And she whose path may Hymen strew with flowers,
 The ' Child of Nature'—pretty Mrs. Bowers."

Mrs. Bowers was then a member of the Company, and had a short time previous made her first appearance as " Amanthis," in the " Child of Nature," when she was Miss Crocker.   Mrs. Bowers' brilliant and successful career as a tragedienne is well known.   She is another happy memory of the by-gone days, and with pride I include her in my list of old and dear friends.

13

During my residence in Philadelphia I formed
many acquaintanceships which time and distance
have severed, and knew many friendships that
death has cut short.   Among the latter I may
name the late John W. Forney, Esq., Pierce Butler, Esq., and Mr. William Savory Torr.   From
the lips of the latter gentleman I heard an anecdote respecting Edmund Kean, which he vouched
for as being, from his own personal knowledge,
absolutely true.   I think it worthy of a place in
my record.

At an evening party given by Nicholas Biddle,
Esq., to which Mr. Kean was an invited guest, a
young lady playfully asked of Mr. Kean during
the evening, what an actor's life was like, to
which he replied, that if she would order the servant to bring him a sheet of paper, he would
give her an answer before the company broke
up, and when she called for her carriage, he put
into her hand a folded paper containing his
answer to her question, which read thus—

> " An actor's life—a sea of ceaseless troubles ;
> An actor's fame—but fleeting, child-blown bubbles,
> Wafted by folly's breath into the air,
> Dispell'd by blasts of envy or despair ;
> Floats on the breeze like Nautill o'er the main,
> Bursts and is gone !—' sans everything ' again.''

I was invited on one occasion to fill the role of
poet, at a celebration of the National Anniver-

sary. Perhaps I may be pardoned for inserting the opening and closing lines of my address in these "Memories." The address was re-written at a later period, with additions, for an anniversary of the San Francisco " Mechanic's Association," and is, I believe, in print :—

" Home of the brave and free, land of my birth,
   Thou fairest, freest, happiest clime of earth,
   Thou glorious refuge of humanity,
   Spread from th' Atlantic to the Western Sea,
   From far Alaska's cold, congealed snow
   To the volcanic hills of Mexico—
   Where mountains rise, whose towering peaks on high
   Piercing afar the illimitable sky,
   Receive and flash the day-god's earliest glance,
   In golden radiance o'er the vast expanse
   That lies around ; where mighty inland seas
   Mount with the storm and ruffle to the breeze;
   Where the huge bison roams the prairie plain,
   And the swift steed, with wildly flowing mane,
   And eye dilated, keenly snuffs afar
   The hunter's lasso on the morning air;
   Where rippling brooks meander on through vales
   That breathe the wild romance of border tales,
   And zephyrs murmur amid verdant bowers
   Rich with the fragrance of perennial flowers;
   Where cavern-cradled tempests madly sweep
   In gusty currents from the mountain steep;
   Where through the fruitful plain majestic on
   Rolls the swift stream, and dashes madly down
   The roaring cataract, 'mid mists that rise
   And paint their rainbows on the o'er-arching skies;
   Where Nature, on her broadest, boldest plan,
   Proclaims aloud the nothingness of man;

Where God hath blent the beautiful and grand
Be thou my theme !   My own, my native land !

*   *   *   *   *   *   *

Home of the brave and free ! dear native land !
With thee my theme began, and so shall end.
If round thy onward path the storm should lower,
Impell'd by traitrous or despotic power,
Should knaves and slaves and demagogues combine,
Fair Freedom's temple walls to undermine,
Thy sturdy yeomen, undismayed and bold,
Unswayed by station, unseduced by gold,
Will at thy summons to the conflict rush,
The foreign or intestine foe to crush ;
Thy banner to uphold, whate'er befalls.
True to the Union, when the Union calls.
In vain the traitor's wiles, the coward's fear
Essay to check thee in thy bright career.
Thou ocean-bound republic ! for on high
Where dwell the stars is writ thy destiny ;
And there those shining orbs have pencilled forth
Thy mission—to regenerate the Earth,
And bid the realm of liberty expand
While floats thy starry flag, my own, my Native Land.

I severed my connection with the Walnut
Street Theatre, at the close of the season of
1849, having received a satisfactory offer from
Messrs. Ludlow and Smith for St. Louis and
New Orleans. I parted from Mr. Marshall with
regret, for I had found him a courteous gentleman, just in his dealings and considerate for the
comfort of those in his employ. I never saw
Mr. Marshall again, but am sorry to know that
ill-fortune darkened his latter years. I do not

know, but believe that he has passed away to the unknown shore.

The prevalence of cholera in the West delayed my departure for some time, and I improved the opportunity to journey as far as Pittsburgh, by a mode of locomotion which steam has made a thing of the past. That summer trip in a canal packet across the great State of Pennsylvania to the Ohio River, is one of my pleasant " memories." The novelty of the conveyance, its adaptedness to the wants of the voyager, the wonderful way in which room was made for everything, in a small ark in which at first sight there appeared to be no room for anything ; the good quality and abundance of the food; the cleanliness of the cookery and bedding, and the discipline and order maintained on those little inland packets, which thridded their way through scenes of rural loveliness, agricultural abundance and natural beauty of valley, plain and mountain, can never be forgotten.

And the trip down the Ohio was equally pleasant; the river was at its very lowest stage— emphatically what John Randolph called it, " a dried up, or nearly dried up ditch;" and I was told on reaching Pittsburgh that it would be impossible to get down the river ; but among the many tied-up steamboats there was one little stern-wheeler that was *not* tied-up, called the

"Exchange," and her master, an energetic young fellow, assured myself and a few more who were anxious to get on, that he would take us through to St. Louis without delay, for the "Exchange" could run and make good time through "damp grass." And he kept his word. I don't think his craft drew more than seven inches of water, and the bars and shoals which had stranded larger boats were sparred over by our little craft with small loss of time. "La Belle Riviere" grew deeper in volume as we advanced. At Cincinnati we took the "Ben. West," a larger boat, soon reached Cairo, and thence made a quick run up the "Father of Waters" to St. Louis.

Messrs. Ludlow and Smith, the well-known western managers, commenced their season in St. Louis on the 15th of August, and I opened as "Sergeant Austerlitz." Mrs. Farren commenced a starring engagement on the 18th as "Lucretia Borgia," and I was the "Genarro."

Mrs. Farren was at that period a great favorite with western audiences. She played the round of tragedy heroines and many other parts with judgment and power. Mr. George Farren was an admirable character actor; his performance of "Sergeant Supplice" in the "Child of the Regiment," and "Captain Cuttle" in "Dombey and Son," were fine examples of his ability and train-

ing.   Mr. and Mrs. Farren played until the end
of the month, acting for their benefit "Much
Ado About Nothing," in which Mrs. Farren
was the "Beatrice," Mr. F. the "Dogberry," and
myself the "Benedick."

I knew in St. Louis Mr. Charles Dibdin Pitt,
who spent a short time in America, and was
esteemed a clever tragedian.   Mr. James Stark
also played an engagement; I knew this gentleman in my early theatrical days; I shall have
occasion to speak of him again.   The "Heron
Family" also appeared; I think that the party
consisted of three or four young ladies; "little
Agnes" was the "precocity" of the organization.
They faded out of sight many a year ago.

During the season there was a grand revival of
the spectacle of the "Forty Thieves."   This old-
time honored melo-drama was always a managerial weakness, so to speak, of Sol. Smith.   He
was very fond of playing "Ali Baba" or "Mus-
tapha," and if he ever saw a chance to have a
"shy" at the "Forty Thieves," he never missed
it.   New scenery on a grand scale was painted
for the piece, and the cave of "Orcobrand," the
evil spirit, in addition to the serpents and dragons
and birds of ill-omen, with which scenic artists
usually adorn it, was embellished with two gigantic demons with bulging eyes, in a sitting
posture on either side of a murky altar.   The

scene on being discovered was received with a murmur of applause which swelled into a roar, when a long-limbed, long-haired, steamboat man in butternut clothes, rose in the pit, and addressing some one whom he knew in the upper tier, cried out, "By G——, Jim, there's Ludlow and Smith counting tickets in the box-office."

The short season in St. Louis closed with the engagement of Mlle. Herminie Blangy. This beautiful danseuse, was a competitor with the no less beautiful Augusta, for the honor of being enrolled as the successor of Fanny Ellsler.

The St. Charles Theatre in New Orleans, opened on the evening of Saturday, November 10th. My trip down the Mississippi on a Leviathan steamer, with all the adjuncts that contribute to the traveler's comfort, was greatly enjoyed—with but *one* drawback; sitting upon the guards one day, my attention was drawn to an intelligent looking, light mulatto, who, to my surprise, had his two wrists linked together with iron fetters about a foot long. I was not at all conversant with the methods of the "patriarchal institution," and was somewhat shocked, when in answer to my inquiry of "why he wore them?" he told me that his *owner* had put them on, not for any offence, but simply as a guard against any attempt at running away, when the boat stopped to "wood up" or for any other purpose. "Who is your owner?" I asked. "Bishop Hawks," he answered; "but he need not have done it, I don't intend to run away." Here was food for reflection. A young man, an intelligent human being *owned* by a servant of God, and *chained* by a servant of God. I *reflected.* On the next day, to my surprise, I was served at table by the same young man; he was an apt and capable waiter; and the captain of the boat had taken off his manacles, upon his word not to attempt to leave. While I am on this topic, I will mention one other incident that caused me to *reflect* on the "patriarchal institution." While in New Orleans, I went one afternoon to some distance below the city to locate, if possible, the range or line of defenses, which were so triumphantly held by Andrew Jackson on the historic 8th of January. I did not have much success, but was pointed to a cluster of trees in the near distance, and informed that underneath their branches General Packenham breathed his last. While I stood thinking of old Hickory and the cotton bales, and of the awful slaughter of that day, in the name of, and for the sake of liberty, I saw working in the adjacent field a negro apparently more than fifty years old, an iron belt around his waist, rings round his ankles, and fetters of very considerable size and weight connecting the two. I was about to speak to him, but a horseman who had the appearance of an overseer, walked his horse slowly by on the inside of the enclosure, and looked at me with a kind of "what are you going to say to that slave?" air; and I was silent. Here was more food for *reflection*. I had come out to view the battle-ground of freedom, and I found a wretched old slave loaded with irons turning up its soil. I *reflected*.

I addition to the stars whose names I have mentioned in connection with the St. Louis season, Mr. Hudson, an Irish actor appeared; Mr. Murdoch played a fine engagement, as did also Miss Cushman, supported by Mr. W. H. Couldock. This gentleman I had known in Philadelphia; he was an admirable actor then, and in his old age now, is acknowledged as one of the truest artists on the American stage. He has made several visits to the Pacific Coast, and is one among others, to whom the writer is indebted for acts of generous courtesy. I had one, and the only opportunity, during that season to see Mr. N. M. Ludlow act. He had been associated for many years in management with Sol. Smith; but had practically retired as an actor. Mr. Ludlow appeared as "Mr. Ferment" in Morton's comedy of "The School of Reform." He had the reputation of being an excellent light comedian in his prime. Mr. Ludlow died within the last year, over ninety years of age.

The season at the " St. Charles" closed on the 29th of March with Shakespeare's "Julius Cæsar," for the writer's benefit—" Cassius," Mr. George Jamison; " Brutus," Mr. James Stark; " Marc Antony," Mr. Walter M. Leman; " Portia," Mrs. J. M. Field. I returned North, and in April re-appeared at the Walnut Street Theatre for a short season with Miss Jean Davenport, when was revived Knowles' play of the " Maid of Mariendorpt."

In pursuance of an engagement to re-join Messrs. Ludlow and Smith in August, I left for St. Louis in time to make the journey by the northern route, and at Buffalo embarked on a steamer which almost rivalled in appointments and size the ocean leviathans of to-day, and sailed by the circuitous way of Lakes Erie, St. Clair, Huron and Michigan, to the city of Chicago— then but the embryo of the mighty metropolis of to-day—and thence by canal and the Illinois River to St. Louis.

That summer trip over the " mighty inland seas," whose shore-line will aggregate not less than twenty-five hundred miles, is a memory of the past which time has not weakened. The weather was delightful, and each long day was too short for the hours of enjoyment. At a certain point off Manitou Island, in Lake Michigan, the water was of wondrous lucidity, and the pebbly bottom was clearly visible at a depth of sixty feet. The company on board the steamer was companionable and pleasant, and among the creature comforts of the table were lake trout of marvellous size and delicious flavor.

As in the previous year, Mrs. Farren commenced the season in St. Louis ; and in the first fourteen nights I played successively "Master Walter," "Beverley," "Huon," "Colonna," "Benedick," "Julian St. Pierre," "Genarro," "Claude Melnotte," "Duke Aranza," the "Stranger," "Black Norris" in Knowles' "Wrecker's Daughter," "Giraldi Fazio," and "Edgar Ravenswood" in the "Bride of Lammermoor." There would have been nothing extraordinary in this, but that four of the longest in the list I had never played before, and what with study—for I sat up nearly all night for most of the time— and the necessary rehearsals, I cannot recall a more exacting two weeks' wear of mind and body during my professional life.

In September, Miss Julia Dean produced Miss Fanny Kemble's adaptation from the French, entitled the "Duke's Wager." This piece drew forth a great deal of criticism at the time, and was somewhat sharply noticed by the press of New Orleans, on its production in that city, as being too broadly "French" for the American Stage. That was nearly forty years ago. The

American Stage, within the few past years, has got bravely over its anti-French squeamishness —perhaps it were better if it had not. Miss Dean's acting as "Gabrielle de Belle-Isle" was remarkably fine. I was the "Duke de Richelieu" of the play.

What son of Momus is this, whose memory comes up to me from the shadows of the past, whose *outré* figure and remarkable features were but secondary factors in the wealth of mirth and merriment that lived in his spirit and found utterance in his speech? Charles Burke. Who that ever saw him can forget him? Who that saw him can remember his superior as a low comedian? Mr. Burke played at that time "Dr. Ollapod," "Billy Lackaday," and some other characters, with an excellence all his own. After a long acquaintance with Charles Burke, I can say—as all who knew him in life will say—that he was the soul of kindness, charity and honor. He was in private life one of the most charming companions imaginable.

Mr. Burke was, I believe, twice married; his second wife was a Boston lady whom I knew in my early theatrical life. The first Mrs. Burke had the character of being a lady of a very lively temperament, so much so, that domestic peace was sometimes in danger of eclipse, at least so said report; that this was true I am inclined to believe from a circumstance that occurred a year later in Baltimore. I was present with Mr. Burke at a large social party for spiritual manifestations; some of the "developments" were considered wonderful; the answers of the "spirits" were very prompt, and every one had some inquiry to make of some departed friend. We were all sitting round a large table, upon which cake and wine had been served, while the seance was suspended; when some one remarked, "Mr. Burke you havn't called up any departed friend to-night; don't *you* want to see any one?" and Mr. Savage, one of the company, who was attached to Laura Keene's Theatre, and had been the powerful "medium" of the evening, added— "No, I've noticed that you hav'nt called on any spirit, Mr. Burke; don't you want to see Mrs. Burke? let me call Mrs. Burke." Charley, with that remarkable expression which defies description, instantly and earnestly answered—"No, don't! don't! I don't want to see her." But Savage was determined, and putting his hands on the table, asked—"Is the spirit of Mrs. Burke here?" when a violent convulsion of the table, which made the tumblers and wine glasses jump up two or three inches, and set everything rattling and breaking, astonished every one but Burke; who instantly exclaimed—"That's her, that's her, I know her; that's her, let her go. I don't want to ask her any questions, let her go."

Another "memory" of that season is the "Bateman Children;" they were two—Ellen and Kate; the youngest was certainly one of the most comical little midgets I ever saw, and was as clever as she was small. Both of these little girls grew up into fine actresses, and one made a noise in the dramatic world. Their father became famous as a manager in England and America.

It is pleasant to remember that the writer's benefit at the close of the St. Louis season was a pronounced and complimentary success. The "Millionaire" was the play. The company again went down the great river, and on the 13th of November, the St. Charles Theatre opened with the "Millionaire," which was played three nights. The "Dimple" of the cast on this occasion was Mrs. Chapman, late Miss Julia Drake, a cousin of Julia Dean, a most piquante and merry little actress, who maintained the reputation of the "Drake" family for dramatic ability. This season was notable for a brilliant engagement of Miss Charlotte Cushman, whose acting of "Lady Macbeth" and "Meg Merriles," impressed the public most profoundly. Miss Jenny Lind sang under the management of the famous Barnum, and packed the theatre to the roof, and Burke and the Seguins added to the attractions of a prosperous season, which came to a termination early in April.   I took the steamer for Louisville, and saw the Queen City of the South for the last time.   At Louisville I first met with Mrs. Coleman Pope; this lady had an established reputation at that time as a capable artiste, but was hardly recognized as a tragedienne.   The feature of that short season in Louisville was the production of the tragedy of "Nina Sforza"— "Nina Sforza," Mrs. Coleman Pope; "Spinola," Walter M. Leman; "Grimaldo," Charles Hill. This gentleman was the father of Mr. Barton Hill, with whom I was afterwards associated in the California Theatre in San Francisco.   Mr. Hill was a very eccentric gentleman, full of the old ways and traditions of the stage; he has been long dead.

From Louisville, with Mrs. Pope, I went to St. Louis, and there met H. A. Perry, whom I had first known as a beginner in the Walnut St.   I knew him subsequently on the Pacific Coast. Harry Perry at that early period gave evidence of his wondrous facial powers, his imitations were remarkable, and he was at home in all he attempted.   I recall the names of Mr. Graham, a tragedian of great ability, who died very suddenly during the season, and of Mr. Charles Bass, the old-time New York favorite; with Silsbee, Mlle. Franck and others; but all, including the manager Mr. Bates, and Mr. Malone Raymond the stage manager, have passed to the " far beyond." At this time I received an offer from the managers of the National Theatre in Boston, and returned to my "native heather" after an absence of ten years. Mr. Pelby, my first manager was dead, and the theatre was opened under the management of Messrs. Wright and Fenno. The opening night presented Miss Fanny Wallack in the character of " Martha Gibbs," and myself as " Stephen Plum," in the comedy of " All that Glitters is not Gold." Miss Wallack is a kinswoman of the Wallack family, but I know not in what exact relation. In speaking of her opening performance, an accomplished critic of the day, after summing up the points of merit, declared that she " astonished every one by the force and brilliancy of her acting." " Martha Gibbs " and " Stephen Plum " were called before the curtain, and speech-making was the order of the evening.

The " Prairie Bird " was produced and ran a week, and this is another pleasant memory, for my old friends up to this period had known me only as an *actor.* At this time I first knew Mr. Barney Williams, of whom I shall have more to say anon. In December the " Millionaire " was presented, and my pardonable pride was again gratified, for it was received well by the audience, and pleasantly spoken of by the press.

After twenty years' absence, Mme. Celeste re-appeared with an English reputation, and was warmly received; and Miss Fanny Wallack played a second successful engagement, followed by one, cut off subsequently in the prime of his powers, who was acknowledged to stand in the front rank among the great actors of his time—Mr. Gustavus Vaughn Brooke. He opened in "Sir Giles Overreach," and made a most marked impression. There was an intensity, a fire of energy in his representations that took captive the auditor, whether he would or no; and he was always so essentially in earnest that he inspired those who acted with him with the same feeling. The magnetism of an earnest actor is more likely to develop what is worthy of development in the histrionic Neophite, than the chilly, arms-length manner and spirit which says, "stand at a distance; be a nonentity; do nothing." The Macready theory was the very reverse of the Booth school; the one said, "I'll do all the acting," the other said, "Act up to me." Brooke was a disciple of the Booth school. His end was a tragic one; he perished at sea.

On the 19th of April the season was brought to an abrupt close by the destruction of the theatre by fire. Mr. George Vandenhoff and Mrs. Sinclair were playing an engagement at the time. Mr. Vandenhoff was a highly educated

gentleman, and had, I believe, in the earlier portion of his life, been a practitioner at the bar.
He would have been thought a great actor, had
he not been preceded by a *greater* Vandenhoff.
Mrs. Sinclair had become famous from the notoriety of the Forrest divorce. She subsequently
became a manageress in San Francisco.

This lady and gentleman had appeared in the
" School for Scandal " on the night of the conflagration, and the piece announced for the following evening was represented on the stage of
the old " Boston Theatre," which was courteously
offered to the burnt-out " Thespians." The destruction of the " National Theatre " was complete. Of all that it contained, nothing was
saved, and the only relic of paper, book, or manuscript found, was a play-bill with a charred border, of the " Prairie Bird," which was picked up
in the vicinity and given to me as a " memory "
of the old " National Theatre " fire.

I accompanied Mr. Vandenhoff and Mrs. Sinclair to Portland for a few nights, which were
supplemented by a few more with Miss Kimber-
ley. This lady aspired to the position of a star,
but she shone with a feeble light.

The manager of this adventure was Mr. J. P.
Addams. Mr. Addams is one of my memories,
and, on the whole, a very merry one. I first
knew him as a handsome page in the spectacle

of " Cinderella," in the time of the " Woods."
He grew up more inclined to be a tragedy hero
than a comic one, but he had the elements to
make a successful comedian. He was a younger
brother of Augustus Addams, who, if he had
lived, would have been the " dramatic Cæsar,"
but he died young. J. P. Addams was always
ready for anything, and equal to anything. I
think he would have been a successful rival to
the most eminent itinerant " Napoleon " that ever
tramped through England in the strollers' palmy
days. With a black cloak and a black wig ; with
a black cloak and a red wig, he was ready for
any tragic or comic part at ten minutes notice.
I met Mr. Addams after a lapse of more than a
quarter of a century, on the Pacific coast. He
had just returned from Australia, where Fortune,
he informed me, had been fickle ; his appearance
confirmed the truth of his words. He returned,
I believe, to the Atlantic coast, and, I think, is
still alive. I hope he is, at any rate, and prosperous, for he is, indeed, a pleasant old memory.

Within the following six months I played
occasionally at Bangor, Belfast, Orono and Oldtown, in the State of Maine, and at Worcester
and Lowell, in Massachusetts. With the exception of Lowell, none of these towns boasted
of a theatre, and the "temple of the muses " was
the town or some other hall. At Orono, the

teachings of the drama were dispensed from the
vestry of the Universalist church, and at Oldtown
from the vestry of the Episcopal church, and the
priestesses were Mrs. English and her two
daughters, Lucille and Helen Western; both of
these young girls became good actresses, and
Helen, especially, made a great reputation in after
years; both are now dead, and their mother, Mrs.
English, is an inmate of the " Forrest Home."

Almost immediately upon the destruction of
the " National," steps were taken for the erection
of a new theatre upon its site, and on Monday,
November 1st, 1852, the new structure, though
far from completion, was opened to the public.
Mr. Joseph Leonard, a well-known auctioneer,
was the head and front of the enterprise, and was
the first manager of the "New National;" he was
a lover of the drama; liberal, but inexperienced
and over-confident, and soon found to his cost
that every man cannot "run a theatre" any more
than a hotel.

The address for the opening was from the pen
of Mr. W. O. Eaton, a brother of Charles Eaton,
and I was selected to deliver it. The programme
included the comedy of the " Heir-at-Law," and
a farce; and the " Dr. Pangloss" of the play was
a gentleman who afterwards rose to fame and
fortune by his remarkable performance of the

most remarkable character of the idiotic drama ever exhibited.

Mr. Douglas Steuart, or Mr. E. A. Sothern (I do not know which was his true name) was announced as from the "Theatre Royal, Birmingham—his first appearance in America," and his debut, which was expected to be a success, proved a sad failure. By mutual agreement with the manager he soon after withdrew from the theatre, and subsequently played juvenile tragedy in Wallack's Old Theatre in New York, and was, I believe a member of Laura Keene's company when a *sketch* part in that burlesque of New England character called "Our American Cousin" gave the opportunity, which with great tact he improved, to build up that most laughable monstrosity, too ridiculous for thought, too absurd for criticism, utterly unlike any creature with the human form ever seen under the heavens above or upon the earth beneath—"Dundreary." Mr. Steuart, or Sothern, affected other characters, but he never played anything but "Dundreary."

Mrs. Vickery and Mrs. Archbold were also new importations by Mr. Leonard. The first was a tragedienne, who did not become popular; the second was a comedy "Old Lady," who did. I last saw Mrs. Archbold some years ago, when on a visit to St. Johns, New Brunswick; she is in my list of pleasant memories.

Mrs. George Barrett, whom I have mentioned in a previous chapter as being *"eternally young,"* re-appeared as "Lady Teazle," and continued as the support of Mr. J. W. Wallack, who astonished the old friends of thirty years before by his acting, which possessed its old artistic finish unimpaired by time. Brooke followed Wallack, and Forrest followed Brooke, and a large amount of money was received, but the expenses outran the receipts; Mr. Forrest demanded and received a clear half. In March, Mr. Murdoch appeared in conjunction with Miss Matilda Heron, who had not yet become famous, but was on the way to fame, and Miles' play of "De Soto" was produced.

At the close of the month the financial pressure caused a disintegration of the large company, and I was among those who left. During the summer I acted at intervals in the New England cities, and first played with Mrs. Anna Cora Mowatt, at Worcester. This lady, whose name was so familiar to the theatrical world of thirty-five years ago, was born in Bordeaux, her maiden name was Ogden; she had been married at an early age to Mr. Mowatt, a lawyer, and was known as the authoress of a number of fugitive poems, and as a public reader, prior to her ap-

pearance on the stage, some ten years before I
met her.   With youth, beauty, a musical voice,
and a fair share of talent, her career had been a
social and dramatic triumph, and her success
upon the stage had been. supplemented by her
success as a dramatist; her two plays "Fashion"
and "Armand the Child of the People," having
a considerable popularity, though since forgotten.
She had visited England in company with Mr.
Edward Davenport—whose subsequent brilliant
career is well know—and was at her zenith when
I acted with her.   She was pronounced a fault-
less "Parthenia" by her admirers, but I have
played "Ingomar" to many I thought her superior.   Mrs. Mowatt soon after married Mr.
Ritchie of Richmond, and left the stage.

Mrs. Melinda Jones is another "memory" of
those summer days.   She was the wife of George
Jones, the "Count Joannes," from whom she had
been a long time separated.   Mrs. Jones was a
very good actress of the *heavy* calibre, but she
was nevertheless fond of playing sylph-like parts.
I think she was a Richmond lady, and like most
Virginians was an expert politician.   I know
that from her conversation in those days, I
fancied she was in correspondence with every
Senator and Representative from the Middle and
Southern States.   She was almost as fond of
what in old days were called breeches parts as

Charlotte Cushman, and played "Claude Melnotte," and "Romeo," and "Richard III," with a great deal of spirit. I met Mrs. Jones many years after in California, and traveled with her daughter, Miss Avonia Jones, who took high rank as an actress, and I think went to Australia with Mr. G. V. Brooke. Mrs. Jones has been long deceased.

Another "memory" of that summer is Mr. James H. Warwick; he was a tragedian, and went to California soon after, I think. I knew him well, and frequently acted with him in the Golden State, of which I shall have occasion to speak in a future chapter.

CHAPTER XI.

MR. HENRY C. JARRETT, at that time
manager of the Baltimore Museum, was in
quest of a stage manager for the ensuing season.
At the suggestion of my friend, James E. Mur-
dock, Esq., a correspondence with that gentleman
resulted in my engagement. During the summer I visited Philadelphia and played for a few
weeks at the "National Theatre"—or rather
"Amphitheatre"—in Chestnut street, under the
management of General Rufus Welsh. Several
grand equestrian pieces were produced, under the

stage direction of Mr. George Harris, the leading lady being Mrs. Gladstone, a beautiful woman and a charming actress.

On Monday, the 29th of August, the Baltimore Museum opened with Boucicault's play of " Old Heads and Young Hearts," and the " Rough Diamond," preceded by an opening address, written and spoken by the stage manager. With an author's, I hope, pardonable vanity, I take an author's liberty to insert here a portion of that address.

    *   *   *   *   *   *   *

" Our cause, the drama ! when the sombre night
  Of barbarism fled before the light
  Of Grecian splendor; in the classic land
  Where art was born, where Homer's mighty hand
  Seized on the magic lyre of poesy
  And swept its chords for immortality;
  There, truth-begotten in auspicious hour,
  To sway the human heart with wizard power,
  To light the heart and lift the soul of man,
  The star-gemm'd goddess first her course began.

  And what has been her course, her teachings ? Say,
  Are they what slander calls them ?　Does she lay
  A snare for virtue's footsteps ?　Is her smile
  That of a siren—only guilt and guile ?
  Turn to her records ; scan them, naught impedes;
  Follow her path and scrutinize her deeds.

  In the long lapse of centuries whose tide
  Has swept o'er systems that have lived and died,
  O'er thrones and altars, dynasties and states,
  O'er kings and kaisers, priests and potentates,
  Through chaos, weal or woe, the drama still
  Survives, her glorious mission to fulfill.

The blind fanatic, who, in righteous zeal,
Breaks his Creator's image on the wheel,
And that more odious bigot who, despite
Of clearer reason and of truer light,
Hates with a holy hatred, everyone
Whose creed a hair's breadth differs from his own ;
The stony-hearted usurer, who rears
His wealth on widows' sighs and orphans' tears;
The shallow empiric, who, with gold in view,
Depletes his patients' veins—and pockets, too;
The demagogue, who, with no selfish wishes,
Loves his dear country—and her loaves and fishes;
The brainless fop, who breaks his stays, and dies
For one dear smile from "darling Julia's eyes;"
The fool of fashion and the idle drone,
Who live by thews and sinews not their own;
The solemn blockhead, big with pompous speech;
The casuist, whose metaphysics teach
That wicked means may serve a holy end;
The perjured lover and the faithless friend—
For these the drama barbs her shining dart,
And sends her arrows quivering to the heart.

But, for the modest maid, the striving youth,
The faithful teacher and the man of truth ;
For stern integrity that walks the road
Of duty, with reliance upon God;
For meek-eyed charity, that thinks no harm;
For honesty that knows no "itching palm;"
For every noble thought and manly sense
The drama pleads with burning eloquence.
When tyrants scourge the brave and bind the free,
The drama's clarion voice for liberty
Talks to the nations, and her tocsin bell
Inspires a Washington, or nerves a Tell ;
Her purpose still, as when her course began,
To light the path and cheer the heart of man.

Mrs. J. Silsbee, the wife of Mr. Josh Silsbee, the Yankee comedian, was the tragedy lady of the company. She was the former wife of a Mr. Gilbert, of the firm of Gilbert and Trowbridge, who were itinerant managers in the New England States when my theatrical life began. She was a highly intelligent woman and a very good actress, and had often played with the prominent stars of the day. I believe Mrs. S. subsequently became the wife of Mr. Chapman, the popular low-comedian of the Walnut St. Theatre.

Miss Marion was a young lady of no great artistic pretentions, but a local favorite. I recall her name with a sad remembrance of the tragic end which befel her some years later, when a dreadful crime committed in New England startled the community.

Mr. William Ellis was the " old man " of the company; with a wonderful study he combined an adaptability for serious or comic roles that made him a valuable acquisition. Mr. Ellis had also a taste for painting, and some of his cabinet pictures possessed great merit. There was a kind of incipient insanity in his deportment at times, that was painfully suggestive of what eventually became raving madness. He died many years since.

Mr. Clifton W. Tayleure, then a young man, though engaged to play *old* parts, is remembered as an old friend, although he did think that in my official capacity I ignored, at times, his just pretensions. What stage manager living or dead ever escaped such a charge? Mr. Tayleure has, I think, in later years, been successful as a dramatist.

Mr. Benjamin G. Rogers, the low-comedian, was at that early day a capable and pleasing actor. For nearly thirty years I had not seen this gentleman; when, in 1883, I had the pleasure of grasping his hand in San Francisco, and renewing the memories of the past. Mr. Rogers is now a valuable member of Mr. Laurence Barrett's company, respected in public and private, a happy, contented man.

The scenic artist of the "Museum" was Mr. Charles Getz, who has since attained to the highest rank as a painter. I deem it unnecessary to dwell upon what transpired during the ten month's season in which I occupied a novel position, and in which Silsbee, who was our first star, played one engagement; Miss Jean Davenport, two; the Bateman Children, one; Mrs. Charles Howard, the lovely woman and fine vocalist, one; Mr. and Mrs. Barney Williams, two; Mr. Wm. R. Goodall, two; Miss Julia Dean, one; Mr. John E. Owens, three; Mr. F. S. Chanfrau and Miss Albertine, two; Mrs. Farren, two; the "Boone" Sisters, one; and Mrs. Melinda Jones, one; and of which the specialty was the production of the "Last Days of Pompeii," to which the manager contributed a liberal expenditure of money, and the stage manager all the skill and knowledge he possessed. It had a prosperous run of three weeks, and the "Millionaire" and "Germantown," each a run of one.

Mr. W. R. Goodall, whom I have mentioned, was a young man of great promise, personally very handsome, and possessing remarkable versatility, in many respects he was not unlike Mr. Harry Perry. His imitative power was great, and if he had lived, I think he would have been eminent. His performance of "Edward Middleton," in the drama of "The Drunkard," was almost painful, in its startling truth to nature. He died young. The "Boone" children were two little precocities in the "Bateman" style, and were clever, and the "Batemans" were more clever than when I had seen them in St. Louis.

Miss Albertine was in those days very popular in many parts which demanded male attire. For some time she had professionally traveled with Mr. F. S. Chanfrau, and the combined attraction made them lucrative stars. She was a little woman, of great physical endurance, and sang and played with spirit. I shall have more to say of this lady when I get to California.

The Agricultural Fair week of the Maryland Society, was an event which then drew (as I suppose it does now) great crowds to Baltimore, and the attractiveness of all public entertainments was somewhat exaggerated by those who ran them, in order to attract public attention. In this race of hyperbole the " Museum " entered for the time, perhaps with questionable taste. I append the heading of one of my bills during fair week :—

AS A FITTING PRELUDE

To usher in the celebration of the

ANNUAL GALA

Which confers on the Free Citizens of our

NOBLE OLD STATE,

Happiest among the Happy Republics which
compose the Brilliant Constellation of
Independent Commonwealth,
the Honorable Rewards

—THAT—

HONEST LABOR,

MECHANICAL INGENUITY,

AND MENTAL PROGRESS

Always command in this

ENLIGHTENED COMMUNITY,

The Management of this Established and Popular Resort offer to the Thousands of

CITIZENS AND STRANGERS

Who are waiting to throng within its portals,
the following bill for the evening:

*   *   *   *   *

The season closed on the 12th of June, and during the nearly ten months of its continuance, successfully held its own against all rivals, among which, a handsome new theatre, erected for and opened by Miss Laura Keene, was the most formidable.

The benefit of the stage manager, which was announced as his " Farewell, prior to his departure for California," filled the house to repletion. The play was Schiller's tragedy of " The Robbers." " Charles de Moor," first time, Mr. Walter M. Leman.

During that winter, as much for a change as for profit, with the approval of Mr. Jarrett, I ran up to the little town of Cumberland, Md., and played three nights. The " Mrs. Haller " to my " Stranger," was Mrs. John Ellsler, whose daughter, Miss Effie Ellsler, was the charming " Hazel Kirke " of the Madison Square combination, so well known, and whose courtesy and professional kindness was evinced at a subsequent date in a manner most grateful to me. The "Charlotte," with a song, was Maggie Mitchell—that was thirty-three years ago, and she hadn't discovered " Fanchon," or " Little Barefoot ;" and the " Peter " was Mr. T. E. Owens, a brother of Mr. John Owens ; this gentleman recently died, an old man, in the " Forrest Home."

15

At the close of the season I spent six weeks in the towns of Frederick and Hagerstown, where, with a small company, a series of performances was given with success. Our orchestra was under the direction—as the bills stated—of the "celebrated leader and composer, Alexander Jamieson, Esq."

I presume that there are not many, even of the musical profession, now alive, who remember "Sandy Jamieson." He was an old man at the time of which I write, and he lived many years longer, being, I think, over ninety years of age at his decease. But in spite of years, which he never made any account of, he was perennially and eternally young—young in heart, young in feeling, young in spirit. Poor Sandy's gone, but if he fiddles in another world, I am sure he'll fiddle none but the liveliest tunes. Pleasant memories are those of my bright summer days in Frederick and Hagerstown; the merry picnics we enjoyed on the banks of the Antietam creek, and the ride over the South mountain were dashed with no vision of the struggle so soon to come, when friends and brothers should meet to shed each other's blood. It is indeed well that we cannot see into the future.

In the month of August, 1854, the good steamer, "Empire City," cleared from New York to San Francisco, with some five hundred passengers, the writer of these " Memories " being one. Among them were grave L. L. D.'s, and wise M. D.'s, merchants and speculators and astute politicians, hardy men of toil, chevaliers d'industrie, scheming widows, and ambitious mammas, and expectant young lady daughters, and curly-headed children, and infants, "mewling and puking in the nurse's arms." We sped over a sunny sea with scarce a ripple on its surface, and most of those who were going to California for the first time, were resolved to make their pile in one year, or two at the most, and go back home to enjoy it.

Those who had been in California had a sententious manner of expressing their contempt for the visionary ideas of some of the new Argonauts, which plainly indicated a doubt of their ever going back at all. An eminent traveler and explorer, afterwards a candidate for the Chief Magistracy of the Union; another prominent politician, who subsequently became Governor of California—now deceased; the wife of a well-known San Francisco journalist; and a young lady of peculiarly strong-minded proclivities, who entertained the idea that she could revolutionize society on the Pacific Coast by delivering lectures on Women's Rights in the mining regions—where there was not, on an average, one female to forty square miles of territory — at four bits a head; together with Mr. and Mrs. Barney Williams and myself, formed a portion of the company allotted to the captain's table; and the conversation at meals, and in the saloon on deck sometimes took a peculiarly ludicrous and entertaining turn.

As usual, in those early days, the "Isthmus" was a common topic of conversation. "When shall we reach it?" and "How shall we succeed in getting across?" were on everyone's lips. Like "Lord Duberly," our Irish comedian's "kakelology" had been neglected in his youth, and I observed that he never ventured a remark about the "Isthmus;" one evening he drew me apart, and plunging right into the core of the subject, addressed me thus:

"I say, Walter, what the d——l is all this about the Isthmus? They're all talking about the Isthmus—what is the Isthmus, any way?"

Amazed, I asked, "Barney, don't you know?"

"Burn me if I do," was his reply. "I know that it's something to get over, somehow or other; they said so when we left New York, and they're talking about it all the time; but what it is, and why they call it an isthmus, by the piper, I don't know!"

Amused at his frank avowal, I got the map from the cabin and explained the knotty problem; and when he got it through his brain, he burst out with an expression of joy: "Oh! by the holy Mother! I see it now; and there's more Isthmuses than one!" And from that moment, to make up for lost time, he talked "Isthmus" all the way down to Aspinwall. I don't know that any geographical knowledge was necessary, however, to a man who, in less than a year, made twenty thousand dollars, playing Irish farces in California.

We coaled the ship at Kingston, Jamaica, which service was performed by women, an endless procession going up one gang-plank, dumping the bucket of coal (which they carried on their heads) as they reached the deck, and returning by another. I thought that the servile and laborious operation of these poor negresses might interest our woman's rights advocate, but she made no sign.

The crossing of the Isthmus was an adventure in those days. The railroad had been completed for about one-half the distance to Panama; we stepped from the cars into mud up to our knees, and we had a lively time getting mules, for which each passenger had been given a ticket by the agent. The famous "military road"—built, as we were told, by Cortez or Pizarro or some other old hidalgo, three or four centuries ago—was nothing but a bridle-trail, worn down in many places by those *patient* beasts, the mules, into a kind of ravine or cañon, where it was impossible for the animals to pass each other, and the rider had to take *his* or *her* chance of being, like Sir Harcourt, "rubbed off," or of backing off his donkey's back, and leaving the two amiable quadrupeds to settle the "right of passage" in their own way.

Those ladies of the company who rode *astride*, made the trip with comparative comfort, and indeed no equestrienne should travel the mountains in any other manner. I enjoyed the whole thing hugely. I had not been in the saddle since my boyhood, and rarely then; but tucking my trousers into my boots, and a bottle of claret in each pocket, with a cry of "hip-la-mula!" I was the second one of our company to ride through the gates of Panama, and the wife of our California journalist was, I think, the third, and she, like a sensible woman, rode astride.

We were told that we should have the steamer "Golden Gate" on the Pacific, but were disappointed in finding the old "California" instead, and were seventeen days to San Francisco, making twenty-nine from New York, but a little more than four times as long as it takes to make the trip now. Of the half thousand souls that came with me over two oceans towards the setting sun, all are scattered. How many survive, how many have crossed a wider ocean—who can tell?

At the time I arrived in California, the drama was, if I may be allowed the phrase, full-born. Only five years had elapsed since the " Eagle Theatre," the first building dedicated to the purpose of the drama had been erected in Sacramento, the earliest and richest birth of the golden age of the Pacific, a building in size, thirty by sixty-five feet, the frame of which was constructed of lumber costing from $600 to $700 per thousand. The roof was covered with sheet-iron and tin, and the sides with canvas, costing one dollar per yard, and sewed together at an expense of sixteen dollars per day to each man employed on the work. Pieces of packing boxes served for constructing the stage, which was sixteen feet deep; the drop-scenes were three, a wood, street and interior view. As an entrance to the second tier a step-ladder was provided on the outside of the building, and in deference to ladies canvas was nailed beneath it. In the parquette the seats were of rough boards, the bare ground serving as floor. It was common between the acts and the pieces, for parties in the pit to indulge in a game of *monte*, using the seats to make their " lay-out " upon. Visitors purchased their tickets in the adjacent saloon, generally pouring out a quantity of gold dust in the treasurer's scales, who took down weight, at twelve dollars to the ounce. For this " comfortable and well-arranged

house," as the " Placer *Times*" called it, including the saloon in front, not less than $80,000 was
expended. In speaking of the opening, the
Times said that the " dress circle was graced with
quite a number of fine looking, well costumed
ladies," and declared "that the sight was somewhat revivifying."

There is living to-day in San Francisco, one
gentleman who was a member of that pioneer
dramatic company of the Eagle Theatre — Mr.
James H. McCabe — during a long life, to good-luck
he has been but a little indebted; in his acting
days his benefit nights were invariably spoiled
by storm or accident. " Douglas " was to have
been done on one of those occasions at the Eagle
Theatre; he had studied the words of the
" Gentle Anna," to be recited in the garb and
character of an old man; Mrs. Ray had grappled
with " Lady Randolph ; " Jack Harris was sober
and perfect in " Glenalvon ; " Atwater and Daly
were all right in " Young Norval " and " Lord
Randolph," and all the indoor elements predicated
a triumphant result, but the storm-king willed it
otherwise; the water rose six inches deep in the
pit before the doors opened, and the play had
progressed but an act or two when the seats
ceased to afford a dry foundation. Half the town
was submerged, and the few second floors then to
be found in the city of canvas, afforded sleeping

apartments for but a portion of its unhoused inhabitants. Fortunately the actors were better bestowed, for the stage was their domicil by day and night.

Mr. McCabe has experienced many reverses of fortune, but has always maintained an equanimity of temper and a philosophical spirit, that have made him, although a poor, still a happy old man, an unpretentious gentleman of inflexible integrity and sterling worth. I am proud to call him my friend.

In October, 1851, three years before my arrival, the "Jenny Lind Theatre," a large and handsome house, rivalling the best theatres in the Atlantic States, and capable of seating 2,000 persons, had been erected opposite the plaza, in San Francisco; but this had been sold to the municipal authorities for a city hall, and in the same year the "American Theatre" had been erected. In 1853 the "Metropolitan Theatre," a massive and costly structure, was built by Mr. Joseph Trench, and at the time of my arrival was open with a full company, under the management of Mrs. Catherine Sinclair. Outside of San Francisco, there were theatres in Sacramento and Stockton, and possibly in one or two other towns in the State; and within the following decade almost every mining town possessed a building devoted to theatrical uses.

The reader will understand how rapidly the drama, like everything else of California growth, advanced in those early days, when he knows that the first theatrical performance in San Francisco had been given in the second story of a building opposite the plaza, known as "Washington Hall," less than four years before San Francisco had left its embryo existence.

In Sacramento, the "Eagle Theatre" had been succeeded by the "Tehama Theatre," and that by the "Pacific" and the "American." In addition to the "Metropolitan" and "American" theatres, in San Francisco, there was a small house known as the "Adelphi," mainly devoted to French performances.

Far away as San Francisco then seemed from the rest of the world, it had already been visited by some of the brightest musical and dramatic luminaries of the age, among whom were found the names of Signora Elisa Biscaccianti, Catharine Hayes, Junius Brutus Booth, J. E. Murdoch, James Stark, Anna Thillon, Matilda Heron, Mrs. Alexina F. Baker, Madame Anna Bishop and many more.

The Metropolitan Theatre was certainly one of the handsomest temples of dramatic art in America. Its general construction interiorly was not unlike that of the St. Charles Theatre in New Orleans. Mrs. Sinclair's stage manager was Mr. James Dowling; this gentleman I knew for many years. Subsequently he met his death at the hands of a variety actor named Tuers, accidently, as the jury declared. The musical director was the renowned Bochsa, with whom Madame Anna Bishop was so long professionally associated. This lady I had been slightly acquainted with in Philadelphia, and it was a pleasure to meet her again; her noble bearing, her grand stage presence, and fine delivery of either recitative or air, claimed universal admiration. She personated the heroes of the "Othello" and "Tancredi" style to perfection. On one occasion in Boston, she appeared in costume in two different musical halls on the same evening, arousing astonishment and applause by her personation of "Othello" in one place, and the freedom of a Spanish girl's manner in the other, as "Desdemona."

She was mistress of every style, and perhaps, as a linguist, her equal was never known, twenty different tongues were by her married to music with purity and grace; whether Russian, French or Hottentot, their roughness became smooth and liquid. Who, that ever heard the duet from "Linda," as given by Madame Anna Bishop and Reeves, can forget it. She died at an advanced age and sang to the last, "fading" from life in "music."

Mr. William Barry, an eccentric and low-comedian of rare merit, was a member of Mrs. Sinclair's company. He was always noted for a rigid adherence to the author, and, I think, was the only actor in his line that never "gagged;" his performance of "Graves" in the play of "Money" and of the "Gravedigger" in "Hamlet," were near perfection. He died suddenly some few years since. Mr. Wm. B. Chapman, a talented member of the numerous "Chapman Family," and his sister Miss Caroline Chapman, a most amiable woman, an exquisite dancer and an actress of protean ability, were in the company; both are long dead. Mrs. Judah stood high in public estimation. Marietta Starfield Torrence, better known as "Mrs. Judah," the name of her first husband, was for the period of thirty years a universal favorite with the people of the Pacific Coast, not only as an actress, but also in private life; four years have passed since she died, and the habitues of the theatre still think, as they will think if alive, when four and twenty have elapsed, that her equal in her peculiar line never *was* or *will* be. I think no "Juliet" ever played in San Francisco that was not over-shadowed by the "Nurse" of Mrs. Judah, and her appearance even in a most insignificant role, was always signalized by hearty applause. She died in March, 1883; it was the writer's sad privilege to participate in the simple ceremonial of her obsequies.

Mrs. Elizabeth Thoman, now Mrs. Saunders, another early California actress, was attached to the company of Mrs. Sinclair—the mantle that Judah dropped fell upon Saunders, albeit precarious health and advancing years make the burthen of active professional life somewhat irksome. Mrs. Saunders is a member of the "Jefferson" family, an admirable artist, an admirable woman, and *is*, as Mrs. Judah *was*, my old and valued friend; one has passed away— may I long be able to say of the other—"She still lives."

Mr. Edward N. Thayer, another member of Mrs. Sinclair's company, I will mention as my associate and friend during a great portion of the period between "fifty-four" and "eighty-four." I think that almost every old Californian has sailed or ran back and forth from "Frisco" to the "States" and from the "States" to "Frisco" as we used to say, from one to a half dozen times, excepting Ned Thayer. I think that he really likes California, although he *growls* a little occasionally, and I know that the public like him, and his private friends like him notwithstanding his *growling*. Mr. Thayer is a son of the fine actor I have spoken of in an earlier chapter, as connected with the Philadelphia stage, and is a worthy son of an accomplished sire.

I have said that San Francisco theatricals in 1854 had passed from the embryo stage, they were in a transition state, as was indeed the case with everything Californian; the city that now numbers three hundred thousand inhabitants, then had but fifty thousand; the time had not so long gone by when a woman walking along the streets was as much of a sight as an elephant or giraffe would be now; where now are miles of lighted streets was then nothing but chapparal and lagoon; and it is almost impossible to conceive the difference between the *then* and the *now*.

The circus ante-dated the theatre in San Francisco early in 1849 and 1850; two had been respectively opened, one by Mr. Joseph Rowe, who still lives in the city which he has seen grow from nothing to empire, in which the easily satisfied populace were content to pay, without a murmur, three dollars for pit seats, five dollars for box places, and fifty-five dollars for the luxury of a private stall. Stephen C. Massett came next, after the circus and ahead of the theatre; and here is a "memory" indeed! Steve Massett! Who is there that does not know him? or rather, I should ask who is there that Stephen C. Massett does not know, from "king and kaiser," to " priest and potentate ? "

In the year 1849, on the evening of Monday, June 22d, what may be considered the first among the regular amusements of the city was given by Mr. Massett ("Jeems Pipes") in a school-room, which was crowded to suffocation, yielding over five hundred dollars. The front seats were reserved for ladies, of whom there were but *four* present; the Collector of the Port loaned the piano used by Mr. Massett (it was the only one in the country), and the porters received sixteen dollars for removing it from the Custom House to the school-room, on opposite sides of the Plaza. These facts are stated on the authority of "Annals of San Francisco." The entire performance was given by Mr. Massett. Tickets three dollars each. I last saw Mr. Massett, I think, in 1881 or 1882; I last heard of him as traveling somewhere in the "uttermost bounds of the earth," and making new acquaintances among the great men thereof.

Everyone who lived in San Francisco for a long time after the date of my arrival, will remember the old Signal Station on the summit of Telegraph Hill. The signal for a side-wheel steamer in the early days was two long blackboards, extended like two outstretched uplifted arms, one on each side of the long, black signal

pole.   Everybody knew this signal, and that the
P. M. S.S. Co's steamships were all side-wheelers,
and one can hardly understand, now, the excitement created by the signal for a side-wheel
steamer.

One night the "Hunchback" was being played
at the "American Theatre;" the house was
crowded, and the play had progressed to the
scene of "Julia's" quarrel with "Clifford," at
the point of "Master Walter's" excited entrance;
the actor's figure, dressed entirely in black, stood
in bold relief against the light-colored scenery of
the drawing-room; throwing up his arms long
and black, he shouted, "What does this mean?"
"Side-wheel steamer!" roared a stentorian voice
from the gallery.   The play was suspended "for
a time."

Another "memory" of Mrs. Sinclair's company
comes back—of Potter—the ubiquitous, the ever-
persuasive, the always-promising John S. Potter.
The man who built more theatres and opened
more theatres, and closed more theatres—I think
he closed twice as many as he ever opened—than
any man in the Union or out of it.   Mr. Potter
was a most remarkable character; he was gifted
with the organ of hope so largely that he could
see a silver-lining to the darkest cloud in the
managerial horizon, and, like Micawber, was
always certain of something "turning up," but

the main difficulty with him was his inability to inspire his actors and actresses with the same buoyant feeling.

. He had opened I don't know how many theatres in the West and in the Mississippi Valley before he reached California, and during his California career he had opened as many more; he was always in management, and I was amazed that he was enrolled only as an actor when I arrived; but he started in on his managerial career soon after; he had the reputation in the West of being able to keep his forces together without any treasure-chest or commissariat, simply by his persuasive tongue.

A friend once found him complaining that but for the *ambition* of his company his "season" would have been prosperous; and being asked what their ambition had to do with his failure, he replied that if they hadn't been so ambitious for their salary he could have made money and kept them all together. Another time, to a poor histrion who begged in vain for a dollar or two of his unpaid salary, he replied: "What, ask for salary when blackberries are ripe!"

He would any time, like Mr. J. P. Addams, play any part in the drama at ten minutes' notice, in a black cloak and wig, and would get the curtain up and down again, shift all the scenes, attend to the properties during the performance,

16

and within five minutes or less after the fall of the curtain would have the receipts from the box office in his pocket, and be out of sight of his "ambitious" actors, who waited around in vain for "salary." I shall have occasion to speak of him again.

Among the new parts that I played during something less than five months in which I was with Mrs. Sinclair, I recall "Ankarstrom" in "Gustavus III," the dual characters in the "Courier of Lyons," "Job Thornberry" in "John Bull," and one or two more. The season was almost a failure; the expenditures much too heavy for the patronage of an exhausted public, and many of the stars had received exorbitant sums, inconsistent altogether with their attraction.

Mr. Samuel Colville was at the time in management in Sacramento, and I joined him in the latter part of January, 1855.

CHAPTER XII.

IN the summer of 1883 there appeared on the
streets of Sacramento a singular figure, clad
in buck-skin coat and trousers, with head surmounted by a time-worn cap, from under which
flowed to the shoulders an abundance of gray
hair, and a full, snow-white beard. This figure
gave to the curious great food for conjecture, and
to the older residents a sensation of surprise that
one who had been supposed dead should re-visit
the scenes of his former trials and disappoint-
ments. This old man was Mr. Wesley Venua,
who, in the year 1852, in company with two other

gentlemen, erected the theatre on Third street, which, in January, 1855, was managed by Mr. Samuel Colville, by whom I was engaged.

Mr. Venua's career was a most remarkable one. A native of England, when a mere boy of seventeen he volunteered into the Portuguese naval service, for what was known as the " Donna Maria " war, and in an engagement had the calf of his right leg shot away. In 1834, he drifted to the United States, and eventually into one of the minor theatres in New York City. He was a member of the company at the St. Charles theatre, in New Orleans, when I was with Ludlow & Smith. From thence he went through Mexico to Acapulco, on the Pacific, and found his way, by a freight-boat, to San Francisco, in the flush times of 1851. He played in the Eagle Theatre, in Sacramento, of which I have spoken, and spoke the first line that was uttered on the stage of the " Jenny Lind Theatre," in San Francisco. In the year 1864, becoming tired of society, he took passage for the South Seas, and resided for four years in the Society Islands, and went thence, on board of a French frigate, to France. In 1869, he was in Italy and the south of France, and was imprisoned in Paris during the Franco-Prussian war, experiencing the privations and perils of hunger and siege. On the entrance of the Prussians into the French capital, he escaped the excesses of the "commune," and went to England, and thence back to California, where he found that his property had been mismanaged, and reduced to one-half its original value. Anxious to get away from society, he purchased a team, and started to find some abode of solitude, and eventually camped among the Cascade Mountains, in Oregon, where he now resides.

He had ridden from his mountain home to Sacramento in fifteen days, using one horse, for which he avowed an almost human affection. I think that I know that horse; it must be "Fox," and yet that can hardly be. In that first visit of mine to Sacramento, in 1855, he owned a horse named "Fox," of which he thought more than of any human being. It was said that he had ridden Fox to the summit of the Marysville Butte, from which he had to be lowered with a "fall and tackle;" but this I will not vouch for. Mr. Venua was a man capable of feeling for a dumb brute, and when he lost Fox, he, without doubt, found another, and attached him to his master by kindness. With his many eccentricities, Mr. Venua is a man to command respect, and the "soldier of fortune," the "wounded sailor," the "histrionic pioneer," the "voluptuary of the South Seas," the "starveling of the Paris siege," the "hermit of the wilds of Oregon," is to me a picturesque and pleasant memory.

I think that I can choose no more fitting place to speak of another old dramatic pioneer on the Pacific Slope, well remembered by the survivors of "the days of old, the days of '49," Dan Virgil Gates. Mr. Gates was, I believe, a native of Rochester, N. Y., where he commenced his theatrical career with Mr. Augustus Addams. He possessed rare imitative powers, but like most young thespians inclined to tragedy. He appeared in the old American Theatre in San Francisco, in support of Mr. James Stark, in 1851, and for some two years thereafter was a member of various organizations, playing in connection with Messrs. Stark, Baker and Proctor. In the winter of '52–53, he was "snowed in" at the town of Nevada with William Barry, David Anderson, Edwin Booth, and others, members of the company of Mr. Willmarth Waller, and encountered with them some of the vicissitudes of early California life, which were not confined to the wielders of the pick and shovel alone.

Subsequently, he traveled the length and breadth of the State—mounted like a distinguished editor of San Francisco—on the back of a mule; a whole theatrical company condensed into one man; a host in himself—rang the bell as he entered into each mining town or camp, posted his own bills, beat his own drum, fiddled, sang, danced, and recited, and gave a ball after

the dramatic performance, to the intense satisfaction of his patrons, who, to this day, tell of
the glorious times they had in the old days with
Dan Virgil Gates. As fortune smiled, he dis-
mounted from his mule and traveled with a team
of *two* horses, and then with a handsome turn-out
of *four*, in company with Mr. Edmon S. Connor,
another pioneer who was, like him, a hunter
for nuggets in the early days. Mr. Connor I
knew when we were both young in Philadelphia;
he had a fair position before he came to California, though he never attained to eminence.
As Polonius says, he was " a good actor," if not
a *great* one. Mr. Connor used to say jocularly,
that "a gentleman was a man who had a gold
watch and forty dollars in his pocket." At this
date he is living in Philadelphia, and upwards of
eighty years old, hale and hearty, as I am informed. I hope that he is possessed of the watch
and dollars, but he has always borne the character of a gentleman. Dan Virgil Gates died in
Leadville, Colorado, in 1876.

Mr. Colville began his short season with Mr.
and Mrs. James Stark. Mr. Stark had been with
me in New Orleans, but in the three intervening
years had made a profitable visit to Australia,
and stood high in the esteem of the public of
California, as well as of the Australian Colonies.
He was an admirable actor, some few characters

were exceptionally fine in the hands of James Stark. I will instance " Richelieu" and " Beverly," in the " Gamester." He was a man of kind and generous feelings, at one time wealthy, but I think lost the bulk of his fortune by unfortunate speculation. He died, I believe, while a member of Mr. Edwin Booth's company in New York.

James H. Warwick was another acquaintance renewed from previous years. I believe that in a preceding chapter I have said he was a tragedian, he was an *aspiring* tragedian. I met and acted with Mr. Warwick many times during his California career, up to the time of his entrance into political life.

In 1862 he was nominated and elected to the lower house of the California Legislature, from the County of Sacramento, and had the opportunity to reiterate before the " assembled wisdom of the State," a declaration that he never omitted to make from the stage when opportunity offered, " that it was his chief hope and wish, to lay his bones in California." It was a question among the miner patrons of the theatre in those early days, how Mr. Warwick could make his bones " go round," for he invariably promised to lay them in every town in which he played. In later years I made a summer trip through the middle mining region of the State with Mr. George Mitchell and what he called his "Equestrian Theatre." Well, it was an " equestrian theatre," for we had a horse, and Mr. Warwick, and Mr. George Peoples, and some others. Mr. Peoples was the tragedian who rode the horse in " Putnam," and Mr. Warwick was the " tragedian " who played " Nick of the Woods," and I can certify, on oath, that Mr. Warwick solemnly swore to " lay his bones " in no less than fifty mining towns and camps during that summer. I have not seen Mr. Warwick for many years, but hope he is alive and well, and still has his " bones " with him.

There was a young man named Folland in the company. I remember him because his sad fate a few months later, impressed itself on my mind. He accompanied Lola Montez on her departure from California for Australia, and was lost at sea.

Dumphries — " Dumpsy," we always called him—was another of the early California actors, and he was a good one. Short of stature, florid complexion, a smiling countenance, bright, merry eyes, brown, curly hair, cheerful temper—such was little " Dumpsy," and he made our traveling tours in those pleasant days, over the " divides," down the " cañons," up the " grades," and through the piney woods all the pleasanter by his presence, but he, like so many more, is " dead and gone."

In the then thriving town of Marysville, which was the main depot for supplying the northern mining region, a pretty, new theatre had been erected, and thither I went, under engagement to Mr. F. M. Kent.   He was a low-comedian, of some merit, and his wife, an exceedingly beautiful woman, was ambitious to play the heroines of tragedy—indeed, any heroines that might be roaming around loose.   It was a pleasant trip, remembered for my first acquaintanceship with young Joseph Wilder, at that time a model of youthful, manly beauty, and giving promise of a great future; all eventually blighted by ill-health, misfortune, and the thousand ills that flesh is heir to.   Joe, too, is dead; peace to his memory.

I returned to San Francisco under engagement to Dr. Spalding, who had leased the " American Theatre," as stage manager, which I resigned at the end of two weeks, and was succeeded by Miss Laura Keene.   I was at this period gradually drifting into the line of old-men characters, and the exigencies of over-study made a stage manager's duty, if properly attended to, almost impossible; and above and beyond all other reasons, Miss Keene was infinitely better qualified. So the change was made, and I was an actor only.   That was a pleasant season; I forget how long we were together, I think some three months. We were strong, too—Miss Laura Keene, Mrs.

Judah, Mrs. Thoman, Miss Julia Gould, Mr. Charles Wheatleigh, Mr. J. A. Smith and others.

Lola Montez is a vivid memory of my early California days. Just after the commencement of our season at the " American Theatre," she sailed in a brigantine for Australia. On the night before her departure, Miss Laura Keene, with some of the company, including myself, went from the theatre after the close of the performance, to her lodgings at the International Hotel, to drink a glass of wine and say " good bye." Lola was in the highest spirits, and full of pleasant and gracious farewell words for all. I think that even as early as that time, she had begun to abate something of the imperious and reckless manner for which she had been so notorious.

The career of Lola Montez was unmatched by that of any female bohemian of our time, and her success was world-wide. An Irish girl of uncertain parentage, her only inheritance was a face full of expression, fine eyes, and hair that a mermaid might envy. As an actress and dancer, even before she had turned the head of that crazy old King of Bavaria—whose weakness, although developed in a different manner, seems to assert itself in his grandson—Lola had won the hearts and depleted the pockets of the half of Paris.

When she had married the art connoisseur, Ludwig, she lived like a "beggar on horseback," and ran him to the verge of ruin, from which he was only saved by his subjects, who threatened revolution if she were not driven from the realm. Heart-broken, he parted from the syren, who tripped it over to London, danced herself, after a fashion, into notoriety, and, after two years, crossed the Atlantic, traveled as an actress, delivered lectures, made money, and lost it all; ceased to attract, became a victim of all who could get a chance to rob her, and finally died in a second-class boarding-house in the city of New York.

One of the husbands of this much-married and eccentric woman was a Californian, and of those who witnessed that marriage two survivors remain, both personally known to me, Messrs. L. R. L. and H. J. C. Near midnight, previous to the morning of the eventful day, one of these gentlemen was told as a great secret, that "in the Mission Church, to-morrow morning, Lola Montez was to be married to Pat Hull, at matin bells."

At sunrise, near the old Mission Church, some fifteen or twenty persons were walking listlessly around, as if waiting for something; among them Governor W. and his wife, the only lady, besides the bride, who was present at the wedding.

Presently the carriage containing Lola and Hull drove up. Lola turned, and on entering the church waved her hand to close the front door; but some forty spectators in all had already got inside.

Lola carried in her hand two vases containing artificial white roses, and presented them to the officiating clergyman at the altar. From the church the party went into an ante-room, where was a spread of cake, wine, cigars and cigarettes. Gov. W. giving Mr. C. a significant wink, approaching Lola kissed her, and C, to "make the occasion memorable," as he said, did the same. Lola made no objection, remarking "such is the custom of my country." She received the congratulations of all who were present and had a pleasant word for all; she then inquired, "where can we get a good breakfast?" Hull replied, "at the Bull's Head;" Lola said "she had rather go to the Tivoli;" and to the "Tivoli" they went.

This strange marriage was but one of the episodes in the strange life of the Countess of Landsfeldt, Baroness of the Order of St. Theresa, and discarded wife of a king, whose life-dream flickered out in obscurity, and who now lies in Trinity church yard in an humble grave, above which is the inscription, " Elizabeth Gilbert, died in New York, aged forty-one years."

The little rose-embowered cottage in which Lola lived with Pat Hull for a short time after her marriage, stood for some period, perhaps still stands, in the pretty town of Grass Valley in Nevada County, California.

I think that my next "memory" of the early California days is connected with Venua's theatre in Sacramento. Mr. Edwin Booth was a member of the company, and in one of the bills I find his name as " Jack Spriggs," in the comedy of " Look before you Leap ; " and in " Twelfth Night " his name for " Malvolio," and my own for " Sir Toby Belsh." I recall the admirable manner in which he played "Malvolio." He also played " Mr. Lionel Lynx " in " Married Life " and " Bucket " the Detective, in " Bleak House." The Misses Adelaide and Joey Gougenheim were the stars; these two ladies had a large popularity for a short time in California, Joey, especially, and went subsequently to Australia. On their return trip from the Antipodes a suit at law was commenced to recover damages from the captain of the vessel in which they were passengers, for an alleged violation of contract. One of the specifications was that he had not, as agreed, furnished any sugar for their limes. It was a funny case, and the minstrels popularized a doggerel song, which the street gamins sung all over town, of "No Sugar on your Limes."

On Monday evening, October 8th, 1855, the new "Edwin Forrest" Theatre in Sacramento, was opened under the management of Charles A. King and George Ryer. Mr. Ryer came to California in 1853, and was a member of Mrs. Sinclair's first company, at the "Metropolitan," in San Francisco. He dabbled in management a good deal during his sojourn on the Pacific Coast, was a very easy going kind of a man, never in a hurry, and never in a worry, and somewhat indifferent to other peoples convenience, of which I remember an instance. A belated actor, when preparing in a hurry for the duties of the evening, found missing at the last moment, a very necessary portion of his costume, his nether garments, or "tights" as they are called; they were nowhere to be found, and no one in the dressing-room had seen or knew anything about them. The difficulty was surmounted by a kindly loan from a brother actor, and at the conclusion of the play, while the actors were disrobing, Mr. Ryer with a chuckle, drew from beneath his doublet the missing "tights," which he had rolled up into a ball and crammed beneath his dress to produce the proper obesity of the character he represented. Mr. Ryer left California many years ago, and I believe became an army chaplain during the war of the rebellion. I think that such a position would have suited him exactly.   Mr. King, or Charley King as he was always called, was a pleasant, genial gentleman, and a fair actor in the line of eccentric and low-comedy.   Like nearly all of the early California thespians he passed away, and his modest monument may be seen in the Sacramento cemetery.

John Dunn, another merry " memory." Surely there are many on either side of the continent who remember that " Rascal Jack ;" what a buoyant spirit, what a careless, reckless, laughing soul. At home, everywhere, he had, as he boasted, hob-nobbed with and slapped on the back the King of the Sandwich Islands, and I think if the opportunity offered he would have done the same to the Czar of Russia or the Pope of Rome. He, too, is long since dead.

And yet another memory of one who was with me at that time—a gentle woman, a loving wife, a noble mother ; and to these *higher* titles may truthfully be added that of an admirable actress —Sophie Edwin.   She was pre-eminently a pioneer of the California stage, having made her first appearance at the old " American Theatre," in San Francisco, in 1850, and had played " Albert," in " William Tell," in the " Tehama Theatre," in Sacramento.   Again, in 1851, she had played at the first "Jenny Lind Theatre." She was married to Mr. W. Stevenson in 1854. For the period of twenty years, I knew Sophie Edwin; commencing at the foot of the ladder, she rose by her own merit to a high rank, and was deservedly popular with every community before whom she appeared. Miss Edwin was born in Sydney, Australia, and was thirty-eight years old at the time of her death, which occurred in San Francisco in 1877. As an emotional actress, she was not far behind the foremost of her profession, and there was a sympathy in her voice that touched a sympathetic chord in the heart of every listener. With a proverbial industry in her calling, she yet found time to rear a family of children, with tender care and solicitude for their moral and educational welfare. Her husband, Mr. Stevenson, survived her some five years, and died respected by the community with whom he had lived so long.

Mr. Woodard—John Woodard—was still another of the early ones whom I then met for the first time. He had walked the trails, and acted in every mining camp and cloth-and-paper town of every county in the State, and later was manager and popular vocalist of several minor theatres in the Bay City. He had much comic ability, and was a gentleman of probity and honor. The old miners who still linger in the deserted

17

placers of the State, will tell with rapture how John Woodard used to sing in the early times,

" The days of old, the days of gold, the days of forty-nine."

He has been long absent from California.

Mr. Frank Mayo was a beginner in that Sacramento corps of 1855. He has since achieved name and fame in " Davy Crockett," and other popular characters.

Caroline Chapman, of whom I have already spoken, was member of the company. Lacking feminine beauty, this lady was beautiful in soul and brilliant in talent.

Another "memory"—a gigantic one—McKean Buchanan. I had known him in New Orleans, where he was a levee cotton broker at the time he startled the South with his advent. This gentleman's managerial and professional career is so well known, that I can hope to add but little to the record. He played with us at this time an engagement of six nights' duration. The " Naiad Queen" was produced with some *eclat;* and at the close of the season a *young* girl, though an *old* Californian, of whom I shall have more to say, appeared—Miss Sue Robinson—the Fairy Star!

I think that pleasant sojourn in the City of the Plains lasted three months, and at its close John S. Potter, the ubiquitous, who had been on

the watch, threw his net and caught me for the
Nevada Theatre, where on Thursday, February
14th, " Romeo and Juliet" was announced for
representation; " Romeo"—Mlle. Marie Duret;
"Mercutio"—Mr. Leman; "Juliet"—Miss Sophie
Edwin.

Madame Duret is a marked " memory" of the
early California days; when younger she had
played in New Orleans and some other southern
cities, and had eventually strayed to the Australian Colonies, where, according to rumor
(whether true or false I know not) she had become the wife of Mr. Gustavus V. Brooke. She
was a capable actress, possessing some emotional
power, and played some of the parts that Madam
Celeste had made famous, with success; later
she turned her whole attention to elaboration of
the character of Ainsworth's Newgate Calender
hero, and was known far and wide as " the only
Jack Sheppard." She was a pleasant and intelligent lady, but was overtaken by misfortune in
her advanced years, and died in straitened circumstances in San Francisco in 1883.

McKean Buchanan had organized a small
company of what his bills called the " finest artists on the Pacific Coast," and we started from
Sacramento for Folsom on the 13th day of May,
1856, to enlighten the central mining regions of
the State with illustrations of the drama, as it

had never been seen before, and as the bills declared, " would never be seen again."

Mr. H. D. Palmer — the Harry Palmer of
" Black Crook " fame, who subsequently, in
partnership with Henry C. Jarrett, made a fortune by that spectacle — was Mr. Buchanan's
advance agent, or rather *avant courier*, combining the position of agent with bill-sticker,
and went ahead with a light buggy and paste-pot
to " bill" the camps.   We had a four-horse team
and carriage with capacity for ten passengers,
were out six weeks, and played in some forty
different towns and mining camps, traveling
about seven hundred miles.

Mr. Buchanan, like Mr. Potter, was a man of
boundless resources, but, unlike Mr. Potter, was
rarely impecunious ; for if business was bad and
the box-office returns meagre, he never would
have told a member of his company who asked
for salary that " blackberries were ripe," but, like
an honest man, would have gone out after playing " Hamlet " and won enough at poker to
square the salary bill the next morning.

We had some very funny scenes during that
trip ; I wish I could remember them.   Among
the euphonious names of the places in which
" the drama as it had never been seen before "
was exhibited, I recall the following : " Tod's Valley," " Yankee Jim's," " Chips' Flat," " Cherokee

Flat," "Smith's Flat," "Woolsey's Flat," "Rough and Ready," "Rattlesnake," "Mud Springs," "Indian Diggings," "Red Dog," "Hangtown," "Drytown," and "Fiddletown." In going from "Smith's Flat" to "Woolsey's Flat," we had to climb the divide between two forks of the American River (I think it was), and the road being very precipitous, a team and span of mules were sent out ahead with the baggage; when they reached the summit, startled at something or other, they went off down the mountain in a "go as you please" style, scattering the baggage and wardrobe on the greasewood and manzanita bushes from the top to the bottom, a mile and a half of distance, with perfect impartiality; Miss Vaux's skirts were dangling from one bush, Jimmy Griffith's russet boots and doublet in one place, my scarfs and other articles of stage attire in another, while Buck's trunk, being the largest and heaviest, had burst and scattered all his regal finery in the dust of the road, from the top of the hill to the bottom.

Any other man than Buchanan would have abandoned the idea of playing that night, for it was dark before we reached the hotel; but he was a man that never lost a night, "rain or shine," and he sent men back on the road to gather up what they could, got the curtain up—the curtain in that particular "temple of the drama," I remember, was composed of four blue blankets basted together—made a speech to the audience, which was a good one, and all the better for the mishap which had befallen us, and after the performance won enough at poker to repair damages.

The old hall in Placerville—better known as "Hangtown" by the early Californians—had a supporting joist sustaining the roof, just in the front centre of the stage. When the room had been altered for theatrical uses, I presume it had been found impossible to remove this square pillar without endangering the safety of the roof. It was a very awkward obstruction for the players, for we had to act round it, and it was a great eye-sore to the audience. With rare genius, Buchanan on one occasion utilized that ugly pillar, in the last scene of the "Merchant of Venice," when as "Shylock" he exclaimed :

> " Nay, take my life and all.
> You take my house, when you do take the *prop*
> That doth sustain my house."

He rushed to the centre, and grabbing the ugly post, delivered the lines with an energy all his own.

Jimmy Griffiths is another merry "memory" of the early days. "Little Jimmy," as he was always called, was dwarfish in stature, and looked as old when I first knew him in Sacramento as he did five and twenty years after. In fact, he always looked old, and always looked just the same. He was shrewd, quick, good-natured and high-tempered. He was property-man, scene-shifter, wardrobe-keeper, played three or four parts, and beat the big drum when we entered the mining-camps, except when, upon particular occasions, old " Buck " beat it himself. The wagon was a large one, and the drum was placed " way astern," as a sailor would say; and on certain occasions Buchanan would take Jimmy's place, and thump the drum all the way to the hotel. I used to expostulate with him for this unnecessary lowering of his dignity; but his answer would be, " Leman, my dear boy, you don't see the thing clear. It makes capital. They say I'm eccentric; and when the miners see me beating the drum they 'll say, ' See, there's Buchanan, the great tragedian, beating the drum ; how odd ! It shows that, great actor as he is, he can descend from his pedestal. Let's all go and see him to-night.' "

I have said Jimmy was high-tempered. Buchanan was a great swaggerer at times, and once he pushed the little fellow to the danger-point. Some over-work had been crowded upon him, and some unjust rebuke had been followed by indications of a blow on Buchanan's part, when

Griffiths dashed to the stage the china vase he held in his hands, and seizing an old rusty sabre, turned, with fury, on his manager, who knew, by the blood in Jimmy's eye, that he meant business, and incontinently fled. He dodged around the wings, half laughing and half afraid, with Jimmy after him for a few moments, until his anger cooled. The scene was supremely ridiculous to the lookers-on.

At another time, Jimmy's promptitude saved us all from a catastrophe. We had wandered away up to Forrest Hill, in Sierra County, I think, and were playing in the upper story of a great wooden shell of a hotel. The hall, lined with cotton cloth, papered, was brimful of people, and the only entrance and exit was by a narrow, winding stairway, which led from the bar. Large kerosene lamps lighted the room and stage. In raising the curtain some obstruction occurred, and Buchanan, always hasty and impatient, seizing hold of the line, and disregarding Jimmy's request to wait until he could clear it, jerked it violently, and in so doing detached one of the flaming kerosene lamps, which fell upon the stage. The audience rose aghast, and Buchanan stood paralized; but Griffiths, with great presence of mind, seized and extinguished it before mischief ensued. Those who know the peril of conflagration that always environed the dwellers in the cloth and paper houses of the California mining-towns can appreciate the calamity that might have ensued if a fire had started in the third story of that flimsy structure, with one narrow and rickety stairway as means of escape for two hundred human beings.

I had some further professional intercourse with Mr. Buchanan, of which more anon. He was most certainly a man of peculiar temperament; but with a deal of vanity and egotism, and a disposition at times to be overbearing, he nevertheless had true and noble characteristics. I always found in him inflexible integrity and honesty. I think his judgment was faulty, for most certainly he thought himself a great actor; but he is, by no means, the only actor whose judgment is misled by his self-esteem. If he could have curbed his dramatic Pegasus within reasonable bounds, he would have appeared better upon the stage; but his steed always ran away with him. He would play some parts of a character, as "Richelieu" for example, admirably; but when he got to the "anathema" scene, in the fourth act, Pegasus would get the bit in his teeth, and "Richelieu" would shout himself hoarse, foam at the mouth, and sweep the circle of the stage in what Walter Bray once very appropriately called a "walk around." One part he played excellently well, as all who have seen his "Sir Harcourt Courtly" can certify.

Mr. Buchanan left California many years ago, and for some time after had a traveling company in the Eastern States. He had learned by experience how to economize, and avowed his determination to engage no more leading actresses for a salary, as there were always plenty of "ambitious novices," who could be obtained for nothing. I don't think his system made him rich. Perhaps it might if he had lived longer; but he died poor. Peace to his ashes!

Mr. Buchanan had a very beautiful daughter— Miss Virginia Buchanan—who became an actress, and, I think, is yet living.

CHAPTER XIII.

ON the fifth day of August, 1856, I embarked
on board the steamer Sierra Nevada, for
San Juan on the Pacific, en route to New York.
There were on board some forty recruits for
Walker, who was then at the height of his
ephemeral power in Central America. Among
them was the son of an old friend, a rash impulsive, generous boy, who within six months died

far away in a strange land, whether in battle or by disease, or treachery, his mother or his sister never knew. This young man during the passage, had a difficulty with the captain of the corps, resulting in a challenge, which was accepted by the captain, and a duel with sabres was arranged to come off on the deck of the steamer at the hour of ten at night. The commander of the steamer put a summary stop to all further proceedings in the little "affair of honor," as soon as the intelligence of their intended meeting reached his ears. On reaching San Juan, the "custom's officials" of Walker's new-born nation came off to the ship with the flag of the Republic at the stern of their gig, and on landing, the squads of soldiers met at intervals; and the knots of natives, male and female, who, with furtive and lowering looks, gazed at the strangers, told of the short-lived power of the so-called "gray-eyed man of destiny," which was so soon to pass away in blood. No event of moment occurred during the safe and pleasant passage home.

Mr. George Ince had become the lessee of the "Baltimore Museum," and on the evening of Monday, September 29, 1856, that establishment opened with the name of Walter M. Leman on the bills as stage manager. The play was "Ingomar," the part of "Parthenia" by Miss Annette Ince. This lady was the manager's daughter, and had for some time held position as an attractive star. There was then, and at a later period, a sort of implied rivalry between Miss Ince and Miss Julia Dean. Both young, both beautiful and both highly talented, adherents were not wanting to maintain the claims of either to pre-eminence. Miss Ince was especially happy in her representation of "Ion," a part which Miss Dean never played; and in very many characters it would have been difficult for the most impartial critic to decide the palm. Subsequently Miss Ince came to California, where she now resides, and, as always, is numbered in my list of old friends.

Miss Ince's sister, Caroline, a pretty girl, danced between play and farce. She, too, is now a Californian.

Stuart Robson! Thou strange, eccentric, odd, unlike-anybody-else actor! Come into Court. It was at this time I first knew Mr. Robson. On the opening night he played "Selim Pettibone" in a "Kiss in the Dark;" he was a very young man then, and I certainly thought I had for my low-comedian the thinnest, queerest, squeakiest little man that I had ever seen. He made everybody laugh who saw him, and has kept them laughing ever since. I don't know whether Stuart Robson was in love before the Museum opened, but I know that he got married during that short season, and I know he'll not be offended at my mention of what has since been a subject for our mutual mirth, his impecuniousness at the time which compelled him to ask a loan from the stage manager to "see" the priest. Mr. Robson is numbered among my old friends.

Mr. Charles Barton Hill I also knew for the first time. Barton Hill, as he is more commonly called, is the son of the gentleman whom I have spoken of as manager at Louisville. Mr. Hill went subsequently to California, and was stage manager of the "California Theatre" during the last years of the lesseeship of Mr. McCullough. Mr. Hill is an actor of varied powers, and is, I think, still living.

Mr. John E. Owens was around—he always contrived to be around Baltimore during the gala, agricultural time, for he shrewdly knew that then the theatrical harvest was ripe—and played for two weeks. Mr. F. Bangs joined the company. This gentleman subsequently attained eminence as a tragic actor.

Mr. and Miss Charles appeared and played a long engagement. On referring to the bills, I find that I announced them as the "only rivals of Mr. and Mrs. Barney Williams." I dare say they might have been, but I honestly confess that I do not retain any remembrance of what Mr. and Mrs. Williams, or Mr. and Miss Charles ever did upon the stage. Some things are stamped on our memory, others are submerged in forgetfulness.

Mr. and Mrs. G. E. Locke also played with us. Mr. Locke was the gentleman who, years before, had such unutterable feelings on witnessing the rehearsal of "Romeo and Juliet." He had now bloomed into a "Yankee comedian." His wife was a quiet little body. They afterwards went to California. Both, I believe, are dead.

The short season at Baltimore closed on the sixth of December, and I was immediately engaged as stage manager at the "National Theatre," in the city of Washington, D. C., where I first became professionally acquainted with Mr. and Mrs. W. J. Florence, whom all the theatrical world knows. This lady and gentleman are still before the public. They cross and re-cross the Atlantic very often—Mr. Florence to get something new in the drama, Mrs. Florence something new in the fashions, and I believe they always succeed, for Mr. Florence is always presenting some new novelty to the public, and his lady is noted as the richest and tastiest dresser on the stage.

Mr. S. W. Glenn was another acquaintance. He was a capital actor in Dutch characters.

Thalberg, the famous pianist, was with us one night, and the Ravels played a very successful

engagement.   Gabriel, though getting old, was
still king of pantomime; and there was a brilliant dancer, a Russian lady named Yrea Mat-
thias, not far behind Augusta or Blangy.

But what I best remember during that short
Washington season, was the production of Mrs.
Sidney F. Bateman's comedy of " Self." It had
been fairly successful in other cities; Mr. Owens
and Mrs. Melinda Jones were in the cast, but it
failed to draw. I think that it was an angry
controversy about Mrs. Bateman's claims to the
authorship of this play that provoked a street
fight in the city of San Francisco.

The season at Washington was brought to an
abrupt close in the first week of February. The
great, barn-like structure, called the " National
Theatre," caught fire in mid-day and was wholly
consumed.

In April I again embarked for California,
reaching San Francisco on the 15th of May, and
greeting my Sacramento friends, in company
with Miss Ince, who had preceded me, in
Knowles' play of the " Hunchback," on the evening of May 25th. The " Clifford " of the cast
was Mr. J. B. Booth, Jr. This gentleman, recently deceased, was so well known to the public,
and so highly esteemed, both as manager and
actor, that I can hardly hope to add aught of interest regarding him. I had known him when a

mere lad, in Boston, where, I think, he first appeared in the old " National Theatre." He came to California as early as 1852, I believe, and had been in management prior to my arrival. His first wife was Miss De Barr and he was subsequently married to a Boston lady—Miss Harriet Mace—whom I had known in my early theatrical days. I believe that he was the eldest son of his great sire and although a good actor, inherited none of the genius of the father. Perhaps I should modify that statement, for there were times when, for a moment, there would appear a flash of *the* Booth, but it would be a momentary flash only. In one scene of " King John " especially this was evinced, and occasionally in other characters ; but it was a very fitful fire, and died almost as soon as kindled. In physique, Mr. Booth was a model of manly beauty ; very fond of athletic exercises, an admirable fencer, and sparred with skill and power ; and in addition to all this, he was of a genial, pleasant temperament, a plain-spoken, upright man. Years later, I acted under his management, and as manager, actor, and friend, I respect his memory. Mr. Booth's third wife was Mrs. Agnes Perry, who survives him. Of this lady I shall have occasion to speak.

In June, Mrs. Julia Dean Hayne leased the American Theatre in San Francisco, and I was

18

again among old friends.   I recall with especial
pleasure that pleasant summer and fall, but I remember no new names among my associates of
that time, if I except Mr. George Waldron, who
rose to favor subsequently; Mr. Frank Lawlor,
who afterwards became known as actor and manager, and is, I think, still living, and a little girl,
Miss Louisa Paullin, who is now a popular vocalist, well known in musical circles, and a member
of the " Mikado Troupe."   The soubrette of the
company was Mrs. Leonard, a little native
Australian nugget, petite, piquante and pleasing.
On closing in San Francisco, we started on a tour
lasting for nearly three months, embracing all of
the central mining region, and combining with
the dust and discomfort of California mountain
travel, pleasurable sights and scenes of novelty
and interest that none but those who have roamed
the mountains of California can ever know.
Many a time and oft, a party of us would antici-
pate the coach departure, and tramp it over hill
and through valley in the balmy morning air, or
leave the carriage and take a cut-off trail beneath
the shadow of mountain pines redolent with spicy
odors, gaining perhaps a half hour's time, which
would be spent upon the grass in company with
a cigar, while we waited for the coach to come up.
In the solemn silence of those forest hills, no
sound would be heard save the woodpecker and

the soughing of the wind amid the branches of the tall tree tops—till anon, a subdued rattle of wheels slowly coming up the grade in the distance. The driver coming in sight would crack his whip, the ladies in the coach wave their handkerchiefs, and on reaching the summit the horses rest and take a drink, and reseating ourselves in the coach we would roll merrily on.

The tour commenced at Placerville, where a new and pretty theatre had been built (without any post in the middle of the stage), and the new "Cary House" just opened. Placerville in the early days, was one of the liveliest towns in California, the center of a very rich "placer" mining region (hence its name, though it rejoiced in another). I remember that our arrival from Sacramento was at too late an hour for performing on that evening, and we had a lively game of "hunt the slipper" on the parlor floor, Doctor and Mrs. Hayne being the leaders of the fun. We played in Placerville ten nights, which was a long time for "Hangtown," but the lady was a prime favorite everywhere in California. That uncanny name of Hangtown was applied to Placerville by the old forty-niners, to commemorate a notable execution under the code of Judge Lynch, in 1850. The large tree which bore such ghastly fruit, stood, perhaps now stands, in the main street of the town. With the exhaustion of placer mining, and the increase of agriculture,. Placerville became one of the most charming inland towns of the State. I have not, however, seen it in many years.

We got as far up in the mountain region of Sierra County as Downieville, which in those days was the "ultima thule" of actors. On my first visit to this place with Buchanan, we had to leave our concord wagon, and go down into town in the saddle, for no wheeled carriage could descend the grade. Downieville was another lively place in the early days, its glory was, however beginning to fade, and I suppose after the lapse of all the intervening years, that it is now, like many of the old camps, where it was thought very dull indeed if they didn't have every morning a "man for breakfast," another "sleepy hollow." We got into one camp away up among the hills—I forget the name—where the hall, in the upper story of a cloth-and-paper house, having no stage, we had to improvise one out of the two billiard tables it contained, covering them with boards for that purpose; there being no room for exit or entrance, excepting by a narrow door on one side, and two narrow windows leading to the roof of a shed on the other, an heroic exit or entrance was out of the question, and in getting before the audience "Master Walter" had to push "Julia" up through the window, the *frame being taken out, and in getting off let her down in advance; the spectators seemed to enjoy the thing as much as the players, and there was a deal of fun if not of tragic fitness. In my previous tour with Buchanan through the mining regions, more than once he knocked "Bosworth Field" all to pieces in his frantic tragedy of the fifth act of Richard III, for want of room to get on and off the stage.

I have occasionally mentioned Mr. Edwin Booth in these desultory "memories." This gentleman, who to-day stands before the public as the representative American actor, has honestly won his spurs. All are familiar with the incidents of his career since he achieved eminence, but his earlier history is not so well known. Perhaps some reference to his early California days may not be uninteresting. As I have already stated, I first knew Mr. Edwin Booth in the old Sacramento Theatre, in 1855; up to May, 1856, he played there, and in the Forrest Theatre, an extended round of characters, with varying success but with constant progress. His first performance of "Richard" was in August, and the Sacramento critics pronounced him "promising." In that same month he played "Hamlet." I remember it because I played the "Ghost," and Mrs. Judah the "Queen," and the *Union* of the next morning said: "Mr. E. Booth portrayed the character of the Prince of Denmark most vividly, and in some scenes 'his acting would compare very favorably with that of Murdoch.'" He also appeared as "Demetrius" in the "Midsummer Nights Dream," and "Antipholis of Syracuse;" but these performances called forth no comment. I referred to his playing "Buckett" the Detective in a previous chapter, and of this the *Union* said: "He showed himself a genuine star." He also played "Marston" in the "Millionaire," and "Wildrake" in the "Love Chase," with many other characters in support of the Gougenheim Sisters. He then took a trip to Marysville, and in November the two companies of the "Forrest" and the "Old" Theatre, were united, and he opened at the first-named house as "Benedick;" he also played "Charles Surface" and "Young Marlow." Mrs. Sinclair was then fighting her way through the notorious "Forrest divorce suit," and going up to Sacramento she took the "Old" Theatre, and enrolled Mr. Booth in her corps, in company with Henry Sedley and others. Here his acting of "Claude Melnotte" drew forth great praise, and a critic declared that "If the subject of this notice will but apply himself industriously, unceasingly and perseveringly to his profession, he will ere long rank himself among the foremost of living actors." This was prophecy.

He made his great success as " Phidias " in the " Marble Heart," which was played nineteen nights, the " Marco" of the cast being Mrs. Catherine Sinclair.

The company then went to Nevada City and Marysville, and on their return the play was repeated for many nights, when a complimentary benefit was tendered him, in recognition, as the bills declared, of the " genius of the man" and " in honor of his great talent." He continued playing constantly in leading and ordinary parts, and always rising in the esteem of the press and the public.

In March, Mrs. Sinclair's farewell benefit was announced—as she was " going East to appear in the second trial of her divorce suit"—and on that occasion he appeared in " The Follies of a Night." That performance was a strange medley of the Classic and Ethiopian Drama—Booth, Sedley and Wheatleigh in the first, Sam. Wells, Billy Birch and Coes in the latter.

The ubiquitous John S. Potter next threw his net and caught Mr. Booth for the Forrest Theatre; but the engagement was not a success.

In April, Mr. Baker was manager, and Mr. Booth was again " leading man." On one night a Sacramento dancing-master attempted " Hamlet," and Mr. Booth appeared as the " Ghost;" Sophie Edwin was the " Queen," and Mrs. Tho-

man the " Ophelia." The dancing-master was
not satisfied with one exhibition of his folly, and
on repeating the play met with a " Shale's " reception, being hooted from the stage amid cries
of " Hands across!"—" Ladies chain!"—" Down
the middle!" etc. A few nights after, Mr. Booth
played " Hamlet" to a splendid benefit, when the
critics again said: " There is nothing now to
hinder his onward march to the highest distinc-
tion in his profession." Prophecy again.

He also appeared as " Sir Edward Mortimer"
in the " Iron Chest," a character in which his
father was superlatively great. Afterwards he
ran through the whole range of tragic characters,
with increasing popularity; and on one night
appeared for the benefit of the family of James
King of William, who was murdered by Casey.
He also appeared as " Richelieu" for the first
time.

In this continuous round of arduous effort, extending over a period of nearly twelve months,
Edwin Booth proved the spirit that was in him;
and after a lapse of more than twenty years,
during which he had achieved fame and fortune,
he returned to California to supplement the triumphs won elsewhere with magnificent and
unqualified success. Most surely, he has honestly won his spurs.

It is quite possible that the reader may feel surprise that recognized and acknowledged artists like Mr. Booth and Julia Dean and others should incur, as they did in those early California days, the discomforts of travel, and the inconveniences of ill-lighted halls and meagre appointments in the pursuit of their art. But, apart from the fact that there was "money in it," there was an amount of intelligence in the audiences of those mining regions quite equal to that which gathered in the pit and boxes in San Francisco or Sacramento. College graduates and accomplished scholars, as well as merchants and artisans, were hunting gold in every gulch and ravine, and rough though their attire might be, they were as well qualified to judge of the merits or demerits of author or actor as a New York or Boston auditor.

Management was shifty and uncertain in the Bay and Capital cities, and a well-balanced organization rarely failed of profit in the interior. When I was out with Julia Dean it was a rare thing to play anywhere, even in the roughest mining camp, to less than three hundred dollars a night; and the audiences were as appreciative, perhaps more so, than in places that boasted more refinement. The mountain tours were healthy, pleasant and profitable.

Between the dates of April 8th and June 17th, 1858, I made the interior tour of which I have spoken, under the management of Mr. George Mitchel, when we were accompanied by Mr. Warwick and his "bones." We started from and returned to Sacramento, playing in fifty-eight mining towns and camps, and traveling a little upwards of one thousand miles. I recall nothing worthy of especial mention.

In July following, Mr. and Mrs. James Wallack, Jr., arrived in California, and I was glad again to meet old friends. Mr. Wallack, fine actor as he was, was not a pronounced success in California. He opened at Maguire's Opera House in San Francisco as "Macbeth," and afterwards took the American Theatre for a short season, where I joined him.

My principal "memories" of that short season are of the production of two "original" plays, one a comedy by Mr. ——, entitled "Fast Folks in California," now forgotten by the public, and by myself, barring the title; and another with the sounding name of "George Washington, or the Trials of a Hero," a tragedy in four acts, by R. M. B. This "tragedy" was certainly an original work, partly in prose and partly in blank verse, though it was hard to tell where either began or ended. I append two short speeches of the "Father of his Country" as specimen bricks:

> "I but approve—that war not conquer all
> Civilities. Enough of wounds are made
> By dire necessity: our cause can well
> Afford to treat polite our foe the English."

Again—

> "As often I advised, my friends, again
> I must repeat to you: When critical
> The times are, people all look with suspicion.
> My worthy generals, and friends farewell!"

The intelligent reader must decide whether this be poetry—or prose—or what? It seems to me like "what."

I soon after made a tour of the central counties, with a small company of which Miss Albertine was a member. This lady was not as prosperous as when I had known her in the East, and the freshness and vivacity of her personations had departed. Her subsequent career was a sad one; in Australia, where she went upon leaving California, adversity overtook her; poor and sick, and partially blind, she was found menially employed in an obscure locality, and given passage to America by the charity of some who had known her in better days. She has long since passed from public observation.

It was, I think, in 1858 that Mrs. John Wood came to California. No more popular actress ever visited the Pacific Coast; her first engagements at the Opera House were a series of triumphs; her songs were whistled and sung in the streets, and the audiences of the interior vied with those of the Bay City in praise of her singing and acting. I played with her in 1859 for a month in various cities, and was with her at the American Theatre in San Francisco on her return to the city in March. Mrs. Wood left California soon after, and never returned. As a burlesque actress, her equal has not yet been seen among those who have succeeded her.

In April, 1859, I played for the first time at Maguire's Opera House with Miss Avonia Jones, and subsequently traveled with that lady in the interior for a short season. Miss Jones was the daughter of Mrs. Melinda Jones and the Count Joannes, and would have been, I think, a better actress if away from the coaching of the mother; Mrs. Melinda taught her to over-act, which propensity is not uncommon among the members of the profession, and was always a marked peculiarity of Mrs. Jones. Miss Avonia Jones went afterwards to Australia, and was reported to have been married to Mr. Gustavus V. Brooke, whether truly or not, I know not; her death occurred not long after that gentleman was lost at sea.

In 1860–61, I was a member of the company attached to the Opera House, but was occasionally drafted for service in the interior. The feverish state of political feeling, foreboding the internecine war, towards which our country was drifting, had an ill-effect on theatricals; and in some localities a free expression of opinion was, if not dangerous, impolitic; my own convictions were so firmly rooted that I never feared to utter them on proper occasions, and in 1862 these convictions found expression in a song, which I wrote for the "Seven Sons"—a sort of twin extravaganza to the "Seven Sisters"—produced in great style at the Metropolitan Theatre; it was adapted to the "Glory hallelujah" air. I will not inflict this song upon my readers, but simply give the concluding stanza, as an introduction to what follows:

> "Swear, freemen, by your mothers' graves
>   And by your glorious sires—
> Swear by your country and your fame,
>   And by your household fires!
> By Ellsworth's—Lyon's—Baker's blood,
>   Be the battle lost or won,
> Come weal or woe—come life or death,
>   The flag shall still march on.
>   Glory, hallelujah, etc."

I knew Col. Edward D. Baker well; and had often sat enraptured by an eloquence, such as is rarely given to men. I recall the impression made on the crowd upon the plaza, by the opening words of his oration at the obsequies of

Broderick—"A Senator lies dead in our midst." He was a born orator and could sway the souls of men. Col. Baker was very fond of the theatre. While traveling with Julia Dean, we were at the town of Oroville, where he was in attendance at the session of court·in a case in which he was counsel, and sat one evening through the play "Old Heads and Young Hearts" with great apparent pleasure. I hope I may not be thought vain, if I say how much pleasure I felt in the compliment conveyed by his words, " Mr. Leman, I think you play "Jesse Rural" almost as well as Rufus Blake."

In the cast of the " Extravaganza" was the name of a lady, one of the earliest among the dramatic pioneers to the Golden Land, Miss Mary Woodward, afterward Mrs. Mary Stuart. She came, I think, in 1852 and delivered the poetical address on the opening of the second Jenny Lind Theatre. In characters of " serious import " and some of the heavy heroines of tragedy, she was a good actress and it nearly broke her heart to have any one proposed for " Lady Macbeth," if she was by. This was certainly a pardonable self-esteem, for she played the character admirably. Mrs. Stuart died in 1872 and lies with others, her brothers and sisters in the mimic art, in the cemetery of Laurel Hill. "*Requiescat in pace!*"

Another name in that list is revealed to me;—what form shall it now take?—then we all familiarly called her "Aggy Perry." When some years before she came, a bright girl, from Australia, she was known as Agnes Land, at a later day she became Mrs. Agnes Booth, and now she is Mrs. Agnes Schœffel; but ever and always she was and is an admirable actress and the juvenile ability so evident, when but a mere girl, has ripened into the full fruition of artistic power. "Father Tom" greets his little "Colleen Bawn" of the old days—across the continent with an All hail!

Two other names are in the programme of that "Extravaganza" and with what melancholy feelings are they recalled: Jenny and Alicia Mandeville. Some years before the Mandeville sisters were great favorites with Californians, I had met them concertizing all through the State. The eldest, Miss Agatha, became Mrs. States and reached the position of recognized prima donna in Italian opera. Jenny was a pleasant singer and lively actress and Alicia, the youngest, almost equally capable. The two latter perished at sea, being victims of the terrible disaster which befell the steamer Pacific off the northern coast of California in 1872. With Jenny were also lost her husband and her infant child. The eldest sister, Mrs. States, had died in New York a short time previously, and the old mother, going on from

California to the last sad rites of her child, sickened and died herself within two or three days; within a twelvemonth the whole family had passed away. The "Mandevilles" are to me indeed a sad and solemn "memory."

My song was destined to create a lively breeze in the town of San Jose a short time afterwards. It was enthusiastically applauded by the Union portion of the audience and hooted by the opposite faction, who loudly called for "Dixie." There was fear for a time of a general row, when it was announced that Jennie Mandeville would sing the song on the following evening—"if the house tumbled down." The theatre was filled in anticipation of the fun; at the proper time Jennie came forward and sang "Our flag goes marching on" in her liveliest style amid the wildest applause.

- In the summer of 1862 an organization was formed, of which I was a member, and the "Union Theatre," (a building now demolished), was opened and successfully run for some three months. Some of the best of the old stock were in the venture and it deserved to succeed. Mr. Mayo was a rapidly rising young man and with Buchanan, Barry, Thayer, Mrs. Saunders, and Miss Virginia Buchanan, the manager's daughter, made a company worthy of praise. Our benefits were all successes; Mrs.

Julia Dean Hayne and Mrs. Judah played for mine and I had an audience up to the roof.

On the 3d of November of the same year I started on what was intended for a short trip, but which eventuated in a successful season of several months' duration, most of the time in Sacramento. I can with truth record the whole of that season as a continuous series of pleasant California "memories." Starting out, as we did, without any great expectations and meeting with almost uninterrupted success, the satisfaction was general. Our hasty manager, the great Buchanan, was, to be sure, frequently in hot water, but he never retained heat or anger long, and I can say with truth, that all of the old fellow's outbreaks were to me food only for mirth.

I remember one particularly ridiculous scene, which occurred in the Capital city. When we reached that point, Buchanan strengthened his force with some additions, among whom were Mr. and Mrs. Charles Pope and Mr. W. C. Forbes; this latter gentleman I had known in the early days of the "Tremont" Theatre, where he had been engaged one season. Although a tragedian, he had a soft voice and an almost womanly manner of expression; his walk was peculiar, the muscles of his lower limbs seeming to move without any sympathy with the rest of his corporeal organization, and with a kind of

19

sorrowful look he always appeared to be in trouble, whether he was or no. Rufus Blake jocularly named him the "king of grief" and called his walk Forbes' "sliding scale." Mr. Buchanan and Mr. Forbes had met when they were both in England. Some unpleasantries had occurred between them, but when Mr. Forbes turned up in Sacramento, whatever their variance was, it was waived, and Mr. Forbes was engaged. It was not long, however, before the old trouble cropped out again and pretty soon grew into open war.

I forget what the *play* was on the evening when it culminated; I remember that the after-piece was the farce of "Family Jars." While I was upon the stage during the last act of the play, to my surprise, Mr. Forbes entered from one side, quite ignoring my presence, and in an excited manner began to talk to the audience, and immediately from the opposite side Mr. Buchanan, equally excited, came on and began to talk. As it was "not my funeral," I got off as quickly as possible, leaving the field to the two angry belligerents, who amazed and bewildered the public with a series of charges and denials—assertions and counter-statements about something or other of which they literally knew nothing and cared less. The more they talked the louder they grew, and while they were jaw-

ing the audience applauded both, thinking the
row was quite as good as any play. When tired
out, they finally went off, and the mirth reached
its climax, as I came on from the upper part of
the stage and exclaimed—"We will now proceed
with 'Family Jars.'"

The biennial session of the State Legislature
occurred that year, and certain charges of bribery
with respect to the election of one of its honorable
members, made a great commotion in political
circles ; the matter was ventilated in the House,
and was for the time the talk not only of Sacramento, but of the whole State. I took advantage
of this public exposure by composing a political
squib, under the title of "King Caucus, or The
Senatorial Muddle," which hit the public fancy,
and filled the theatre for a week. This little
extravaganza was arranged in "four sessions,"
and the characters were "made up" and recognized as prominent members of the Legislature.
The bill was headed with the couplet—

> "Scheming Rogues with forms to mock us,
> Straggling one by one to Caucus."

And to enhance the effect, the "original wardrobe" in which one "honorable gentleman" hid
himself, to listen to the bribe which another
"honorable gentleman" was charged with pro-
posing to a third "honorable gentleman," was

brought from the "Golden Eagle Hotel" and used for the same purpose on the stage. The squib answered completely the purpose for which it was intended, and caused a good-natured laugh all around.

CHAPTER XIV.

OUR prosperous season terminated about the
middle of April, and on the twenty-second of
that month we crossed the Sierra Nevada Mountains to Carson City, via Placerville, over the grade
that Hank Monk made historic when he let out
the lines over his six-in-hand, and assured Horace
Greeley that if he'd " hold on " he'd have him in
Placerville " on time."

At Carson, Silver City and Gold Hill we filled
up the time until the 10th of May, when we got
into Virginia City. This was in the flush times
of the " Comstock," and the wild town on the
slope of Mount Davidson was crowded with men
who were there to make their fortune—or *had*

made it, in "feet." From the edge of Carson Valley, up through Silver City and Gold Hill, over the ridge between the latter place and Virginia, where sometimes the "Washoe Zephyrs" blew with sufficient strength to overturn a stage-coach, along the whole line of the city to far north of the Ophir Mine, was, or was supposed to be, one vast repository of gold and silver, and from North, South, East and West the seekers for wealth had come to get it.

The wonderful produce of the "Gould and Curry," the "Imperial," the "Ophir" and other leads that had then been opened, had made men wild, and holes in the ground were dug and "salted" and new "leads" discovered every day, which, with all their "dips, spurs and angles," were put on the market; and men with mining "shares" in their pocket representing a value of $50,000 would frequently borrow four bits, if another equally wealthy friend had it to lend, to get a dinner at the restaurant. It was the commencement of the wild game of speculation which, at a later day, was transferred to San Francisco, making a few rich and beggaring thousands.

Our first performances were given in a hall, the name of which I forget, and we had powerful rivals in the minstrel and hurdy-gurdy establishments. But a fair patronage was secured. The ground had been obtained for the erection of a new theatre, which was commenced soon after our arrival, by Mr. Thomas Maguire, and rapidly hurried to completion. Our company formed the nucleus of a new organization, which was filled by additions from the Bay City, and on the evening of July 2d, 1863, the new theatre was opened with Bulwer's Comedy of "Money," preceded by an opening address by Walter M. Leman, spoken by Mrs. Julia Dean Hayne.

In speaking of that first night, the *Territorial Enterprise* said: "There was scarcely space to move throughout the theatre, it was so densely filled. A strong wind blew during a portion of the evening and there was considerable agitation visible in the fairer portion of the audience; the most decided sensation of the evening was that produced on Mrs. Hayne—by a mild shower of gravel-stones, which rained upon the building. Large as was the audience, its magnitude was surpassed by it's beauty and manliness. Well, we'll just bet, that if there's a marriageable actress in the company with winning graces and matrimonial inclinations, she never goes over the mountains unwedded." I append a few lines from my opening address, as a "memory" of the drama on the Comstock:

Where the Sierra's rugged mountains show
Their peaks aloft—amid the drifted snow,
Skirting the vale, where Carson's placid stream
Flows onward to the desert—where the gleam
Of God's own sunlight shines in fervid power
On rocks of gold, and hills of glittering ore;
Where thunder-smitten mountains lift on high
Their rifted battlements against the sky.
In this fresh clime, a youthful empire springs
To life and vigor upon freedom's wings,
Nevada !—soon her starry gem to set
Upon our Union's glittering Coronet.

*   *   *   *   *   *   *

Amidst her rocky hills, of verdure shorn
A young and gay metropolis is born
Sudden as from the brain of mighty Jove
Minerva sprang—or, as the Queen of Love
Rose blushing from the Adriatic Sea
In beauty radiant and in fancy free;
And here is reared a rich and gorgeous dome
Of taste, the temple and the muses home,
And here, obedient to Thespian laws,
We stand to-night to plead with you our cause.

*   *   *   *   *   *   *

The "mild shower of gravel stones," of which
the *Enterprise* speaks, not only produced a "sensation" upon Mrs. Hayne, but upon every one in
the house; I am sure it did upon me.   When the
"Washoe Zephyr," sweeping up the cañon,
"rained" that stony artillery upon the rear of
the new building, which creaked in the tempest
like a ship at sea, I thought for a moment that
the opening and closing of "Maguire's New

Opera House" would occur on the same evening, but it was reserved for the *usual* fate, which befel it years after; it went up in a cloud of fire, and took a good portion of the city along with it.

Virginia City was rather a wild "metropolis" in those days—"new discoveries" were reported every day, and speculation ran mad. There were two stock boards in operation, and it was only necessary to dig a hole, "salt" it a little, and put the "shares" on the market to become a capitalist or a beggar in four-and-twenty hours, dependent upon whether one *bought* or *sold*. Some of the sharps dug a hole upon the top of Mount Davidson, and within a day or two elegantly engraved shares of the "Mina del Alta," the mine on the mountain, were put on the board. Speculation on the "green cloth" of battle was also at its height, and the "tiger" walked abroad night and day. Law and order had the "best hand," as the sporting gentlemen allowed; but still, it was thought a dull week when there had not been one or two "men for breakfast." I have found by experience, that a quiet man can get along very well, generally—even in a stormy community, by minding his own business—yet, sometimes it is risky to be in the vicinity of the unsettled spirits. I will mention an instance. I was living at "Wimmer's Virginia House." Wimmer was an old San Franciscan whom I had

long known, was a popular landlord, and his lodg-
ing-house was the best in the city; he set no
table. My room was one of many on either side
of a hall, beneath which was a large saloon on
the ground floor, where, when day drifted far into
night, and men with angry antagonisms (for
it was the time of civil war), met together, each
one with a pistol in his hip-pocket, a sharp word
was often followed with a sharp report. My custom was to go home from the play and quietly
up to bed, which having done, one evening, as I
sat on the edge of my couch undressing, with
my head leaning forward, up through the floor
came a pistol bullet, just grazing my ear, and
buried itself in the ceiling of the room. I heard
a rapid step in the corridor, and Wimmer pale as
a sheet burst into my room, with "My God,
Leman, are you alive?" I was, but I was undoubtedly quite as pale as Wimmer. He told
me that he had been trying in vain to compose
the angry disputants, and when the pistol was
fired, knowing the position of my room and bed,
he feared the worst. I didn't sleep very well
during the rest of that night.

The antagonistic feelings engendered by civil
strife were very bitter in Virginia City at that
time, but the Union spirit was greatly in pre-
dominance. A big meeting was held in the
Opera House on one afternoon, where, in less

than an hour, $5,275 were subscribed for the sanitary fund, and the historic " sack of flour " was sold and resold, producing, I don't know *how* many, but very many thousand dollars. I, myself, had the pleasure of owning that sack of flour for about three minutes.

I was in acquaintanceship and on friendly relations with gentlemen, from whom, in political sentiment, I was as far as are the poles, apart. On one occasion, one of these friends met me as I entered the hotel, saying, with a satisfied tone, " Leman, old boy, I'm sorry to hurt your feelings, but we've got great news from Vicksburg, and Pemberton has knocked h—l's bells out of Grant's wheel-houses." Within five days the truth came, and meeting my secesh friend, I said, " Mr. ——, old boy, I'm sorry to hurt your feelings, but *we've* got great news from Vicksburg, and Grant has knocked h—l's bells out of Pemberton's wheel-houses."

In that era of sectional bitterness, happily now passed away, the utterance of disloyal sentiments was painfully prevalent, and spoken as they were in favor of men who upheld the " *Patriarchal Institution*," which claimed the right to manacle men because their skins were black, aroused in me the same feelings which caused me to *reflect*, when I saw the bright mulatto boy fettered for no crime, on the deck of the Mississippi steamer, and the poor old negro toiling in chains on the plains of Chalmette, and again I reflected on the so-called " Patriarchal Institution " which made our Declaration of Independence a *living lie* in the face of all the world, and felt that it did not perish from the land an hour to soon.

The season closed in the latter part of September, and I re-crossed the mountains by the grade (the name of which I now forget), but I remember that it led by the edge of the beautiful little Donner Lake, where, in the early California days, the wretched, snowed-in party perished one by one, the bodies of the dead feeding those who survived, and was in San Francisco, at the "Opera House," until the last week in December, when I again found myself with our old friend Buchanan, in Sacramento.

On February 16th, the " Millionaire " was played for the author's benefit, to a crowded house. " Marston," by Mr. Charles Pope, "Emily Larcelles," by Miss Virginia Buchanan, and " Swift," by Mr. Albert Hart. Mr. Hart was a well-known citizen of Sacramento, and had, in his early days, some experience of theatrical life. He appeared to advantage on this occasion. He has been in political life since then, having filled successively the offices of Governor's Secretary, State Librarian, and, I believe, Pension Agent. Mr. Hart still lives in Sacramento.

I again crossed the Sierras, for a second season in Virginia City, where the theatre opened on the second of March, 1864, and during that period made the acquaintance of one of the remarkable women of the day—Adah Isaacs Menken. She was a thorough Bohemian, possessed wonderful beauty of face and form, and with these, accomplished triumphs which her indifferent stage ability would never have achieved. She was a rattle-brained, good-natured adventuress, born of Jewish parents, somewhere in the Southern States. The conventionalities of society were quite disregarded by the " Menken," and she smoked and rode astride, and gambled with a freedom that was delightful to the men on the Comstock, who hailed her arrival with joy, for they adopted her at once as " one of 'em." " Mazeppa," " not over-dressed, nor wholly bare," but nearly so, was in her element with these men, for she had the faculty of adaptation to all kinds of men, and after the nightly exposure of the "Tartar Prince," " naked to the pitiless storm," and the eager eyes of admiring miners, she might be found in T. P——'s, or some saloon where the red and white chips passed merrily from hand to hand, and where she said she went because T. P—— played a " square game."

Miss Menken played nothing else but " Mazeppa "—if I except the part of " Katharine

Kloper," in the musical trifle of "Lola Montez," but this was feeble to the last degree—and faro, which she played with skill and success.

The career of the "Menken" was almost as remarkable as that of her great predecessor, Lola. Her first husband was John C. Heenan, the pugilist, then she captured Orpheus C. Kerr, and left him for a California gambler, with whom she went to Europe. When on the Continent, she was familiar with Dickens, Dumas and Swinburne, and boasted that "beginning with a prizefighter, she would end with a prince," reversing Lola's course, who began with a king and ended with a miner, and she came very near succeeding. Fair and false, and fast and faithless, her soul might possibly have gone to heaven—as she said it would—through the "gates of Paris," if it could have got out of that gay city, where her body lies buried beneath a monument inscribed with, "Thou Knowest;" unsatisfactory as to its meaning, which nobody knows.

Adah Isaacs Menken is a vivid "memory" of the drama on the Comstock, as is also T. P——, in whose saloon she used to fight the tiger. T. P—— was a man of daring personal courage, and was, I think, a civil officer at the time. Subsequently, in an encounter so common in those days among men of his class, after receiving a mortal wound, while his life-blood was

ebbing rapidly away, he had the desperate determination to raise himself on his elbow and shoot
his slayer dead; both were buried together.

On the evening of May 13th, the writer was
tendered a complimentary testimonial benefit
when the "School for Scandal" was acted.
"Charles Surface," Mr. Charles Pope; "Lady
Teazle," Mrs. Charles Pope; "Sir Peter Teazle,"
Mr. Walter M. Leman. The house was brim-full,
which, perhaps, is the pleasantest among my
"memories" of the Drama on the Comstock.

On the conclusion of the season, Mr. Charles
Pope and myself resolved to spend a day or two
at Lake Tahoe and catch trout, before we re-
crossed the mountains from the land of sage-
brush to California, the land of fruit and
flowers; in pursuance of which plan we took the
stage over into Lake Valley, and put up at the
old tavern near the lake shore; I forget the name
of the house, for it was nearly a quarter of a
century ago. I remember it was one of those
comfortable old roomy log houses, with a fire-
place in the great bar-room large enough to hold
a whole load of wood; and the flaming logs were
piled upon the fire with reckless profusion.

Mr. Pope was, as I supposed, a skillful angler
and anticipated a great deal of pleasure from the
splendid "catch" on the morrow. I hadn't

much confidence in my own abilities, for generally, when I went fishing, I got many bites and few fish; but we were certain of a pleasant day on the lake, whether successful or not, and after breakfast the next morning, supplied with an ample lunch, we took seats in the boat, with trolling lines all prepared, and our boatman plying his oars, were soon out on the bosom of one of the loveliest sheets of water in our broad land. Pope had been anxious to get a bet on his catching the first fish, which I didn't want to take, but finally accepted—he lost the bet. We kept on, all earnestness, and presently I caught another, and after a little while a third. These were all small, which made Pope laugh, and declare that he didn't want any sardines, but he'd soon show me the kind he was fishing for. Our boatman slowly skulled the boat, with our lines extended perhaps a hundred feet or more, when suddenly came a pull at my line, as if a shark had taken the hook. The boatman told me to keep cool and haul steady and, all excitement, I succeeded in landing a beautiful trout, which seemed to me to be twice as large as any shad I ever bought in the Philadelphia fish-market. Charley looked on with interest and was as much excited as myself, for fear I should lose my noble prey, but when he was safe at the bottom of the boat, I think he began to feel chagrined at his ill-luck, but he put a good face on it and swore he'd " have the next big fellow." I think that I caught one more before lunch time, when we put into the little cove of Emerald Bay and enjoyed our meal and a cigar.

Charley, certainly, was attended by ill luck. Up to this time he had not got a fish, although he had hooked several ; but the afternoon was to redeem his piscatorial reputation, and I hoped that it would, for I had a kind of guilty feeling, as if I were doing him a wrong by being so lucky. Well, we put out again on to the lake, and from that time up to the hour, when it was necessary to draw in our line and return to shore, Pope never caught one fish and I had got five or six more, for when we got to land and counted them, there were thirteen in all. Charley, certainly, took his ill fortune with great good nature, but said little or nothing to the inquiries of the men, who came to the beach, as we landed, and wanted to know who caught that big fellow. We had a hearty supper and adjourning to the bar, I went up to the Register, which lay on the counter, where visitors, in addition to their names, had added memoranda of their fishing experience, as thus—" May 25. J. J. and party, Sac. City, went fishing ; fine luck ; caught a dozen trout, one pretty large one,"—and turned over its leaves. I saw Charley looking at me, as if in wonder what I would write about our day's fishing, and taking the pen, I wrote thus after the name and date: "Went fishing with Mr. Pope; had excellent luck; caught one seven-pounder." After a moment or two Pope went up to the book, read what I had written and taking a pen, wrote underneath with a quizzical look at me before doing it: "Charles Pope went fishing with Mr. Leman; had d——d bad luck; caught nary pounder."

That splendid trout was boxed up and sent to Mark Twain, for the delectation of the newspaper fellows of the *Enterprise*, with a letter from Charley Pope, and I fully believe that he told them he caught it; if he did, I forgive him, as I trust he will forgive me for revealing his want of skill —(I beg pardon) his want of luck—the day that we went gypsying and fishing on Lake Tahoe, in the pleasant days of the long ago.

I have sometimes thought that in returning to California from Nevada at that time, instead of going over into Utah, I made a mistake. Mr. Selden Irwin came to Virginia City during the season and played a few nights with us. He had been with his wife for some time in Salt Lake City, where he was quite a favorite; indeed, I think he was the first professional player that reached that then isolated metropolis of the Saints.

Mr. Pope and his wife and myself had seriously entertained the idea of going from Virginia City to Salt Lake, and Irwin especially encouraged the scheme; clapping me on the back, with enthusiasm he exclaimed: "Go! by all means, go! Leman, you are the very man they want—you'll be a Bishop in three months!" After some correspondence with Mr. Clason, Brigham's son-in-law, our plan was abandoned. Perhaps it was for the best, for with that Mormon Bishopric and the attendant harem of wives, I would hardly have survived to celebrate my golden wedding with *one* wife, which I did two years ago.

On Saturday, July 16th, 1864, I embarked on board the bark "Onward," Captain Hempstead, for Honolulu, Hawaiian Islands. After a pleasant passage over a calm ocean, we sighted the eastern point of Maui, and passed along the northern coast of Molokai in the afternoon of the 31st, and on the following day were moored at the pier in Honolulu. It was the anniversary of the Hawaiian Restoration, and I found the city decked with flags, the military on parade, and the population in festive attire; the gala terminated with a grand ball in the evening, attended by most of the notables, foreign and native, to which I was an invited guest.

On board the "Onward" I had as fellow-passengers, two gentlemen, residents of San

Francisco, an old school-fellow whom I had not previously seen in many years, and a lady who had won the title of "Queen of Bohemia," and was perhaps the most marked specimen of her peculiar class—Ada Clare. She was of Southern birth, and had a reckless, devil-may-care spirit within her that made her as utterly indifferent to criticism as Lola Montez or Menken ; she had a lithe form, a clear complexion, a nervous expression, and a superabundant wealth of massy blond hair. She had written for the journals and had written some things *worth* remembrance though now forgotten ; she was pleasant company on shipboard, and made the trip to the Volcano, riding astride, as the Hawaiian women invariably do, and as every sensible woman should do, in mountain travel. Miss Clare met with a painful death in New York, some years later, falling a victim to hydrophobia from the bite of a pet dog.

On Thursday, August 16th, a pleasant party of six in number, the writer being one—three ladies and three gentlemen—embarked on what had been the Royal Yacht "Naheniena," for Hilo, Hawaii. This "royal yacht" was an Oldenburgh brig, which had been confiscated to the Hawaiian Government for some violation of maritime or commercial law, and his Majesty Kamehamea V, having no navy, resolved to indulge in a yacht, and had her cleaned up, a crew of some forty seamen put on board, and made the voyage around his Island Kingdom in her, in the summer previous to my visit. She was a lumbering old tub, drew as much water as a more modern vessel of three times her tonnage, and with an immense spread of canvas could, I think, have won any prize in a regatta where the victor was the one who came in *last;* but though slow, she was sure, and as strong as wood and iron could make her.

The third day found us becalmed between the islands of Maui and Hawaii, but catching a breeze, we beat a long way to windward, and on Monday morning sailed into Byron's Bay, at the head of which is situated the pretty town of Hilo; its neat white cottages nestled among the cocoanut and pandanus trees, each residence a fairy bower of taste and comfort.

All our preparations completed, we started from Hilo on the morning of Wednesday, the 24th of August, for the volcano of Kilauea. I will not detail the events of that interesting ride, but touch only on some salient points. The whole face of the country was a kind of green desolation. Mauna Kea, the highest peak of the Islands, was on our right hand, 13,000 feet above the sea, to the southwest the long ridge of Mauna Loa rising to nearly the same altitude. At 5 P. M.

we reached a native grass hut, where the residents, with the assistance of our attendants, three in number, prepared the evening meal, which we ate with sharp appetite and went to our repose on pallets of fragrant grass, while far in the southwest a fiery cloud hanging in the still heavens told us where burns—

"Pele's unquenched fire."

On the next morning we rose at 5, were in the saddle at 6, and reached the crater at 10 A. M.

The crater of Kilauea is of gigantic dimensions, oval in form, upwards of three miles in length by two in breadth and with almost perpendicular walls or sides of from 500 to 800 feet in height. The bottom is a black flooring of hardened lava. In the center of this great crater is the ever-living lake of fire, which, in the daylight, shows from the outer bank of the large crater only a slumbering pit and surrounded by jagged walls of desolation. By a rough trail or path, we all got down upon what might be termed the first bench of the crater, where stunted trees and ferns contended for a foothold on the very borders of eternal fire and ruin. Here, also, we found the Ohelo, a juicy berry, abundant in the bushes and wild strawberries ripening in the sun.

The weather, until the 27th, was unpropitious for our night visit to the burning lake. A thick mist began falling, as we commenced the descent, but, following our guides, we scrambled down into this immense bowl in the Earth, the depth and dimensions of which cannot be realized by looking into it from the bank above. A walk of half or three-quarters of a mile brought us to the lava floor. What, from above, appears an almost level surface, proves to be rough and billowy, as if a sea of molten iron had rolled up in huge waves and cooled upon the gravelly shore. Stepping upon the adamantine surface, we advanced over this floor, rifted into a thousand tortuous forms, and crossing deep chasms and seams varying from six inches to four feet in width and of unknown depth, towards the Stygian lake in the center, passing cones and pinnacles of lava, thrown up, sometimes in ridges, like a mountain chain, sometimes in isolated singleness. One remarkable representation bore a strong resemblance to a chapel in ruins, with its towers and pinnacles still standing and looking as if scared and blasted by fire. To this the guides had appropriately given the name of "Pele's Church."

The day declined; but long before we came to the brim of the abyss, we were made aware of its activity by the noise of the terrible cauldron. Language can hardly describe what may be said to be indescribable. For the last half century travelers have at various times visited the "Crater of Kilauea" and hardly any two visitors have agreed in their description. This is not strange, either, for this ever-burning and unquenchable lake, this awful valve for the pent-up flames of the globe's center, is ever changeful in aspect, ever grand, mysterious, terrible!

On the night of our visit, the surface of the lake appeared to be about forty feet below the rim on which we stood, which rim, or bank, seemed to be of calcerous matter mixed with lava and of exceedingly irregular formation. As we stood facing the northeast, from the rifts and chasms of a depression on our right, masses of sulphurous vapors arose and along with the clouds of smoke from the burning lake were swept away to the northward.

On our left hand the bank rose into a cliff some fifty feet higher than the level of the rim elsewhere. Part of this cliff, or precipice, had broken off some few weeks previous to our visit and fallen into the lake; the part remaining had, from a stand-point a little to the right, the severe outline of a human face gazing down into the boiling cauldron, whose flaming surface cast upon it, through the gloom of the night, a spectral illumination, as of a lava Sphynx. The lava flood was, with slight interruptions of a few minutes, in continual action during the five hours

that we remained. Around the whole edge of
the lake, where the lava impinged against the
bank, a circle of sheeted flame and molten fire
glowed with intense brilliancy, and like a bright
belt, encircled the black island in the centre;
while every few minutes, in one or the other part
of the surface, the lava cauldron would commence
to heave in fiery throes, momentarily accelerating
in force, propelling the jets of crimson metal or
lava in cascades up to the height of ten, twenty,
thirty feet, indeed, often higher than the bank on
which we stood. These fiery jets would run, one
into another, until frequently as many as six or
eight were in furious action together, when their
united power would suddenly open a blazing
seam across the blackened surface of the lake,
which cooled quickly after each convulsion.
And then the liquid flood, released from the
hardening crust that kept it down, would roll in
flaming combers across the whole surface of the
lake and dash itself upon the Stygian shore.

For five hours we remained, gazing mute
and awe-struck on this magnificent scene. High
in the air a tropic bird floated slowly across the
heavens, the flames of the crater gilding him
like a meteor. Our blankets were unpacked,
and refreshments taken, after which one of our
ladies—Miss Charles, of Hornelsville, N. Y.—
sang the songs of home and Fatherland. Never,

I think, was "Sweet Home" sang to such an accompaniment—the music of woman's voice, at what might appropriately be termed the very vestibule of Hell, while above and around

> "Fiercely the spires of volcanic fires
>   Steam on the sulphurous air."

As the night advanced the activity of the volcano increased; but the surface of the lake seemed to lower somewhat during •our stay— this was not unlikely; tourists at different times have found its elevation variable, sometimes a hundred feet down, sometimes within a few feet of the bank. We judged it to be about forty feet down, and it certainly appeared to recede somewhat during our stay.

Once or twice the momentary shifting of the wind blew the suffocating vapor partially upon us, and an immediate retreat was necessary; it was, however, but momentary. The contingency of a change of wind blowing strongly upon the visitor when partially asleep, or dozing, seems to be the greatest source of danger, but no casualty of that kind has ever occurred.

The banks of the lake are more or less covered with a fibrous substance, somewhat resembling threads of flax, and brittle as spun glass; it appears upon the lava boulders like cobwebs. The appropriate name given to these fibres, found so near the abode of the dread divinity, is "Pele's hair."

Our return was against the advice, and in spite of the opposition of our native guides—who rather dislike tramping the floor of that awful amphitheatre, except by daylight. The night was intensely dark; we started in Indian file; one guide preceding us with a lantern, another in the center of the column, and the others skirting the flank of our march; when we came to the chasms and difficult points, our guides would concentrate and light us over. Only in one or two instances did they diverge from the safe path, and then only for a rod or two, and the trail was easily found again. It was 11:30 when we started, and two in the morning when we reached the little grass hut dignified by the sounding title of the "Volcano House"—thus occupying two and a half hours on the return.

Tradition and the observation of intelligent residents of the Islands, all prove that the volcano is in a constant transition state, sometimes more active, sometimes less; although for the past few years its general activity has undoubtedly decreased, notwithstanding its occasional fiery outbursts. An old gentleman of Maui, who had visited it thirty years before, assured me that the burning lake then occupied fully one-sixth of the whole area of the crater. Estimates of its extent vary at different times—we thought it not less than one thousand feet in diameter.

The dark mythology of the Hawaiians has invested this appropriate arena with additional horror; it is the dwelling-place of their awful goddess, Pele, the prime divinity of their Pantheon; here, in company with her subordinate demons, she bathed and disported in its sulphur waves.

Christian courage here subdued supernatural terror, when, in 1825, the converted chieftainess, Kapiolaui, braved the anger of the goddess and the attendant horrors of the path by descending alone into the crater, and casting with her own hands, into the seething gulf, the sacred berries, as an open and avowed act of desecration.

Our party spent five days at the "Crater of Kilauea" and our return to Hilo was as delightful a ride, as our departure thence. Mr. Hitchcock and all our friends rode out to meet us on the approach to the pretty town, where we found another plan had been organized for a grand picnic up the Wailuku, with a party of eleven, ladies and gentlemen, on the following Wednesday morning. I will not attempt a description of that ever-remembered day, or of the surpassing loveliness of the scenery with its cascades and torrents; the Rainbow Fall of 70 feet; the Upper Fall, a grand cascade of 120 feet; the Pools, or

Bowls; the Circular Rainbow, and the thousand
natural charms, that rival in beauty, if not in
grandeur, Yosemite itself and which, if known
to the traveling world, would throw most of what
is now known far into the shade. In order to
reach the proposed point for our picnic ground, it
was necessary to send out a gang of natives on
the previous day to cut a path with Matchetes
through the dense undergrowth, and even with
this preparation, our horses were with difficulty
forced through the green obstruction.

The Wailuku falls into the sea a little north
of the town of Hilo, and the southern bank,
which is at this point a verdure-covered bluff of
sixty feet in height, was a favorite bathing place
and toward evening the youth of both sexes
assembled to indulge in what to a Hawaiian is a
necessary part of existence : with shouts of mirth
and laughter they would dive or jump from the
cliff, cutting the water like an arrow, and sometimes re-appearing on the surface three or four
hundred feet from where they made their plunge.
I think that in this lively diving and swimming
the girls were, if anything, more expert than the
boys. They were of all ages from eight years to
sixteen, and all quite nude, with the exception of
a cloth around the middle, and most of the girls
were in form models of feminine perfection ;
what, with the merriment, and shouting, and

leaping, and the wonderful aquatic gymnastics, it was a cheerful and pleasing scene.

In the charming little hamlet of Hilo, there were, at the time of my visit, about fifty white, or as they were generally termed, foreign residents, and most of these were Americans. I believe that I was the first actor, that ever landed on the lava strand, which fronts that little town in the " sun-down " sea and Mr. Cony, the Sheriff, Mr. Hitchcock, Mrs. Capt. Spencer and others had determined that I should do what had never been done in Hilo—give an entertainment. If I had been disposed to offer objections, they would certainly have been out of place, where so many courtesies had been received. To be sure, I had neither books nor memoranda to draw from, but Mr. Cony, in his beautiful little cottage, had a well selected library, which was at my disposal. I was told, that they only wanted me to appear; they didn't care in *what*, or *what* I did; they would make every preparation and all be present to honor me.

So, in a beautiful moonlight evening, I walked down the little tree-embowered street, and sàw through the foliage the picturesque, white-painted school-house (which was Court-house as well), gaily lighted, every window thrown up and surrounded by an eager crowd of natives, and the seats within occupied by every American lady and gentleman, with their children, resident in Hilo. With such an audience and on such an occasion, I felt like doing my best.

My programme for the evening was a series of recitations, serious and comic, and the reading of the fifth act of "Hamlet." As the papers say, my audience was "appreciative and enthusiastic," and the Hawaiians on the "outside" seats greeted the comic recitations and the humors of the "Gravediggers" with unanimous and hearty applause. A charming collation at the cottage of Mrs. Capt. Spencer terminated the evening, where Miss Charles sang "When Stars are in the Quiet Sky" in a manner to make it one of the most delightful "memories" of a series never to be effaced.

Mr. Cony left the next morning at an early hour, on official business, for Lapahoihoi; but I found an envelope to my address with a gracious note and a handsome sum in current gold coin, the voluntary offering of friends whose kindness and liberality can never be forgotten.

On the evening of August 11th, previous to my trip to the Volcano, I gave a lecture at the Nuanee Hall, in Honolulu—subject, "The Drama;" and on my return, upon the evening of September 16th, a "Reading" at the same place. Both of these entertainments were well attended.

On the night of Monday, the 19th, in company with several American gentlemen, I attended by invitation of the Hon. David Kalakaua—then Chamberlain of the Palace and Postmaster-General of the realm, but now "his Majesty Kalakaua I, King of the Hawaiian Islands"—a grand "Hula-hula," the wild native dance, which, I think, is the more dear to the Islanders the more it is proscribed.

Mr. Kalakaua was very courteous to me during my visit to Honolulu; and I had the pleasure of meeting him, after a lapse of many years, on American soil, when he was a King. I think in the higher rank he is, as he was in the lower, a true gentleman.

On Wednesday, the 21st, I bade the last farewell to my Island friends, and left the charming Hawaiian Islands, where I had spent three months among the pleasantest of a long life. And full of happy "memories," I arrived in San Francisco on Tuesday, October 11th.

CHAPTER XV.

I SAILED from San Francisco on the 19th
of October, 1864, crossed the Isthmus of
Nicaragua on November 2d, and arrived in New
York on the 13th. I recall the anxiety among
the passengers, as we neared the end of the
voyage, respecting the result of the presidential
election, and I think I won a small bet on "the
rail-splitter"—

"That true-born king of men."

On the 21st day of June, 1865, I again started
for California, on the steamship "Morning Star,"

and on the 29th we passed the wreck of the "Golden Rule," stranded on Ran-cador, in the Caribbean Sea. I had made the voyage from Greytown to New York in the "Golden Rule," and felt sorrow for the loss of a noble ship, and some I knew on board. We made the transit safely, and I was again in San Francisco on July 21st, 1865. After a vacation of nearly a year's duration, I re-appeared at the Opera House on the night of the 26th as "Sergeant Austerlitz."

I found in Mr. Maguire's company at that time an actor with whom I had a slight acquaintance some years before, and who, some years later, won the title, and maintained it to his death, of being, if not the best, certainly among the very best representatives of the intense emotional school, which has to some extent supplanted the older methods—and produces its effects more by what it refrains from doing than by what it does—not but that Mr. Thorne could act on the "old lines" as well, but he adopted the new method and became a proficient in it. Of a manly person and expressive face, and with a well-rounded voice, Mr. Thorne had all the natural qualifications for success—and study, aided by good judgment, placed him eventually at the top of the ladder. I was his professional companion for several seasons on either side of the continent, and recall some sad, but many pleasant memories of a deceased friend — Charles Thorne, Jr.

Mr. George Pauncefort was another member of the Opera House Company at that time. Mr. Pauncefort was an Englishman of a peculiar temperament. He had been, I think, a member of the Boston Theatre Company with Mr. Thomas Barry, and remained but a short time in California ; long enough, however, to get married to Miss B——— D———, who had been a California actress from the early days. After many years, Mr. Pauncefort was heard from, traveling through the wilds of Washington Territory with a horse and wagon, giving itinerant performances all by himself ; and still later I read an account of his turning up as an Eastern potentate away off in Syria or Asia Minor, with a Harem, and Chibouks, and all the surroundings of a Persian Caliph. Mr. Louis Aldrich was another member of Mr. Maguire's Company. I can hardly call him an Old-Californian, though he is not so young, as when one of the famous "Marsh Troupe." He used to astonish the people by the exhibition of talents far beyond the "*juvenile*" order. Mr. Aldrich was a good actor then—I mean, when I met him in 1865—he is a better one now and deserves the good fortune he has achieved with a successful play, the principal character of which is, in his hands, a fine dramatic portrait. Although not a member of the "Young Men's Christian Association," he has many Christian virtues. I hope he may live long and prosper to the end.

I also found Mr. Pierrepont Thayer with Mr. Maguire at that time. This gentleman was, I believe, a native of Boston, possessed of much capability for the stage, and, but for an unhappy tendency competent to make an honorable record as an actor, he had fallen away and resolved, again fallen away and re-resolved so often, that his best friends could see no other end than that which eventually came. A few years later, this gentleman's lifeless body was found, and, lying on the table near by, a paper, on which, in his own handwriting, were these words: "I test the problem."

What problem? of existence? Life and death, though mysteries, are facts and not problems—of existence hereafter? It would seem, that the mind of that man, who would test the problems of future existence or non-existence by self-immutation must be warped by insanity. I believe that poor Pierrepont Thayer was insane. .

On the 16th of August, the New Theatre in Marysville, a handsome and commodious building, was opened by Mr. Maguire with the company from the San Francisco Opera House. The opening address for the occasion was from the pen of Mr. Walter M. Leman and beautifully spoken by Miss Sophie Edwin. A few extracts are appended:—

Where erst a few months back, devouring fire
Made of the Muses' Fane a funeral pyre,
Whose tongues of flame shot madly forth on high,
Mounting fantastic to the midnight sky
And sending thence their red reflection down,
Like a volcano, o'er the sleeping town ;
To the proud duty, which he knows so well—
Starting the fireman by the alarum-bell ;
Here, where the prosperous city spreads amain
With living energy athwart the plain ;
Here, where its busy marts and crowded streets
Show how the healthful pulse of commerce beats
'Mongst pleasant homes, by Yuba's golden sands,
Our new-born temple of the Drama stands.
Perfect in structure, radiant to the view,
To virtue dedicated—and to you.

*   *   *   *   *   *   *

Friends of the Sage, upholders of its laws,
The suppliant Drama brings to you her cause ;
While to the Drama's teachings we are true,
Her cause, before the curtain—rests with you.
If you shall nod, or give approving smile,
To prurient actions, or to words of guile,
Oh, *you* and *us* shall be the double sin ;
But if with wisdom's maxims we shall win,
And mould your plastic sympathies of soul
With Thalia's mask—or with Melpomene's bowl—
To acts of truth, and virtue's true regard,—
To *you* and *us* shall be the full reward.
And here the weary hours shall you beguile
'Neath the bright radiance of woman's smile—
And when your labor's done, at evening hour,
Own the full influence of her magic power.

Here shalt the Drama's glass to you impart
The dark recesses of the human heart,
And show the silver-lining to the eye
That gilds the clouds of human frailty.
Old Lear, in accents wild shall rend the air
With the loud wailings of his blank despair;
Hamlet, the heavens majestic roof shall scan,
And show you—"What a piece of work is man!"
Here Juliet shall barb Love's quivering dart
And send the shaft to Romeo's bleeding heart;
And Lady Teazle, with her scandalous school,
Hold poor Sir Peter up to ridicule.

And Rosalind in masculine bravery
Lead young Orlando to a willing slavery.
And here your hearts shall pay the ready boon
Of pity for the hapless Octoroon;
And be again with grief and sorrow torn
For the confiding, artless, Colleen Bawn.
When floats the black-flag on the scenic breeze—
Here mimic Farraguts shall sweep the seas;
And in new battles for the rights of man
New Grants and Shermans lead the glorious van,
Along with Hooker bold—and gallant Sheridan.
And here shall drop the willing tear for those
Who died to assuage their struggling country's woes,
As the just Lincoln fell amid his bloody foes.

In September we were all back to the Bay
City, where "Vestvali," of whom much was
expected, made her first appearance before a
"Pacific" audience. Mlle. Felicita Vestvali had
been a notability in opera in the *Old* World, but
abandoned the lyric stage when she came before
the public in the *New.* She was a lady of pon-

derous proportions and moderate talent, and made little or no impression.

In October, Mr. Daniel E. Bandmann, who was announced as "the great Anglo-German Trage-dian, appeared and played on alternate nights with Vestvali—and Mr. Bandmann's impression was like Vestvali's. I presume that this arrange-ment was made in order that the public might have forty-eight hours to get over "Vestvali" and forty-eight to recover from "Bandmann." Fortunately, there was no epidemic.

In the latter part of December, while at re-hearsal, a lady clad in plain attire, plain almost to the verge of poverty, if appearances were a true indication, strolled through the front en-trance of the Opera House and sat down in the rear of the pit. I thought that her face seemed familiar; all wondered who she was and why she was there. Being accosted as to her busi-ness—she wished to see the manager, and the manager appearing, the lady announced herself as Miss Charlotte Crampton.

I was not wrong in thinking I had seen that face. Charlotte Crampton, *née* Wilkinson, *née* ———, had turned up in San Francisco, utterly unheralded and unknown; from where I never heard—by what means of conveyance I never knew; and during the short and fitful engage-ment of three or four nights, I hardly think any one knew from whence she had come or whither she was going.

She was engaged instanter, for there were many in the theatre who knew her wonderful ability; a proper costume was spoken for—for she absolutely had nothing in the way of wardrobe—and on the evening of the 27th she appeared as "Margaret Elmore," and electrified the audience with her wonderful feeling and power. "Hamlet" was the next character, and rarely had a more philosophical Shakespearean Prince of Denmark been seen.

The way was open to favor—to success—to more, perhaps to fortune—one other appearance —"Marguerite of Burgundy," in "La Tour de Nesle," when—Fate! Shall I call it "fate?" No; folly is a better term—"Folly" assumed its baleful power, and all was lost. The lady appeared no more.

In the cast of "Love's Sacrifice" I remember the names of Mr. and Mrs. Harry Jackson. This popular couple had lately come from the Australian Colonies. Mrs. Jackson, *née* Annie Lockhart, was a fine actress in parts requiring pathos and Harry Jackson was a good character actor, especially in the line of Jews and "rustic" ruffians. The lady had a sad experience in California and died some time after in Salt Lake City. Mr. Jackson went to London in the month of July, 1885. I dined with him at his handsome residence on Russell street, Bloomsbury, said good-bye with a promise to see him as soon as I got back to London and returned in three months from the Continent to find him—*dead!* Sad "memories" of both.

And Harry Courtaine! What "memory" of him? Courtaine, until he had willfully spoiled himself—the capable, facile, versatile, admirable *Actor!* Courtaine! By his willful spoliation of himself—the vascillating, unrespected, degraded, unmanly *man!* I saw *him*, too, in London—on the strand—once, twice, thrice! and he was— Courtaine! swayed and ruled—not by Fate, not by fatality, but worse—by folly and by madness.

In the spring of 1866 the "Extravaganza" of the "Seven Sisters" was produced, mainly for the purpose of introducing a new third act, which, at the request of the management, I had written under the title of—"An Allegory of the Union." This sketch embodied a series of symbolic tableaux—illustrated by dialogue, in which "Columbia," the "Genius of Liberty," "Uncle Sam" and all the "States" took part. In this dialogue "Massachusetts" and "South Carolina" were the principal talkers and "Uncle Sam" had hard work to keep them apart, even with the threat of a spanking. Sophie Edwin was the

"Massachusetts," Aggie Perry the "South Carolina" and Walter M. Leman the "Uncle Sam." It ran sixteen nights.

In the text of "Uncle Sam's" part in the "Allegory of the Union" was the following apostrophe to Baker, the last line of which is a repetition of his closing apostrophe to Broderick in the funeral oration delivered on the plaza in San Francisco, when Broderick was slain by Perry :—

And thou !

The Soldier-Senator of spirit proud,
Whose manly form " wrapped in a bloody shroud "
Will soon, alas !—" lie dead within our midst."
What thy heart bravely thought, thou bravely didst;
Thy clarion voice, upon Potomac's shore
Was hushed—thy eagle eyes will glance no more !
Farewell ! Thy race is run ; thy course is spent.
Baker, farewell ! Thou "Old Man Eloquent !"

The grief, that chokes my words,
Thy words may truest tell ;
Brave heart ! Good friend ! True hero !
Hail and farewell !

On the 28th of March, the "School for Scandal" was played for the writer's benefit, on which occasion Miss Emily Thorne appeared as "Lady Teazle." This lady is not to be confounded with the American family of Thespians of the same name. The press differed in their estimate of her abilities. Of her kindness I entertain a lively " memory." I had the pleasure of meeting Miss Thorne in London in 1885, after a lapse of twenty years. She is now a member of Poole's Company in that city and a great favorite.

On Monday evening, May 14th, Edwin Forrest made his first appearance in California as "Richelieu." In the fourth chapter of this work, I have spoken of my earlier acquaintance with this distinguished gentleman and touched upon the adverse surroundings of his visit to the Pacific Coast. I think that to ill-health, more especially than to any other cause, may be attributed his failure. His engagement was shortened for that reason and he did not play in the state outside of San Francisco. Mr. Forrest was supported by Mr. John McCullough, and as a female second he brought with him Miss Lilly. Mr. McCullough will long be remembered. Miss Lilly was instantly forgotten.

On Tuesday, June 15th, I sailed for the third time from San Francisco, bound to New York, and had for fellow passengers several professional associates. An incident which occurred on the Nicaraguan Isthmus is worthy of mention. Either the San Juan River was at a lower stage than usual, or our stern-wheeler drew more water than usual, for on going down that sluggish tropical stream we were frequently aground, and several times the little steamer touched at the bank where portages of a quarter of a mile or so, would be made to the next stopping place. A large number of the male passengers availed themselves of these opportunities to foot it from point to point through the dense woods, where superabundant vegetation wreathed the trunks of the great trees with a living green to their summit, and monkeys leaped from branch to branch, chattering and *mowing* at the unusual presence of man. The paths were *rough* ones, and often crossed muddy little inlets, with a rail or branch laid across to assist one in getting over. There was a general desire to make the short transits as quickly as possible, to be in time for the boat, and the intense heat made these walks in the wilds of Central America, short though they were, very fatiguing, but still it was a novel experience and enjoyable notwithstanding the discomfort. As Mr. Thorne and myself were getting over one of these inlets, rather larger than the rest, leading to a small lagoon a short distance from the river, we were astounded by a tremendous splash within six feet, and a shark six or seven feet long pushed his head and a third of his ugly body out of the water, half turning over in the act, and wallowing in the muddy stream. I think that if he could have got near enough to our legs or feet for a bite, he'd have taken it ; it was a rather startling and not very pleasant acquaintance. We were amazed to see a shark in a fresh-water stream ; but these ravenous salt-sea monsters go up the San Juan River constantly, as far as the Machucha Rapids, for " plunder and prey."

On Wednesday, the Fourth of July, we were off the Island of Cuba, and had a celebration of the holiday, with the " Santiago de Cuba " decked in flags and streamers. The programme included—

" Reading of Declaration of Independence,"
                              Mr. HARRY WALL.
Song—" Flag of our Union," . . Mrs. SEDLEY BROWN.
Address . . . . Rev. Mr. ELY.
Poem—"Our Country," . . . . . . Mr. W. M. LEMAN.
" Drake's address to the American Flag,"
                              Mr. CHARLES THORNE, Jr.

We wound up that " Independence Day " with song and dance at night.

> While o'er the seas the tropic breeze
>   Drove on our rapid keel—
> With favoring gale and swelling sail,
>   And swift revolving wheel.

Mrs. Sedley Brown is the daughter of my old associate and manager in the early days, Mr. W. H. Smith, who was well-known to the public on both slopes of the Union. She had been in California but a short time, but has visited it often since. I had the pleasure of her company in 1884, at my home in San Francisco; she was then a member of Wallack's Company, a part of whom were playing there at the time. I believe that Mrs. Brown is now the widow of Mr. —— Smith, a son of another old manager, who has been mentioned in previous pages—Mr. Sol. Smith. Mrs. Sedley Brown is a true and good woman, and an excellent actress; with pride I rank her among my friends. I arrived in New York on the 8th of July, and was greeted with intelligence of the disastrous fire that had swept away one-half of the city of Portland, Maine. I read with painful interest the newspaper accounts of how that conflagration " burnt back " against the wind for a mile and a quarter from the point where it started, to the very base of the " Old Observatory," which, sixty years ago stood, perhaps now stands, on " Mount Joy." I used to roam all round about that vicinity, while studying my " parts " in those long-gone days, and into the old cemetery, where side by side lie Burroughs and Blythe, the American and English naval heroes of the sanguinary fight between the " Enterprise " and " Boxer," enemies in war, reposing in amity in the peace of the grave. I recall a distich that the patriotic gamins of " Bunker Hill Town " (as Charlestown was often called when I was a boy), used to sing about that sea-fight—

" At length you sent your ' Boxer '
   To box us all about ;
We had an ' Enterprising ' Brig
   That beat your ' Boxer ' out.

She boxed her up to Portland
   And moored her off the Town
To show those sons of liberty
   This ' Boxer ' of renown.''

But this is digression. On landing, I was immediately met by Mr. J. B. Booth, Jr., then connected with Messrs. Tomkins and Thayer in the management of the " Boston Theatre," and engaged for that establishment, to commence with the opening in August.

When the company assembled in the green-room, preparatory to the first night, it was in truth called a "California crowd," no less than seven of its members—nearly one-half—hailing from the Golden State. Bulwer's comedy of " Money " was the opening " bill ;" Mr. Frank Mayo was the " Evelyn ;" Mrs. Agnes Perry, the " Clara Douglas," and Mr. Leman, the "Sir John Vesey " of the cast.

I have heretofore spoken of Mr. Frank Mayo. He commenced his professional career, I think, in California. I remember him first in the "American Theatre," San Francisco, during my engagement with Julia Dean Hayne. He played with us later, in the " Union Theatre," rose rapidly, went East, and made a phenomenal hit in

Boston in the part of " Badger," in the " Streets of New York." From that time his career has, I believe, been a highly successful one. The play of " David Crockett " made a great deal of money for Mr. Mayo, and he now has a new play, entitled " Nordeck," which is reported to me by those who have seen it, as being one of the best American plays yet written. Frank Mayo is a handsome, stalwart man and an actor of whom California may be proud. He resides, when at home, somewhere in the State of Pennsylvania.

In writing these desultory reminiscences of a long theatrical career, the use of the " first person, singular," becomes perhaps too often, a necessity. I have simply endeavored to keep the record consecutively, so far as I am personally concerned, without referring to what perhaps partial friends have said respecting myself; but I confess that if I were tempted to transgress the rule of a becoming modesty with regard to any period of the more than fifty years in which I was in theatrical harness, the three and a half years which I spent with my old Boston friends would be the time, but I forbear.

Among the stars of the first season, I remember Mr. Edwin Booth, who played a long and brilliant engagement; Mrs. Scott-Siddons, Miss Kate Reynolds, Mrs. Lander, Mr. Forrest, Lotta and others.

Lotta, thou midget! come into my mirror of memory as I first saw thee, away up in the foot-hills, at Ione City—was it? Yes, I think it was at Ione City. I forget the county, but the State was California. A little girl with a banjo, which thou did'st play with grace and skill, hopping and skipping and kicking—how thou did'st kick —at everybody and everything, and when there was nothing else to kick at, thou would'st kick out into space; how thou did'st squirm and do a "walk-around," and do all with an impunity and a vim that defied all opposition and criticism, for thou wast bright and merry, and everybody loved to see thee, laugh at thy capers, enjoy thy fun, and toss into thy lap the coins and nuggets of the land of gold.

Miss Charlotte Crabtree (Lotta) had grown older but not much bigger than in the California era, and though her acting, judged from an artis-tic standpoint, did not call for much comment, she was always pleasing and wonderfully attract-ive. The idea of Lotta being serious in any-thing, seemed an absurdity, and yet in "Little Nell" she was serious, and played with feeling; but she was born to make us laugh, and not to weep, and she has fulfilled and is fulfilling her mission. John Brougham called her a "dramatic cocktail," for the following reason—

> Because in Lotta we can see
> Artistic concentration
> Of sweetness, strength and piquancy,
> A pungent combination.

In the company of the " Boston Theatre " was a gentleman who subsequently became the victim of a terrible calamity—Mr. Henry L. Bascomb. I had known his father, who was the landlord of the " Boylston Hotel," which stood upon ground now occupied by the magnificent " Parker House," in School street. The " Boylston " was a great Thespian resort, and was the legitimate successor of the " Stackpole House," on Milk street, and " Bradstreet's," on Atkinson street, where, seventy-five years ago, Hodgkinson and Fennell and Snelling Powell and Barrett and Tom Cooper and the other worthies of the old Boston stage were wont to gather. Mr. Bascomb, a few years since, lost both of his feet by exposure to intense cold. It would seem as if his was a case that demanded recognition by the government of the " Forrest Home," but I do not know that it was ever brought to the notice of the trustees. I think that he now holds a position under the municipal government of Boston.

Another friend, whom I shall always remember—John Scott—not John R. Scott—not as good an actor as was John R. Scott—but as good a man, as good a man as ever lived was in that company. I have seen that old friend within a twelve-month in his happy home, near Boston; he is now cashier of the Dorchester National Bank, and his name is S. J. Willis. The name of Scott was but a *nom de théâtre.*

Mr. Edward L. Davenport, one of the finest actors that the American Stage has ever known, played a very successful engagement. I had never had much professional association with this gentleman since the third or fourth year of the old "Tremont"—with the exception of one year at the Walnut Street, Philadelphia. His career in England had been a prosperous one, and there were not a few good judges who thought him, twenty-three years ago, the equal of any tragedian. There was no man who so closely approached the grandeur of the elder Booth in the character of "Sir Giles Overreach" as E. L. Davenport. There were always pleasant ties of personal friendship between him and myself. I honor his memory.

During the first season at the "Boston," detachments of the company played occasionally in some eight or nine different towns in Massachusetts; in Providence and Newport, in the State of Rhode Island; Hartford and New Haven, in Connecticut; Portland, in Maine; and Albany and Troy, in New York. And during the two

following seasons these excursion trips were repeated, but not so often.   They were pleasant in
many respects, for they gave me an opportunity
to renew old friendships and revive the memories
of "lang syne;" and sometimes there was a great
deal of fun extracted from them, especially when
Charley Thorne and Louis Aldrich were with us
—the first has passed away, but my old friend,
Louis Aldrich, yet lives, and he will recall the
merriment (wicked merriment, sometimes) that
we used to extract from a much-married man,
now deceased, who had an ardent devotion to two
objects: his black bottle and his "little wifey-
pifey," as he called her, though she was twice
his size, and always got the better in their
matrimonial combats, which were of frequent
occurrence.   Poor J——! Well, he is gone.
Peace to his memory!

On one of these excursions an incident occurred, which has drifted into the newspapers
as happening in various places, but which really
happened in the city of Lowell, Massachusetts.
I had been sent up from Boston with Miss Kate
Reignolds and a portion of the company, to play
"Dora."   Mr. Leslie, the deputy manager, having everything to attend to, had neglected to
procure the little child—which is a very important factor in the interest of the play; and at the
last moment went out and brought in a great

lubberly boy from the street, with dirty clothes and shoes, uncombed hair and unwashed skin, to represent " Dora's " pretty " four-year-old."

Miss Reignolds and myself protested against sending this great lubber before the audience, as he was sure to turn the whole play into a ridiculous burlesque. But Leslie had too much on his hands to get a substitute, and Miss Reignolds took the *Infant* before the audience, who gazed in wonder and astonishment. As " Farmer Allan," I had to take the child, fondle him, and ask his age, as he sat upon my knee.

With the hoodlum standing between my knees (I couldn't take him on my lap, for he was as big as his mother), and the audience by this time in unsuppressed laughter, I yielded to the current which I could not stem—and instead of saying, " How old are you, my little man ?" to which question the child's proper answer is, " Four years old "—I asked, " And how old are you, my strapping boy ?" to which, in a harsh, hesitating, fish-market voice, he answered, "Four —to-to six." " Forty-six !" I replied ; " You look it, my boy—you look it !" As a burlesque, " Dora " was that night a complete success.

The little drama of " Dora " was wonderfully popular; during a series of summer excursion trips, combining relaxation with business, I think Miss Reignolds and myself played it more than half the time, and I had the same experience with Miss Ada Gray. The regular season of 1869 opened on the 20th of September. Boucicault's play of " Formosa " was produced and fell flat before the public, which was not strange,— for certainly, mighty as is its author's name, it is but a common-place, coarse and stupid affair. I made a final tour of a month's duration, among the New England cities, and terminated my engagement at the Boston Theatre on the 12th of February, 1870. During the three years, in which I was an employee of Messrs. Orlando Tomkins, Benjamin F. Thayer and Junius B. Booth, Jr., not an unpleasant word or occurrence ever marred our friendly feeling. All three of these gentlemen are dead.

On Monday, the 14th of February, 1870, I left Boston on my fourth trip to California, and this time overland. On reaching San Francisco, I found there my friend, Mr. Thorne, who, like myself, had been anxious to return to the Pacific Coast. Early in March we opened at the Opera House in the " Three Guardsmen." Mr. Mayo soon after came out, and an unsuccessful season lingered along for some months, against the superior attractions of the " California Theatre," then in its second season under the management of Messrs. McCullough and Barrett. With Madame Methua Scheller we made a pleasant tour in the interior. This lady was a pleasing Anglo-German actress, who played in comedy, drama and tragedy with less force than the Janauscheks and Modjeskas, but still with skill and power. She fell a victim to the cholera a few years later, while playing in one of the Mississippi River towns. I withdrew from the Opera House on the advent of a company of " British Blonde Beauties," as they were termed in the bills, and on the 7th of July started, in company with Professor Wolcott Gibbs of Harvard University, the Rev. Clarence Eddy, S. N. Roberts, Esq., of Boston, and three ladies for Yosemite Valley. At Stockton, our party was augmented by a gentleman and his sister, from San Francisco, making us nine in number. It is not my purpose to enter into a description of the wonders and beauties and sublimities of Yosemite, with which the world has already been made familiar. Five years before that time, with San Francisco two hundred miles distant and the great plain of the San Joaquin intervening, with but a few towns and villages scattered over its vast expanse, there seemed little probability of the rushing army of civilization reaching the Yosemite by any other method than the tortuous bridle path, which our party took soon after leaving Mariposa. In 1865, only 147 tourists visited Yosemite Valley; in 1869, the year before our visit, when the

Overland Road had been completed, 1122 tourists registered as visitants. I believe that I was the second "actor," who ever stood upon the grassy floor of Yosemite, Mr. Joseph Proctor being the first.

While it is not my intention, as I have already said, to describe "Yosemite," I will briefly speak of an adventure, which occurred to us while enroute:—As I have stated, our party selected the Mariposa Route to the valley, as a portion of them wished also to visit the Mariposa Grove of Big Trees. This motive had no weight with me, however, as I was already familiar with these monarchs of the forest—having, while with Buchanan, played one act of the comedietta of "Used Up" upon the stump of the "felled-big-tree" in the Calaveras Grove.

From Mariposa we were accompanied by two attendants, to act as guides in the valley, with two extra horses in addition to those they rode, and they occasionally relieved the team, by giving some of us gentlemen passengers a spell in the saddle. When we were a little more than half way to Clark's Ranch, I thought I would try it for a mile or two, as a kind of preparative for my equestrian feats in the valley, but I was so well pleased with my Bucephalus and we got *on* with such accord—he never once trying to get me *off*—that I made the remainder of the distance in the saddle, along with one of our party and the two guides up and down the grade, over the Conchilla mountain to the romantic spot on the south fork of the Merced River, known as " Clark's Ranch," whence we were to start on the morrow for Yosemite.

As the day closed and the balmy night came on, we wended our way over an excellent road far in advance of the stage wagon, up and down among the gigantic and picturesque pines ; each turn and change on our ever-changing way opening a new vista of beauty ; the moon sending her silvery beams through the branches, each new turn forming a new development of " Fretted Roof" and " Gothic Aisle " far surpassing all that I had yet seen of man's architecture.

Sometimes one of us, and sometimes the other, would be in advance, but we generally kept pretty well together for conversation and companionship, and it was well that we did so, for we came almost directly on a she-bear with her two cubs. Two of our party, who chanced to be a few paces in the lead, stopped not more than fifty paces from Mrs. Bruin and her family. We reined up suddenly, turning and backing away a little ; it was almost impossible to hold our steeds in hand. The bear and her two young ones, after a minute or two, made tracks down the mountain side, expedited by our shouts and a flambeau, which our guides kindled with match and papers found in their pockets.

If we had got more close to her, there might have been trouble; a grizzly or cinnamon bear with two cubs is very likely to bite and tear, if molested; but I confess, that my first thought was not so much of the danger of being chased by the bear, if she should pursue us, as of being tumbled off my horse in the chase; for a man, who gets on the outside of a horse only once or twice in ten or twelve years is not likely to be an accomplished rider. I was very glad, when we came in sight of the house, far beneath us, and still gladder, when we reached it in safety—eight long hours from Mariposa. The balance of our party came up in the stage wagon an hour later.

I certainly lost no time in getting to the haven of rest and safety, especially for the last two or three miles down the mountain; for in the moonlight every white stump and old log looked like a bear. We started from Clark's on the following morning, reaching the vicinity of the Valley after the hour of noon, and as we progressed down, down, down, beneath the overhanging rocks from "Inspiration Point" and along the brabbling Merced; in the cool of the evening; at the base of the great cliffs, upon whose summits we had stood in the morning; the glistening blue California sky, tinged with amber and sparkling with a million stars over our heads; " El Capitan " and the " Sentinel " and all the great pinnacles and domes looking down upon us; with gigantic pines towering up all around and the air fragrant with sweet-smelling wild herbs, we realized the surpassing grandeur of nature, combining the beauties of torrent, and river, and mountain peak, and forest in a marvelous and perfect panorama. But, faithful to my word, I will attempt no description of " Yosemite." We lingered in the grand and lovely valley a week and our visit was made doubly pleasant by the company of a lady we met there, and who, though now no more, lives with all of us as one of the pleasantest " memories " of " Yosemite "—the Hon. Mrs. Teresa Yelverton.

In the year 1860, a remarkable trial occupied the attention of the Dublin Courts. The celebrated suit was brought by a gentleman against Major Yelverton for a sum of money due for the board of his wife, Mrs. Teresa Yelverton. After making the arrangement, the Major deserted his wife and married again. He denied that he had ever married her, and claimed that she had lived with him as his mistress; that he went through the forms of the ceremonies to " ease her conscience," and that he had no thought of making her his wife. It was thought that his family caused him to take the step he did, and that his marriage to Mrs. Forbes was also the result of their efforts; she had a large fortune and Major Yelverton had nothing but his pay, as an officer of the English army. The Major was the son of an Irish peer, who was himself a British officer.

Miss Teresa Longworth, the lady he thus stigmatized, had been twice married to him, once by the Scotch, and again by the Irish law. Their marriage was kept secret, lest his family should learn of it and disinherit him. He was the heir apparent to the Avonmore peerage, and an officer in the artillery, and Miss Longworth was not a member of the nobility. He was simply Captain Yelverton when she met him, but in a few years he became a Major, and previous to his death he assumed the title of Lord Avonmore; but if not noble, the lady was of high position; her mother dying when she was very young, she was sent to Paris to be educated in a convent, her family being of the Roman Catholic faith.

The acquaintance between the two commenced on the English Channel in 1852, where the lady, who was returning from France, was introduced to Captain Yelverton by some friends on board the steamer. The acquaintance was kept up in London, and by correspondence afterwards, both being evidently greatly attached to each other.

Miss Longworth spent two years in Italy, and when her education was completed, she returned to France, in a memorable year, 1855, when young ladies of rank went as Sisters of Mercy to the Crimea to nurse the sick of the Allied Armies, and she went with a party of ladies on this errand, being at Malta six months or more.

In all this time she had not met Captain Yelverton, who was stationed at Malta, but was in England at the time. When he returned to his regiment he offered his hand to her. For a time there was a happy companionship between them, for the beautiful girl was deeply attached to the young officer. He proposed a secret marriage, on the ground of opposition from his father, on whom he was dependant. Miss Longworth was not to be led into this arrangement, and broke the engagement. She went to the Crimea with an officer's family, and again met Major Yelverton, whom she had not seen for some months. He again proposed a secret marriage, and was again refused, and Miss Longworth returned to her sister in Wales. At this time she was in the heigth of her charms, and known for her beauty where she was unknown personally. Major Yelverton desperately enamored of her, and unhappy in his exile, obtained a leave of absence and followed her. During the winter season she was at Edinburgh, and he was constantly at her side, and persisting in his appeal to be married secretly. She refused again and again. One day he induced her to let him read the Church of England marriage service to her, and when he had completed it, told her that in Scotland that constituted a marriage.

She returned to her sister in Wales, and was claimed there by him as his wife, and induced to go to Ireland to be re-married by a Catholic Priest. Up to this time, and subsequent to the marriage, which was performed by the Parish Priest of Rosstrevoir, with the consent of the Bishop, she believed him to be a Roman Catholic. Miss Longworth made her first mistake in agreeing to keep the matter private. They traveled through Ireland together, and went to Scotland, and at the trial the various travelers' books in public places were produced as evidence, to prove that he wrote her name everywhere as Mrs. Yelverton.

Their passports were taken out in his name, and they introduced each other to their friends as husband and wife, as the case might be. The letters written by Major Yelverton to her when absent were read, and created a profound sympathy for her, and a great array of witnesses came from far and near to testify against the defendant.

The jury were out only an hour, and on the rendering of their verdict, which was in Mrs. Yelverton's favor, the excitement was of the wildest description. Outside the courts thousands of people had congregated, and as soon as the news was announced, the horses were taken from the coach which was to convey Mrs. Yelverton to her hotel, and down the quays, lined with people, was drawn in triumphal procession; the efforts of the police were unavailing, and the little lady was carried up the stairs of the hotel and on to the balcony, where she could be seen by all. She was weeping, and had to be supported, but soon realizing the generous kindness of the people, she advanced to the railing and in an eloquently pathetic manner, thanked them for their kindness.

In the meantime, Major Yelverton had married Mrs. Forbes, and he appealed the case. It was reversed in an English court, and the verdict of the Irish court was set aside.

Broken-hearted and ruined in health, Mrs. Yelverton left England forever, and came to America. She was at this time twenty-eight years of age, highly accomplished, a superb pianiste, and had a rich contralto voice which, in conversation, was music. From New York she went to Missouri, where she purchased a stock-farm, and for some years lived almost entirely alone.

It was said that she never saw a piano while in Missouri, but this was untrue, for her log-house contained, in addition to a piano, other musical instruments and a great many books. Anxious to get still further from a world where she had suffered so much, she sold her Missouri farm and went to New Zealand, where she had a cattle-ranch, and shortly after died there.

Such is the story in brief of the lovely lady I met in Yosemite Valley. Her conversational powers were wonderful, her affability was endearing, and her lovely face was a pleasure to the sight, albeit the great sorrow of her life had saddened and subdued it to a painful degree. She was a companion in our rides and walks, an associate in our junketing and pic-nicking, and will ever be a sweet and gentle "memory" of our visit to the Valley of the Yosemite.

CHAPTER XVI.

IT was on my return from Yosemite that I first met with Mr. Joseph Proctor. This gentleman, although he had been connected with the drama in Boston for a part of the time in which I was engaged there, I had not personally known, or known only as the most casual acquaintance.

At the time of our meeting, he had leased the " Metropolitan Theatre," in Sacramento, was gathering his company, and was in quest of "just such a man as me," to use his own words, and it took but a few moments to come to an understanding which was mutually pleasant, and without a single ripple of discord during the two years of our connection.

Mr. Proctor had an unquestionable right to be called a California actor, for he was among the early comers to the Pacific Coast. He was, I think, a partner of Mr. Venua in the building of the " Sacramento Theatre," in 1852 ; but I believe that he did not remain long at his first visit.

Mr. Proctor was a forcible and capable actor in the line of tragedy, and was—shall I not rather say, *is?* for he still lives—infinitely more pleasing and satisfactory in many of the classic tragic roles than some of those who claim a higher reputation. He *knows* his business thoroughly, and if he plays the "Jibbenainosay " more frequently than Shakespeare, it is not that he loves the immortal bard the less, but that the multitude love the "Jibbenainosay " the more. His performance of " Damon " and " Virginius," of " King Lear" and "Alexander the Great," are admirable representations of thespian power.

In private life he is unimpeachable ; as a manager just; and in all the relations of life, an honest man.

On the 30th of November, 1883, Mr. Proctor was the recipient of a testimonial benefit from his Boston friends, to celebrate the fiftieth anniversary of his professional life, which was largely attended. No man more worthy of such a compliment ever came before the public.

Mr. Proctor commenced his campaign on the 10th of September, just prior to the commencement of the State Fair, thereby availing himself of the advantages which that great gathering offers to those who cater for public patronage. The weather was intensely warm, but the week's business was very lucrative, and his season had an excellent " send off."

The stage manager was Mr. J. F. Cathcart. This gentleman came to California not long before with some organization which got stranded in San Francisco; he was a good general actor, and had been through an English Provincial experience. Mr. Cathcart subsequently visited California, playing the seconds with Mr. Charles Kean.

Miss Sue Robinson was our leading lady; she had grown up from a child on the Pacific Coast, and was known far and wide, in every mining camp of the early days, as the " Fairy Star" brim full of natural talent. If she had been taken when young and given the culture and training of a proper dramatic school, I can think of none more likely to attain to the highest grade of her profession; but when nuggets and handfulls of gold-dust were thrown to the little girl who twirled the banjo and danced the clog and sang the topical song, those who controlled her were too eager to gather the spoil of the present to think very much of her future. When she joined Mr. Proctor she was a very good actress, in spite of very bad training, or rather of no training at all; and in the two seasons which she remained with us her development and improvement were wonderful; her performances in some of the higher characters of comedy would have done credit to any first-class theatre; and the vocal and terpsichoreal extravagances of her earlier youth, modified by good judgment and taste, were powerful adjuncts to her attractiveness. Towards the close of the season she was in treaty with a prominent New York manager, and getting ready to start for a new field, when death intervened, and she was suddenly cut off at the threshhold of what I believe would have been a great artistic future. Poor Sue Robinson! Her picture hangs in my chamber—a not altogether sad "memory" of the past.

Mr. Proctor had very few stars during his managerial career in Sacramento; nor did he need them. He had a working company, and there was a very generous response on the part of the public to his efforts.

I recall the name of one young actress, whose appearance, both in the Bay City and Sacramento, was a pronounced success. Petite in figure, with a finely-moulded form and childishly beautiful face, she had nevertheless an astonishing amount of nerve and power. Among her other characters, I remember "Nell Gwynne," "Mrs. Oakley" in the "Jealous Wife," and, above all, "Juliet." This latter character in her hands was superb; in form and feature she was the typical "Juliet" of our imagination, and in her wild bursts of passion, not behind Neilson. She, too, is dead. ("Whom the gods love, die young.") Her name was Rose Evans.

Miss Jenny Mandeville was a member of the company, as was also Mrs. Stuart (*née* Woodward) and Mr. Robert Fulford, who subsequently married Miss Annie Pixley, another California girl, who has made her mark in dramatic annals.

Mr. Proctor crossed the mountains with his troupe, I think, in December, and some time was spent in Carson and Virginia City, where Miss Leo Hudson played an engagement as "Mazeppa." This lady had a shapely form, and was rather a pleasing actress within her sphere—a narrow one. She was seconded by Miss Eva West, a young lady who could, if need be, take her principal's place, if for any cause disabled, and, strapped to the "wild steed of the Ukrame," make all the "runs," utterly insensible to personal fear. Miss West was a far better actress than her leader, and has since then been oftener before the public, and always to their acceptance and gratification, and has had to encounter ill-health and many of the hardships which await the members of a profession where the most deserving are not always the most successful. I hope her future may be prosperous.

There were many changes in the company for the second season of Mr. Proctor's management. Among the new-comers was a young man, a perfect novice, who commenced low with a determination to "fly high," and who, from that hour, never faltered in courage to *do*, what he had the will to *resolve*, and stands to-day one of the foremost of young American actors—Eben Plympton. Mr. Plympton is favorably known in England, where he has played with great acceptance the seconds to Edwin Booth and Miss Adelaide Neilson.

Miss Sue Robinson was succeeded by Mrs. F. M. Bates, who is now (1886) a member of Mr. McKee Rankin's "California Theatre Company," and Mr. Crosby, now (1886) with the "Bunch of Keys" company, was the low-comedian. Vivian, the carricaturist, was with us. Mr. Vivian was called in the "bills" the "Great Vivian," but he was not, to speak truth, very large. Mrs. W——, a "society lady," backed by a gorgeous wardrobe, appeared as "Lady Gay Spanker" and two or three other characters, evincing a capacity for the stage, which, with study, promised success; but I never heard of her after.

With the possible risk of being called mercenary, the writer of these " memories " confesses that the two most pleasant remembrances of that season are associated with the evenings of October 4, 1871 and March 15, 1872, when his name was on the bills as a beneficiary. The complimentary card, tendering the first one, was signed by one hundred and fifty prominent citizens and the audience numerous and brilliant. The play was Morton's comedy of " Speed the Plough." At the second, the beneficiary essayed for the first time the character of " Falstaff," which was thrice repeated.

About the middle of the month of April, I got a dispatch directing me to meet Mr. John McCullough at the railroad station, and the result of that brief interview was my engagement for the California Theatre in San Francisco ; where, early in May, I appeared for the first time as " Adam," in " As You Like It ; " the " Rosalind " being Miss Carlotta Leclerq ; the " Orlando," Mr. John McCullough ; the " Touchstone," Mr. Williamson, and the " Banished Duke," Mr. Henry Edwards. Perhaps I may be called presumptuous in the assertion that with respect to perfect appointment, fitness of all the surroundings and appurtenances, beautiful sylvan scenery and appropriate music, never since *time was* has Shakespeare's charming idyl been better put upon the stage. The exquisite song, sang by that most exquisitely sympathetic tenor, Mr. Joseph Maguire, now deceased, of—

> " Blow, blow, thou winter's wind,
> Thou art not so unkind
> As man's ingratitude.''

Lives with me, and will live ever as a sweet and melodious " memory."

The death of my old associate, Mr. W. H. Smith, with whom I had played in Boston nearly half a century previous, opened the way to my connection with the California Theatre, which, under the direction of the late John McCullough, maintained for a period of nearly nine years its claim to be the best managed and most prosperous theatre in the Union, the *best* theatres in New York, or any other city, not excepted.

John McCullough is no more ; his lamp of life went out in mist and darkness. It is not for me to comment on his status as an actor, but it is wholly proper and congenial to my feelings to say of him : That, as a generous and just manager, as a kind friend, ever ready to relieve the distressed, not alone of his professional associates, but of all who needed aid, he was indeed a " man of men." Who, of the large number of prominent actors and actresses, who for many successful seasons played at the " California;" who, of the still larger number of the supporting corps, who from year to year aided in the work, will not certify to the liberality in business, and kindness in intercourse, of John McCullough? I venture to say, Not one!

In pondering on the recent afflicting termination of a career so full of *promise*, as was Mr. McCullough's; nay, rather of fruition than promise, for fame came before *death*—the "memories" of many departed associates come up to me like sombre shadows—and "so depart." At the obsequies of very many of these I assisted, among whom may be mentioned Frederick Glover at Sacramento, William Leighton, Harry Perry, Nathaniel Bassett, James Kendall, Mortimer, George and Caroline Chapman, Mary Stuart, Mrs. Judah, William Barry, Sophie Edwin, Montague, Samuel Piercy and others. To these brothers and sisters of the mimic art the end has come; may those who are left be just, without fear or guile, realizing that

> "It is not all of life to live,
> Nor all of death to die."

The season at the "California" terminated in about six weeks from the time of my joining the Company and in the latter part of June I went East overland once more to my "native heather" and with my old manager, Booth, played for my more recent manager, Mr. Proctor, in the drama of " The Red Pocket-Book," which had been successful in California, but was only moderately so in Boston. This engagement of two weeks, terminating on the 15th of September, 1872, closed my career in Boston, which had commenced five-and-forty years before.

On the 19th day of September, I left Boston to cross the continent for the fifth time, and availed myself of the opportunity to visit Salt Lake City. Brigham Young was then in the plenitude of his power. He was courteous to strangers, and received a little party, of which I was one, with all the coolness and *a-plomb* of a man of the world—which, indeed, he was. There was an intensity of expression- in his steel-blue eyes, that pierced into the thoughts of men, and after seeing him, I hardly wondered at his power. Salt Lake was—and is still, I presume—a pretty city. The early Mormon residents were very fond of the theatre and had constructed a handsome building, where Brigham used to sit on a Boston Rocker in the center of the pit, with his numerous family in the lower tier of boxes on either side. Payment, at first, was taken in produce,—a bushel of potatoes or a fat turkey for a box ticket, or pit admission, as the case might be. He talked freely of the theatre and was high in praise of Mrs. Hayne, who had recently played in Salt Lake City. I confess, that the general appearance of the gentle sex at Salt Lake did not make me much regret the opportunity I lost of obtaining a bishopric and a harem, by refusing to act on Irwin's suggestion at Virginia City, nine years before.

The " California Theatre," altered and re-decorated, opened for the season on the evening of Monday, September 30, 1872, with Lovell's comedy of "Look before you Leap."

The record of the " California," under the administration of Mr. McCullough, was, from its commencement to within a year of its termination, one of almost unexampled prosperity, but towards the end the clouds began to lower. The erection of the " Grand Opera House " and the " Baldwin Theatre " would not necessarily have jeopardized that prosperity, apart from other causes. The first, as a business venture, had been conceived in folly, lingered to a slow, half-completion, after months of delay, and was an elephant on the hands of its builders ; the latter was backed by wealth, but persistent ill-fortune attended its earlier management.

The increased competition of two large theatres in addition to the two already existing, called for increased energy, and some of the manager's best friends thought he made a mistake by leaving the field in San Francisco to his lieutenants, to fight his battle for fame and fortune in distant fields. A discussion of the cause and the result would be profitless and uninteresting in these pages.

In each successive season of my continuance at the "California Theatre," "star" followed "star" in rapid succession; piece after piece was produced with lavish expenditure, and the dramatic and orchestral force were kept up to the public requirement. Some changes were made in the stage department, but the personnel of the company remained, on the whole, the same.

The leading gentleman and lady of the first season were Mr. George Chaplin and Miss Annie Graham. In 1873, Mr. Lewis Morrison and Miss Ellie Wilton held respectively those positions, and in the Fall of the same year, Mr. Barton Hill became stage manager. The next year, Miss Belle Pateman was leading lady; Mr. Morrison was succeeded by Mr. Thomas Keane as leading man, who held the position until Mr. Mc-Cullough's retirement. The successive low-comedians of the company were Messrs. Williamson, Pateman, and C. R. Bishop, and the orchestral department was under the direction of Mr. Charles Schultz.

To the names of all these ladies and gentlemen, I might add those of Henry Edwards, John Wilson, W. A. Mestayer, Owen Marlowe, Eben Plympton, Stephen W. Leach, E. N. Thayer,

Fred Franks, William Barry, J. N. Long, Nelson Decker, Frank Kilday, W. B. Curtis, J. P. Burnet, Louis Harrison, and J. Tighe; of Mrs. Judah, Mrs. Saunders, Helen Tracy, Minnie Walton, Carrie Wyatt, Nellie Cummings, Rellie Deaves, Louisa Chambers, Sophie Edwin, Georgie Woodthorpe, Louisa Johnstone, Kate Denin, Maggie Moore, Alice Harrison, Belle Chapman, Eleanor Carey, Frankie McClellan, and very many more who were in the " stock " during the palmy days of the " California Theatre," some of whom are now " stars " in their own right, and some have passed away, never to return.

Among the stellar luminaries I recall the names of Lawrence Barrett, Chanfrau, Boucicault, Sothern, May Howard, Shiel Barry, Adelaide Neilson, John Raymond, Wm. Hoskins, Mrs. Bowers, Rose Eytinge, Edwin Adams, Charles Fechter, Mr. and Mrs. W. J. Florence, Lizzie Price, Catharine Rodgers, Modjeska, Owens, Rose Evans, Augusta Dargon, De Bar, Edwin Booth, Alice Dunning, Ada Cavendish, Frank Mayo, Janauscheck, Fanny Davenport, Jeffreys-Lewis, and yet the half not told.

Of all these the writer has pleasant " memories " because, as my friend Mr. Henry Edwards truthfully says, in his feeling oration at John McCullough's tomb, " there was a something in the atmosphere of thoughtful kindness that pervaded the place, that made everyone who came within its influence feel the calm comforts of a home;" and we both of us speak

"Of that which we do know."

One of the pleasant outgrowths of those happy days in the California Theatre was the organization of the "California Theatre Boat Club." Among the leading spirits of the club were Messrs. Wm. Mestayer, Thomas Gossman and John Trueworthy; the somewhat unsylph-like frame of the first was unfitted for continuous effort with the ash, but the two latter were powerful members of the "California Crew," which generally captured the laurels from all opponents.

The organization was composed mainly of attachees of the theatre, reinforced by a few gentlemen from the outside, among whom was my old friend Dr. Knowlton, so well known to all San Francisco for superior skill in his profession, and for his websterian faculty of combining the elements, which, when in proper combination, make a fish chowder a "feast for the gods."

The club utilized this faculty at their merrymakings, and the Doctor was always a willing volunteer. I append a few lines, which, at his request, I wrote for one of those festive gatherings—

SONG OF THE CALIFORNIA THEATRE BOAT CLUB.

No fairer sight beneath the light
 Shed by the god of day
Was ever seen by mortal e'en
 Than San Francisco Bay.
No stouter arms or truer hearts
 In all the Union wide
Than those that skim its crested waves
 And stem its restless tide.

Chorus—

Then raise on high the joyous shout
 And let the chorus swell—
The California Boat Club! hip, hip, hurrah!
 With lapstreak or with shell.

Enthroned in state by the Golden Gate
 The queenly city sends
Her crowds of youth and beauty forth
 To greet their stalwart friends—
Whose manhood with the bending blade
 Was never known to quail;
Whose muscle in the sharpest "spurt"
 "Knows no such word as fail."

*Chorus—*Then raise on high, etc.

Then clear the track, craft all aback,
 The racers now are placed,
Each oarsman grips the sturdy ash
 And every nerve is braced.
The signal gun—they're off! hurrah!
 The stake-boat soon is reached,
The California's round it first;
 They're on the homeward stretch.

*Chorus—*Then raise on high, etc.

The line is crossed, the flag is won,
 The rattling contest ends,
The vanquished know no bitterness,
 True oarsmen all are friends.
And the victor California's boys
 No sordid triumph feel,
For they honor every foeman
 Who is worthy of their steel.

*Chorus—*Then raise on high, etc.

During Mr. McCullough's management many eminent personages visited the theatre, of whom, one especially eminent, not only as a ruler, but as a man, may be individualized—the Emperor Dom Pedro of Brazil. · He attended a matinee performance on the 28th of April, 1876, the play being "King Lear," selected by himself. No extraordinary preparations were made for his reception; with one or two attendants he came as a private gentleman, and the only recognition of the illustrious visitor's presence was the trophy of Brazilian flags twined over the mezzanine box which he occupied. His Brazilian majesty seemed greatly interested in the performance, paying, I think, quite as much attention to the book of the play, which he held in his hand, as to the actors on the stage. Between the fourth and fifth acts a little girl entered the box and presented him with a bouquet, when he took the little one upon his knee and made her proud with a kiss—truly is it said, "One touch of nature makes the whole world kin." And when the play concluded, walked quietly through the lobby to a coach in waiting, with no notice of his rank from any one, other than that of courtesy, as he passed.

A word or two more, and the "California Theatre" and all that pertains thereto is dropped from my pages. The Patemans are in England;

Mr. Morrison is traveling with his own company; Mr. Thomas Keane is also traveling with his own company; Mr. Williamson has been for some years a successful manager in Australia; Bishop — Charley Bishop, "too handsome for anything," and whose look alone is enough to put a "soul under the ribs of death"—is still playing in San Francisco; Harry Edwards has been for many years at Wallack's Theatre, in New York; John Wilson has gone to a better land — as have Owen Marlowe and William Barry. Mestayer has been his own manager for many a year, and made a fortune; and so has Curtis; Eben Plympton has risen to high rank, and commands his own terms; Stephen Leach lives in Oakland, California, and nurses the musical talent of the Bohemian Club in San Francisco; and Louis Harrison is his own manager, and banks his own money.

Of the "stars" whose names I have enumerated, seven have paid the "debt of nature," and the rest still gleam in the theatric horizon.

Mr. Barton Hill and Mr. Robert Eberle still live; the former is acting in the eastern cities, and the latter is the efficient manager of Mr. Hayman's company, at the Baldwin Theatre in San Francisco. Of the ladies named as being members of the stock company, I think all but four survive.

24

Mr. John Raymond, whose name is in my stellar list of the California Theatre, was the low-comedian of the company, I believe, during the first season, when Mr. Lawrence Barrett was associated in the management. He has been eminently successful—and, indeed, deserves to be, for where shall we find his *match ?* I am reminded here of a ludicrous incident which occurred when he was manager; perhaps he has forgotten it—I had almost forgotten it myself; but I think it was in 1871, in San José, where he opened a theatre, a new one, and made "his pile" in a week.

The play was "Richard III," and the "Richard" was Mr. McCullough. Of course, Manager Raymond could not lavish so much money on the appointments and scenery of his new theatre as if he had been the lessee for a *year* instead of a *week*, and the armies of the representatives of the contending houses of York and Lancaster were somewhat spare in numbers and meagre in dress and armament; to tell the truth, although I suppose John would deny it, he sent "Richmond" on the stage with an army of *one* man. "Oxford," in addressing the Earl, says—

> "Your words have fire, my lord, and warm our men,
> Who looked methought but cold before—disheartened
> By the unequal numbers of the foe"—

"Oxford" looked round, and seeing "Richmond's" gallant army of one man, ill-dressed, with a tin-foil helmet on his head, standing "all forlorn," he took in the situation at once, and changed his speech to—

"Your words have fire, my lord, and warm *this* man," etc.

It was a judicious departure from the text of Shakespeare, and the San José critics never uttered a word of censure.

One ludicrous thing reminds me of another—which occurred in the Old Theatre in Sacramento. A certain member of a company then in occupation of the theatre was addicted to occasional intemperance; he was naturally of a serious deportment, and in excuse for his indulgence always avowed that the propensity was a disease—that it was, in short, a fiat of the Almighty that he should be drunk, and he had to submit. On the night in question he went before the audience so inebriated, that their displeasure was shown by a general hiss, when, staggering to the front of the stage, he laid his hand on his heart, and throwing a look of drunken solemnity around, exclaimed, "La-ladies and gent-gent-lemen, a visitation of God!" and staggered off. For some time after, the irreverent men about town were wont to invite to the social glass by suggesting "a visitation of God."

Mr. McCullough was for a short time the lessee of the " Baldwin Theatre," and it was opened with the " School for Scandal," introducing Mrs. John Drew. This lady was, and I believe, still is, manageress of a Philadelphia theatre; and her " Lady Teazle" was pronounced by the critics " perfectly delightful in grace and movement and gesture, and all the qualifications which bespeak the true artist." Mrs. John Drew was the little Miss Lane whom I remembered in the Tremont Theatre, nearly fifty years before.

In August, 1878, I was engaged at the Opera House, and there met Mrs. Scott-Siddons. This lady reminded me in her style and method of Mrs. Mowatt; she possessed grace, but lacked power. On the 16th of November, the " Semi-Centennial Testimonial tendered by the public of San Francisco to Walter M. Leman, on his completion of fifty years' service on the stage," took place. On this occasion, I had the volunteer assistance of a large number of ladies and gentlemen connected with the theatre, and of several gentlemen prominent in social life. It was a brilliant financial success, the great theatre being absolutely full. In point of fact, the semi-centennial date had passed, for I had commenced in 1827.

A poetical address, written especially for the occasion, was spoken by the beneficiary, of which the following lines are a portion :—

    '' The old man links the present with the past,
       His step is firm, although his locks are white ;
       You have met him often amid scenes of mirth,
       Yet scarcely happier than he is to-night ;
       You have often seen him in his mimic life,
       Play the sad semblance of a dark despair ;
       You have seen him, when reality most real,
       Found echo only in the listening air.
       His cup is full—this last most welcome boon
       His grateful heart fills brimming full—and cheers ;
       But why assert in words ? since I am sure
       His face an index of his heart appears.''

This neat and friendly offering was from the pen of B. P. Moore, Esq.

On the first of December, I left San Francisco on the Steamer "Great Republic" for Portland, Oregon, under engagement to Mr. John Maguire, then manager of the "New-Market Theatre" in that city. His acting manager was Mr. Marcus R. Mayer. The season commenced with Miss Ada Cavendish and was one of moderate success. My visit to Portland is one of happy memories, for I met old friends, and the continuation of my tour made me familiar with some of the grandest scenery on the continent. At Vancouver, which was for many years the principal trading-post of the Hudson Bay Company, and is now one of the prominent military stations of the great Northwest, I found in the garrison some gentlemen of my acquaintance, who became soldiers at their country's call, and remained in the army after peace returned.

The post was under the command of General Sully, a scar-worn veteran, who was, I think, a brother of the famous painter of that name. He must have imbibed some of his brother's tastes, for the pretty little theatre in the garrison was decorated with scenes, most of which were painted by him. The General died not long after my visit. From Portland, a small company, of which I was one, started for the thriving town of Walla Walla, the center of a wonderfully rich grain region, where but a few years back the painted savage held undisputed sway. At Vancouver, the boat took on board General Howard and Aid, and our trip up the Upper Columbia was one to be remembered. I had not then seen the Rhine—I have since. There are no old feudal castles on the first-named river and none are needed to make it what it is, in every point of grandeur and beauty by far the finer of the two. At Wallula, another novelty awaited me: the chiefs and head men of a small Indian tribe, I forget the name, were to meet General Howard for a "talk" and I was present, with some ladies and gentlemen of our company, in the dingy room where the talk was held. The principal spokesman was an old chief, "Homily," who, as General Howard afterwards assured me, had always been a friend to the whites and a "good Indian," in spite of the growing opinion, that no Indians can be "good," except dead ones. The General told us, that all of these red men would want to shake hands, and would take offense if refused, and so we went through the proffered hand-shake with each one in succession. The council, or talk, broke up in about an hour.

At Wallula we took the railroad for Walla Walla, a distance, as I remember, of some thirty odd miles. Walla Walla is a beautiful town, full of life and energy, with spacious houses of business and elegant homes. In this pretty town where we contemplated a stay of but three weeks, we remained six; and went for three or four nights to "Dayton," thirty or forty miles distant, through a grain region where a yield of from forty to forty-five and fifty bushels to the acre is, I believe, the *rule* and not the exception; the wheat of the Walla Walla country is world famous.

I spent a pleasant day while in Walla Walla at the Cavalry Post, some three miles from the town, where I had an opportunity to see for the first time an exciting series of cavalry maneuvers, and I remember a funny object which, however, was looked upon with indifference by the soldiers—one of their number walking about within prescribed limits, enclosed in a barrel minus its two heads—the culprit seemed to care as little for his disgrace as the lookers on. One of the men told me that he lived in that barrel half of the time, "for he would get drunk, barrel or no barrel."

We returned to Portland, and on the 8th of April, recommenced with the engagement of Miss Rose Eytinge, which continued for two weeks, and thence started for another section of our wide-spread republic, which I had long wanted to see—the Puget Sound region, and who so does not see it, misses the sight of what I think is in the near future destined to be the "promised land." Puget Sound, our beautiful Mediterranean of the Northwest, indented with bays and inlets deep enough to float the largest iron-clad; its shores skirted with mighty forests, above which "Tacoma" towers with his 15,000 feet of glistening snow—can hardly be described by description—it must be *seen*. We played in Olympia at the head of the Sound, where the hotel—a good one—was kept by a colored woman, a refugee slave who had escaped, and found a far-away home among the free, and ate oysters abundant in quantity, minute in size and sweet in flavor. From thence by steamer to Seattle, beautifully situated like an amphitheatre on the shore of the Sound, and hoping to be, like many other places, the " great city of the Northwest," in which race it seems thus far to have the advantage ; and again by steamer over that beautiful inland sea to Port Townsend, and across the straits to the quaint and interesting city of Victoria, within the realm of her gracious Majesty of that name, where we remained for a week, which was moderately remunerative and infinitely enjoyable, and returned to Portland, where we took steamer and sailing down the river crossed the angry bar in safety, and so to San Francisco.

CHAPTER XVII.

IN the middle of October, 1879, I again left the
Pacific metropolis, playing in the cities of
Oakland, San Jose, Stockton, Sacramento, Reno
and Carson, and thence to Virginia City, where
Miss Ada Cavendish joined us for a week, and Mr.
Frank Mayo for another, and returning home-
ward, closed at the " California Theatre " my last
engagement, and practically terminated in San
Francisco a theatrical career which commenced
fifty-two years and four months before, in Boston,
Massachusetts.

There have been since then, occasional renew-
als, as for the benefit of a charity, or to serve an
old friend, or assist in the production of a new

play, the last of which occurred in February, 1886, at the "Bush Street Theatre," in Boucicault's comedy of the "Jilt," fifty-nine years from the time I tumbled over "Petruchio's" legs as "Nicholas," in the "Taming of the Shrew."

There were with me, in my visit to Portland and Victoria, three individuals who deserve mention in these reminiscences, the first of whom should by no means be omitted in any record that treats of "old Californians" connected with the stage.

Dr. Robinson, the father of "Sue Robinson," the "fairy star," of whom I have previously spoken, was one of the early comers to the land of gold. He had played in all the mining regions of Oregon and California, and the lavish favors of fortune had been followed by her frowns so often that he had become indifferent alike to frown or smile. The dilapidated old theatre in Victoria, in which we played, had been erected by him twenty-five years before. I do not think that Dr. Robinson had ever received anything like regular theatrical training, but, like John R. Potter and J. P. Addams, he was "up" in everything, and some parts he played well. When I last saw him, eight years ago, he was poor. Perhaps fortune has changed and made him rich; I hope so, with all my heart.

Miss Georgie Woodthorpe was a little San Francisco girl, who made her first appearance on the regular boards some few years before, at the " California Theatre," as "Arthur," in "King John." She had developed into an actress, and made such improvement that the leading parts in juvenile tragedy and comedy found in her a fair representative. Miss Woodthorpe went East subsequently, and I am unaware of her present residence, or whether she is still on the stage or not. She had all the elements for success, if industry was not wanting.

The third name I recall is that of Mr. Samuel W. Piercy. This young man was a native of California, had commenced as an amateur when quite young, and obtained some little recognition during the early years of the " California Theatre." He went East, making rapid advancement, and returned to his native State a very fine juvenile actor. Mr. Piercy married a lady of San Francisco, and lost her in Philadelphia within two years, but had a daughter on whom to bestow the love that had been a wife's, but not for long; for ere a twelvemonth had elapsed, he followed the wife and mother to the tomb, far from home and kindred, but not from friends. For Samuel Piercy there was a great future, had he lived, but death came to him in loathsome shape and suddenly, by small-pox, in the city of Boston, in

1880. Many months after his decease his remains were brought to San Francisco, and re-interred in the family vault. It was my sad privilege to participate in the burial ceremonies. I may be pardoned for inserting here a short extract from my funeral eulogy.

"Samuel Piercy sleeps, calmy, at rest; separated — not divided—by a few rods of our common mother, earth, from the wife he fondly loved. Nature and humanity recognize neither prelate nor council, nor consistory, nor dogma, nor creed. The gentle zephyrs of the Pacific will blow sweetly over both, and the soft dews of heaven will descend alike upon the graves of the husband and the wife; in death they are not divided."

In the month of August, 1879, I had received the nomination in convention of my fellow citizens, for the position of one of the "Justice's of the Peace, for the City and County of San Francisco," and in the following October election had been chosen to fill the place, as "Col. Sellers" says, "by a large majority." This was previous to my last theatrical engagement, and in January, 1880, I took my seat on the bench as one of the minor magistrates of the city and county. It can hardly be said of me that I filled the "great bard's" picture—

> "In fair round belly, with good capon lined,
> With eyes severe, and beard of formal cut"—

for I had but little belly, and no beard at all; nor was I—

> "Full of wise saws and modern instances"—

for all I knew of law was gathered from a very
cursory reading of " Blackstone" and a tolerable
acquaintance with the requirements of the Civil
Code of California.

My pleasantest memories of that judicial term
are of the "happy couples"—presumably happy,
at least — whom I united, amounting to one
hundred in all.   Two hundred "souls with but
one" hundred " single thoughts"—two hundred
"hearts that beat as one" hundred !   The reader
will be careful to make the proper numerical
distribution—outside of Brigham Young's kingdom—one a piece.

During the summer of the year after the close
of my official term, I was called upon to occasionally lecture, or deliver an address, and found
myself at Los Angeles, where Captain Jack
Crawford—or "Captain Jack," as he was usually
called—was playing with a small theatrical company.   I had known this gentleman in San
Francisco, where as a kind of semi-professional
actor he had been connected with several organizations not over successful.   He was a whole-
souled, generous, noble-spirited fellow, had been
in service on the frontier as a scout and on
Crook's staff, and rode a horse as if born in the
saddle.   He could write very fair verses, and
was a pretty good actor.   Now, whether *my*
" Captain Jack " is the Captain Crawford whom

the Mexicans have recently murdered in Arizona
or no, I know not; I think he is; but, if not, *my*
Captain Jack is still a pleasant memory.

And still another memory of that summer I
recall; one in conjunction with whom I gave a
musical and literary entertainment in the pleasant burgh known as R—— C——y. The lady
was Mrs. L—— S—— C——. She was the
daughter of one of the most beautiful women
ever seen on the London boards, who, fifty years
before, had been the reigning toast among the
bloods of the British metropolis. Mrs. C——
had made an unfortunate marriage, and was
engaged in an honorable struggle with fate and
poverty to rear the two dependent children that
had been left upon her hands. She sang and
played well, though with some exaggeration of
style; was extremely impulsive and erratic, but
had a thoroughly good heart, and had sufficient
confidence in *herself* to attempt anything. Our
joint programme of readings, recitations and
musical selections produced some profit, and
was repeated in S—— M——o.

From a western magazine I copy an article, of
which this fair lady was the heroine :

"There came, one day, from the railroad into
Deer Lodge Montana, a solitary freight team,
part of the burden of which were two broken-
down show people. The freighter brought them

up more through sympathy than for compensation, for when they landed in the suburbs of the town they had but a lone half-dollar between them to commence business with.

"The man looked anything but a showman—a little pinched-up fellow, with face to drive rather than draw an audience; but the rascal had been fortunate in striking a partner. (The ways of an actress are past finding out!) Broke, like himself, it is true, but possessing a fair wardrobe and any amount of confidence in her abilities, this lady of the stage, when the kind-hearted freighter set her down in the suburbs of our town—dirty and dusty, her unartistic garments faded and worn, unkempt hair floating in the evening breeze, her shoes too much worn to afford protection from the prickly cactus—was more an object of pity than of curiosity.

"There was no similarity in the names of these show people. Professor —— and Laura Agnes sounded strangely when they traveled in one firm, lived in one wagon, and owned but one pair of blankets; but stage people come and go in their own peculiar way, and we must take them as we find them.

"Laura Agnes made good use of the river that flowed by their camping-ground, for in the morning, when she strode into the office of the *New Northwest*, in good attire, her complexion brilliant as a rose, and her face full of smiles, I did not at first recognize her as the woman who sat on the ground by the freighter's wagon the evening before, crunching slap-jacks and sipping coffee from a tin cup.

"Well, Laura Agnes found the editor in his den and bearded him; she interviewed him as to the prospects of getting a paying audience in town, the price of hand bills, local blasts, etc., and was in ecstasies when she learned that no first-class troupe had played there since the immortal Jack Langrische had swept the town of its last dollar; as luck would have it, a new hall had but recently been completed for banquet and ball purposes, and altogether Laura Agnes' star, that had set in the unappreciative Sierras, was beginning to rise in glory to shine forth 'mid the valleys of the everlasting Rockies. She made an impression on the editor, I think (those actresses are such winning things); he was a bachelor, and a long way from home, and he told Laura Agnes that if saying good things of her would bring her good-luck, then she might count on a house that would do her eyes good.

"When Laura posted off to see about the hall, I took occasion to mention the little history of her, that I had from the freighter, that I thought it my duty to inform him of the state of Laura Agnes' finances, and that I believed that she was owner of just a half dollar. The editor was a man noted for his kindness of heart, and his desire to see everybody prosper, and he only replied—that if she was *down* we must help her on her feet again.

"Well, Laura Agnes returned to the office with the cosmetics fairly running from her face, bearing the announcement that the hall was secured, and that we could go on with our good words, and then returned to the wagon to gather her little baggage and wait the appearance of the paper, which was to come out in the afternoon, satisfied that she had found friends in a strange land. Then we went to work and got up the posters; they were immense; they could be seen afar off. There had never been seen such an artist on that side of the range before (so the bill said), and probably never would be again. It was the only opportunity, now was the accepted time to see and hear the great Laura Agnes—Come one! Come all!

"In the meantime Laura and her tag had taken rooms in the highest-priced hotel in town, and was treading majestically to and fro on the balcony where she could be seen to the best advantage from the street.

"When the paper made its appearance that afternoon, Laura must have been astonished to learn that she had played before all the crowned heads of Europe; had crossed the ocean and startled the greatest cities of the East with her wonderful acting, but above all, must have been surprised to learn through the local columns of the *New Northwest*, that to her money was no object, that, having already a large bank account laid away, she had come to the mountains merely to recuperate and get away from the excitements of the stage for a time, and had only consented at the earnest request of a few who had heard of her fame to give an entertainment at Deer Lodge. That evening, nearly every man in town, married and single, took supper at the hotel (ostensibly, to get a square meal), but in reality, to get a square look at the wonderful Laura Agnes.

Opera Mad—Opera Mad;

or,

Romeo and Juliet,

Greeted the eyes of the Deer Lodgers at every turn next day, and some of the bills found their way into the nearest mining camp, ten miles away. The theatre was all the rage, the price of admission was fixed at one dollar, which was next to nothing in those days, and the large hall was jammed long before the curtain rose.

"At last, the bell tingled ' all ready;' the curtain slid hurriedly to one side; for a quarter of a minute after you could have heard a canary feather drop, then came one spontaneous outburst that shook the very ground on which the building stood; there was nobody on the stage but Romeo; he was the most forlorn looking lover that ever appeared on any stage; he stood slantwise to the audience, a wild vacant stare in his eyes, like a dead man looking off into the other world.

" Romeo was a cheap man in every sense; his foundation was a block of wood, in which two sticks were inserted for legs, on which rested a bust of some kind, and on this a block for a head, and over this a false face and one of Laura's wigs; a hugh mustache set around on one side of his mouth did not help his looks; he was dressed in a red cambric gown, and this was the Romeo—a perfect blockhead in every respect. 'That's a wooden man, too dead to skin,' said some one in the crowd; this brought forth another roar of applause; when this was over, a miner rose up on a back seat and shouted, 'We've seen Romeo, now bring on your Julio!' which was followed by cheers and cries of 'Julio! Julio!'

" After a minute or two, the curtains of a little dressing room in the farthest corner of the hall parted, and 'Julio' strode majestically across the stage and made her courtesy amid the wildest uproar.

" When the audience had calmed down a little, she explained that she was supposed to be a young lady, who had gone opera-mad, and was practicing with an imitation Romeo, preparatory to going on the stage. A lady in town had lent a piano for the occasion, and Laura sang and played in a manner that surprised the natives, after which she made love to Romeo after a style that kept the house in a continuous roar. But Romeo couldn't be prevailed upon to return her demonstrations of love, and when she would rush at him with outstretched arms and beseech him to speak to her, to embrace her just once, he would only stare at her with those frightful eyes —but it invariably brought down the house. Once, when she rushed at him, threw her arms about his neck and called upon him to embrace her, a man on a front seat became so impatient at Romeo's indifference, that he sprang to his feet and shouted 'Go for her, Romeo, or let some one there that can !'

" Between acts, Laura Agnes sang and played, and spun strange yarns until near midnight, and it was only with the greatest reluctance that the seats were vacated then. If ever an audience got the worth of their money invested, it was that one. Laura announced an entire change of programme for the next night, but on the following day a petition was presented to the successful

Laura, requesting her to repeat the programme of the previous evening, and give them ' Romeo and Julio ' over again, and her fame went out into the mountains that day, and the second house was even greater than the first.

" But Laura Agnes' success didn't end in Deer Lodge. She made a tour of the Territory and was everywhere greeted with the best of houses. It was at Pioneer, however, where the admiration for her acting swept the whole town off its feet and brought downfall to Romeo. At that time, there were in Pioneer seven or eight hundred miners and not a stingy one among them. The mines were rich and everybody made money, but they only made it for the fun of spending it. Some of the miners had been to Deer Lodge, when Laura played there, and when she passed through Pioneer on her way to the Missoula country, a committee of miners waited on her, and promised her, that if she would play there on her return, every man in the diggings would go to hear her. Laura fulfilled her promise and was on hand at the appointed time. The people went wild; mining and business of all kinds suspended and Laura Agnes realized what it was to play to an audience of gold miners, who didn't care for expense, so they had fun. The hall was filled and men climbed on top of each others' shoulders to see Laura, when she made love to Romeo.

Between the acts the house was emptied and the saloons were filled, and when the last scene was over, the town was in a glorious state of intoxication. In the excitement of the closing scene, Romeo got separated from 'Julio' and was borne by the boys to a saloon, where he was stood up at the bar, and made to take part in the midnight orgies of the miners. He was drenched with whisky, until the paint came off his face and not a dry stitch was left upon him. While in this condition, he was pushed against a man too drunk to know the difference. He imagined he was assaulted by one of the boys, and pitched into Romeo, while the crowd stood back and urged him to 'give it to him' for insulting him. Romeo went down in the battle and when his adversary had done with him, he was completely demolished; his red coat was torn to shreds, his nose bit off, his eyes gouged out and his cheeks smashed in. The pieces were gathered up and laid behind the bar and the miners went on with their drinking and carousing.

"In the meantime, Laura Agnes had become uneasy about Romeo, and had sent a man to look him up. The man found him lying all in a heap in the saloon. Some one suggested that the fragments of Romeo be gathered together and returned to his mistress with a suitable apology. He was stretched on a board and carried by two men to the hotel, while a crowd followed at their heels to see the fun.

"Laura was at the breakfast table with a good many others, when her dead Romeo was carried in and deposited in the center of the hall; then one of the pall-bearers addressed her in the most solemn tone:

"'Madam, it becomes my most painful duty to present to you the remains of your beloved Romeo. He *would* run with the boys last night, and *would* drink, and *would* fight, and this is what is left of him.'

"Laura gazed at the figure a moment, then rose up, and with a scream that brought a rush to the breakfast room, fell upon Romeo. 'Dead! dead!' she exclaimed; 'my Romeo—my dear Romeo, speak to me this once! tell me you love me! it cannot be that he is dead! Romeo! Romeo! my darling Romeo! Yes, yes, he is dead! dead! Oh, Romeo, Romeo, Romeo!' and with tears streaming down her cheeks, tumbled over on the dilapidated remains of Romeo, to all appearances, as dead as a mackerel.

"The miners couldn't stand this last act, and made a rush for the door, their solemn faces and glistening eyes telling their suppressed emotions.

"No sooner was the room cleared than Laura Agnes sprang up from the floor, wiped her eyes, and sat down to the breakfast table again, laughing at the manner in which she had "played it" upon the boys.

"The miners returned to the saloon, a sad-looking set, where they raised among themselves a purse of dust large enough to buy a regiment of Romeos.

"When the stage called at the hotel that morning to take Laura Agnes on her way back to Deer Lodge, the miners gathered round to bid her good bye, and as she took her seat, the purse was tossed into her lap and Laura was 'gone from their gaze.'

"This remarkable woman left the mountains with many regrets and many dollars."

Since Mrs. C——'s profitable adventures in Montana, she must have experienced severe reverses, for she was very poor. I honored her for her perseverance and courage in fighting the battle of life, and for her fidelity to her children, who were entirely dependent upon her, their father, the little "pinched-up" fellow who rode with Laura Agnes into Deer Lodge in the freight wagon, having deserted her and them.

I have now to record an event which is one of the most grateful "memories" of a long life. It will be stated in the most succinct manner by copying the heading of the "California Theatre" bill, of June 22d, 1881 :

SPECIAL WEDNESDAY MATINEE.

JUNE 22, 1881.

GRAND BENEFIT

Tendered by the members of the Madison Square Theatre Company, and the resident dramatic profession

— TO —

WALTER M. LEMAN.

The programme included selections from the " School for Scandal," the opera of " La Mascotte," and two acts of " As You Like It." To all of the ladies and gentlemen who zealously participated in this gracious offering, I felt and still feel grateful—a gratitude of the *heart*, rather than of spoken or written words.

In August, of the same year, I received the nomination in convention of my fellow citizens, for the office of " Public Administrator of the City and County of San Francisco." The result of the election may be briefly told in the following editorial, copied from the columns of the San Francisco *Evening Bulletin:*

" THE HIGHEST ON THE TICKET.

———

"It has turned out just as though it had been a play. The ' good man ' of the play, if it be not a tragedy, always comes off nicely with his audience. He thwarts villainy, protects innocence, and is assured of sympathetic applause. Moreover, great is his reward, generally, in the drama. When the curtain falls, it falls upon the fullness of his night's honors.

" Perhaps he imagines himself for the time being, the actual character that he personates. Mr. Leman has for years without count been the 'good man' of the stage. How many mimic rascals he has brought to deserved justice in his long career as an actor he could not approximately number himself. His efforts and successes on the boards, excellently rendered, have brought to him great popularity; no political services have given him nominations and votes.

" Theatre-goers of all parties know him in a pleasant way, and have assisted him in his candidacies. Although nothing of a lawyer, yet he has made an acceptable justice of the peace for this city. His decisions have been formed on the plain principle of right between man and man ; they have not been misguided by such legal technicalities as commonly have weight in the lowest of our courts. His success in that public capacity warranted his party in tendering him this year the nomination for the far more important office of Public Administrator. He is elected, and both his vote and his majority are greater than those of any of his associates on the ticket. It is the 'good man's·' special victory. He was popular with Democrats as well as with Republicans. If more of the voters had seen him act frequently, it is quite probable that his majority would have been even much larger. As it is, it must be to his sufficient gratification. If he shall make as good a Public Administrator as he did a Justice of the Peace, he may never have occasion to return to his old profession."

The result of the election in the following year was disastrous to the political party which had my allegiance. The tidal wave which swept the Union and the State swallowed up all opposition in the city and county—and not one candidate on the ticket whereon was printed my name was chosen; all went down together. I accepted the situation, without loss of appetite, or sleep, or spirits. I hope that I may not incur the charge of self-adulation, by saying that all the estates that came into my hands, during my incumbency, were settled and closed within a twelvemonth from the end of my official term. This is to me a pleasant memory, and all the more so, that it is justly complimentary to the legal ability and promptitude of my attorney and friend, Frank J. French, Esq., of the San Francisco Bar.

Nearly four years have passed, and six have already been added to man's allotted "three score and ten." If on the active stage of the Drama or in the arena of Politics I may no longer live and move, I still may and do feel a deep interest in the honor and purity of both.

The uses and abuses of the stage have been defended and anathematized since the dawn of the drama, and will be to the end of time. In our own land there are very many who, if not opponents of the drama and the stage, still take a pessimist view of the theatre and its influence on society.

They shrug their shoulders and say, "Oh! if we could have a pure drama, an American drama untainted with the leaven of vice! If we could have a moral stage!"

These are without doubt very suggestive *Ifs*, and carry weight in view of the questionable imbecilities which a class of modern translators and adapters have inflicted on the public.

The revolution in the control and conduct of the theatre, which has been effected within the last two decades, has been attended—especially in our own country—with great detriment to the best interests and influence of the drama.

The disbandment of regularly organized theatrical companies, where the young actor was by a proper training fitted for his calling, and taught how to play subordinate parts before being entrusted with leading ones, and the unlimited extension of the starring system (which in its inception was vicious) have been most disastrous.

We shall have a pure drama, an American drama worthy of the name, when playwrights cease to write plays with *one* part only; when managers relegate the transplanted drama of the demi-monde to the place of its birth, and have sufficient judgment to discover merit, when the playwright possesses it, even if he should have the misfortune to be born on this side of the Atlantic.

And the American Theatre will have a better moral standing when municipal magistrates have sufficient consideration for the youth who are destined in the immediate future either to honor or disgrace their country, and sufficient official firmness to close the filthy "dives" of our cities where men are degraded, women debauched, and the Drama bastardized by the manager (God save the mark!) who calls his *den* a theatre.

And when elderly gentlemen, with scanty hair upon their heads, take their wives and daughters to the boxes to listen to Shakespeare, instead of going *solus* to the front-orchestra seats, with opera-glass exactly focused to see the Queen of the Ballet.

> "Fair Angiolini bare her breast of snow,
> Wave her white arms and point her pliant toe."

I dare to hope that the time is not far distant when the genius and spirit of our land will be as ably illustrated in the field of dramatic com-position as they are now in every other branch of literature; as they are at the bar, in the pul-pit and forum; as they have been, and are, by all her victories in the arts of peace, no less than by her triumphs on the slippery deck and bloody battle-field.

With brief reference to a short tour in the British Islands and Central Europe, this record of the remembrances of an old actor may prop-erly close.

On the 23d of June, 1885, I landed from a Cunard steamer at Queenstown—the Cove of

Cork—one of the finest harbors in the United Kingdom, and from the city of Cork went, without stopping to kiss the blarney stone, to the Killarney region, where lakes and fells and mountains are hallowed by romance and legend and story, and celebrated in poetry and song.

With a glance at the Currah of Kildare, I next found myself in Dublin, and learned to know how false and unjust our impressions may sometimes be, for Dublin is a beautiful city, embellished with costly public and private edifices, with every evidence to the stranger of municipal good government.

My stay in the Green Isle was necessarily brief. It is a lovely land, where the blessings which God vouchsafes to his creatures seem ever destined to be marred by the perversity of man. Whose perversity is most responsible for the evil I will not undertake to say; why Lord Kenmare and Mr. Herbert, with their vast and magnificent estates in the Killarney region, should be unable to collect twenty per cent of their rental, and are made practically poor by their great wealth; and why the Killarney mountaineers should be in abject penury beneath a sky and in a land so bright and lovely, is beyond my ken.

Perhaps the " Irish problem," as it is called, is near solution; let us hope that it is.

I met a pompous " Binney, the Butler," in the hotel at Killarney, and was bored by an ignorant prig in attendance at the " castle," in Dublin, but I found the women of Ireland modest, gentle and attractive ; the men frank, honest and sincere.

Across the Irish Channel, rolling on by the ruins of Conway Castle, grand in decay, to Chester, with its walls and battlements that have stood a thousand years ; thence to the great mart of Liverpool, in all things the antipodes of Chester, to Glasgow, the industrial and commercial metropolis of Scotland, with its grand cathedral (now restored), whose history would be an epitome of the ecclesiastical history of Scotland, and its grand necropolis ; down the Clyde to Greenock ; thence to Ayr, the " land o' Burns," where I met the last surviving relative of the poet, his niece, Miss Begg, a bright, intelligent lady, 73 years of age ; and wandered amid

> "The banks and braes o' Bonny Doon."

On the banks of the Frith of Clyde, ten miles below Greenock, I visited the old ruin, Rothsay Castle, with its legend of the Norse warrior and the Lady Isabella—

> " And oft in the murk and midnight hour,
>   When a' is silent there,
>   A shriek is heard, and a ladye is seen
>   On the steps o' the bluidy stair. "

From there, up the Frith to Dunbarton Castle, to the summit of which I mounted—this fortified rock contains the sword of Wallace—and so to Loch Lomond, skimming its surface by steamer, and returning by rail to Glasgow.

I came suddenly upon the monument and tomb of James Sheridan Knowles—spoken of in a preceding chapter—in the Glasgow necropolis; the memories of fifty years and more came back as I looked upon his grave-tablet, and I could hardly realize that the dust of the genial Irishman—the brilliant dramatist—the energetic actor—and, strange to write it, the controversial clergyman—was at my feet.

From the walls of Stirling Castle I looked forth upon six battle-fields, and climbed the massive tower surmounting the Abbey Craig, which tells of the glory won by Wallace and Bruce on Bannockburn beneath.

Edinburgh, the most picturesque city I saw while abroad, held me enchained by its mighty memories. I sat in the chair of the " Wizard " of Abbotsford and held in my hand the ivory and mother-of-pearl cross, that Mary Stuart held in hers, when she mounted the scaffold. I roamed in Melrose Abbey, and lingered in Rosslyn Chapel, and explored the vaults of the mighty old Norman Keep, that stands on the banks of the Esk.

26

Edinburgh Castle — the Canongate — Holy Rood! The very names bring back, not to me only, the memories of a *visit*, but to all mankind the " memories " of seven centuries.

I found myself in London in July, where within the national place of sepulture—whose monuments "epitomize a people's history," where kings and queens, warriors and statesmen, and the intellectually great of the past lie side by side in eternal silence—I sat, when a high dignitary of the Church in the presence of hereditary nobility and the representatives of royalty, rank and power, paid a noble tribute to the strength, self-control and magnanimity of the simple soldier, whose deeds have become his country's heritage, in these words:

"Such careers as Grant's are the glory of the American continent ; they show that the people have a sovereign insight into intrinsic force. If Rome told with pride how her dictators came from the plough-tail, America, too, may record the answer of the President, who, on being asked—"What should be his Coat-of-Arms?" answered, proudly mindful of his early struggles: "A pair of shirt-sleeves."

" The answer showed a noble sense of the dignity of labor, a noble superiority to the vanities of feudalism, a strong conviction that men are to be honored simply as *men*, not for the prizes of accident and birth."

No more trenchant words were ever uttered in Westminster Abbey and we, who sat in the place of honor, looked in each others' eyes, proud that we were born in a land, that produced a man worthy of such a eulogy in such a place.

I lingered on my way from the Scotch metropolis long enough in York to see the great Minster, and in Durham to inspect its famous Cathedral —" Half house of God, half castle 'gainst the Scot."

From London to Paris, to Basle, to Lucerne, to Interlaken, Berne, Lausanne and Geneva ; thence by Chamounix, via the Tete-Noir Pass, to Martigny and Brieg on the Swiss frontier ; over the Simplon to Pallanza on Lake Maggiore, through the chain of Italian lakes to Como and from there by rail to Milan and thence to Venice.

When I left Venice, I doubled on my route for the short distance between Venice and Verona, where, within the mighty circle of that heathen temple, erected two hundred and forty years before Christ was born, I sat, where the beauties of Verona once sat with smiling faces and cruel hearts, and, like their sisters in Vespasian's still mightier temple, turned down their thumbs as a signal for the slaughter of the conquered gladiator—

"Butchered to make a Roman holiday,"

And lingered for a while in contemplation at the Apochryphal Tomb of Juliet. From Verona I went northwardly, via the Tyrol, to Innspruck, and from there to Munich, next to Strassburg, Heidelberg, Frankfort, Mayence, down the Rhine to Cologne, Amsterdam, The Hague, Antwerp, Brussels and Ostend, and, recrossing the Channel to Dover, sped by rail again to London. On leaving the great city, I crossed central England —in order to visit Stratford-on-Avon, Warwick and Kenilworth Castles—to Liverpool and met the steamer for home.

This tour, which, in addition to the British Islands, embraced a part of France, Alsace, Switzerland, Northern Italy, the Tyrol, South Germany, Holland and Belgium, is crowded with a myriad of sweet and bitter memories.

I had stood upon the floor of Notre Dame, and the Saint-Chapelle, of Les Invalides, and the Pantheon, of the cathedrals of Milan and Strassburgh and Antwerp and Cologne, of the wondrous Basilica of St. Marc, in wondrous and

“Beautiful Venice—the Bride of the Sea.”

I had mused and pondered at the tombs of Scott and Burns and Shakespeare, had roamed through Holy Rood and Hampton Court and Windsor palaces, and wandered through the gorgeous Salons of the Louvre, the New and Old Residenz in Munich, the Doge's Palace in Venice, and other royal dwellings.

I had gazed on some of the masterpieces of art, which can never die, while roaming through the grand museums and galleries, with which the great centers of Europe are crowded. I had mounted triumphal pillars, erected to commemorate the glories of the great, and had thridded —candle in hand— the crypts of Chillon, the dungeons of the Doge's Palace, and the horrid vaults of the "Stein" in Antwerp. I had climbed the Alps and floated on the Irish and Scotch and Swiss and Italian lakes.

I had strolled through many a gorgeous pleasure-ground, and trod the marble floors of many a baronial hall and castle, but I had been in no land in which, as in my own, the humblest and poorest citizen can easily acquire and hold a castle of his own. I had seen the grandeur of of Nature—for God's work everywhere is grand —but I had seen no mountain higher or whiter than "Tacoma," no lake more beautiful than "Tahoe," no stream so mighty as the "Mississippi," no valley so sublime as "Yosemite," no cataract so grand as "Niagara."

Realizing, as an American, our own shortcomings—that we have too little respect for the restraints of law, and too little regard for moral obligations and the sanctities of home,—I yet returned home an American in every fiber of my being, with small respect for the American who, whether his sojourn abroad be brief or otherwise, comes back with a real or pretended admiration for foreign institutions over those of his native land.

On looking back over the years that are gone, I call to mind scores of dramatic luminaries of either sex, with whom at various periods of my career I have been on terms of more or less social and professional intimacy; and also many prominent personages whom I have known without the dramatic pale, whose names are unmentioned in this volume; but at seventy-six years of age our mnemonics lapse somewhat, and were it otherwise, the briefest individual reference to them would swell the book to unreasonable limits.

The great master has told us that—

> "All the world's a stage,
> And all the men and women merely players."

If in these desultory memories of a long life, the greater portion of which has been spent within the inner circle of the mimic world, and now in the course of nature rapidly drawing to its close, the writer has penned aught that will interest or beguile the tired hours of one weary struggler in the great drama played on the world's stage, his object has been attained. And so hoping, he bids his Readers courteously farewell.